Mission to Kabul

Mission to Kabul

H. Ronken Lynton

*Mapin*Lit
AN IMPRINT OF
MAPIN PUBLISHING

First published in India in 2006 by
MapinLit
An Imprint of
Mapin Publishing

Mapin Publishing Pvt. Ltd.
31 Somnath Road, Usmanpura
Ahmedabad 380013 India
T: 91-79-2755 1833 / 2755 1793 • F: 2755 0955
E: mapin@mapinpub.com • www.mapinpub.com

ISBN: 81-88204-72-2 (Mapin)
ISBN: 1-890206-95-4 (Grantha)

Jacket Design: Siddharatha Das
Designed by Janki Sutaria / Mapin Design Studio
Printed in India

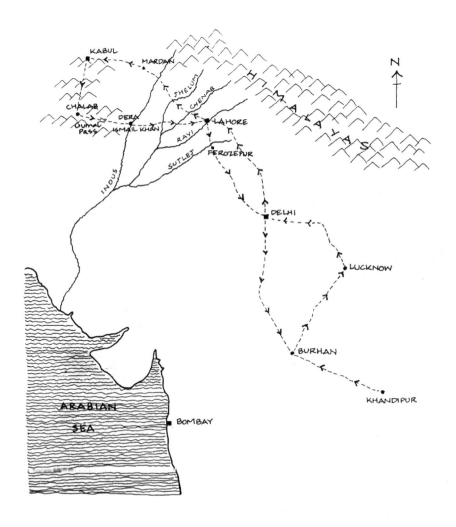

Routes of Sayed Mahmood's Travels

1

Khandipur, Central India
August, 1879

Hamidullah leaned forward and patted his horse's shoulder. "Good canter, old boy. Nice going. Now let's gallop a bit." The horse responded. As the stride lengthened and the fields and huts sped by ever more rapidly, Hamid waved exuberantly, his crop describing circles above his head, and shouted out his high spirits. People working in the fields or driving buffaloes along the road smiled and waved back at the young man. The monsoon over, the earth rested and refreshed, it was time to start again the immemorial round. The scent of new-turned earth, the delicate green of paddy ready for transplanting, the bursts of colour as flowers volunteered their perfumes in unexpected places—nature and people together rejoiced in the renewal of life.

Once more Hamid leaned forward and patted the sweaty neck. "That was lovely. Now let's go home."

Home was clearly a word the horse knew, for his stride became even more rapid. They passed the outlying houses, reached the bazaar area. The streets were crowded, so that customers trying to enter the small shops ran a gauntlet of pushcarts. Piles of fruits, vegetables, garlic and spices, vegetable pakoras or sweet jalebis just out of the boiling oil, tempted passers-by with fragrances as bright as their colours. Coming to the main street, man and mount swerved around the corner onto it without slackening their pace, galloped on down the street and through their own gate, unaware of the cart they had upset.

"Budmash!" the furious fruit-seller shouted at the retreating horseman. While fruit rolled in the dust, the wheels of his pushcart buckled and the whole thing collapsed in a worm-eaten heap. "Haramzada! You and your tribe of bastards! Budmashes all!"

At home, not much later, Hamid's elder brother Mahmoud heard the story from an old family servant who had been in the bazaar. Mahmoud's jaw tightened. "Not again," he exclaimed. He was growing rather tired of his happy-go-lucky younger brother's exploits. He couldn't seem to get through to Hamid how fragile the family's position was. Their prestige depended on the respect accorded to them because the community still remembered their father, who had been that rarity, a magistrate who was not only incorruptible, but who actually cared about the people in his jurisdiction. That respect could be squandered by Hamid's kind of thoughtlessness. Budmash, haramzada, bastard, these were not words a lower-class man could be allowed to apply to a family that guarded its honour. First he had to correct that, then tackle Hamid again.

Without another word, Mahmoud left the house and went into the street of the carpenters. Having completed rapid and detailed negotiations there, he appeared before the fruit-seller, who was sitting dejectedly by the small pile of bruised fruit that he had been able to salvage.

"Here is money for the fruit that was spoiled," Mahmoud told him, holding out some folded notes. Paper money, not coins; that showed the sum was not niggardly. "Moreover, I have stationed a new cart for you in the next street," he went on. "That is now your position; you will sell there from now on."

"But Sahib," the Peshawari protested, "this is the main street. I won't sell nearly so much over there."

"Those who don't mind dealing with a crude fellow will soon find you. As for the better families, they will choose to buy from someone more respectful. If you wish to claim the new cart, you will go there now." Mahmoud walked off as the man began to gather up his remaining fruit, all the while muttering under his breath about the injustice of life.

That evening Hamid found his brother in the mardana, the section of the house reserved only for men. Its outstanding feature was its carpets, mostly Persian, though some of the newer ones were from Kashmir; all of them were good, but some showed the wear coming from generations of use. Pillows and bolsters were scattered around, some with mica embroidered in their covers, some of iqat, others block-printed with bright colours. On a table made from an elephant's foot stood a bronze hookah, the water pipe that the British had dubbed a hubble-bubble. Hamid folded his long frame onto the carpet in a single easy motion, and relaxed against the bolsters.

Mahmoud sat up straight, legs crossed in the lotus position. "I've told you this before, Hamid. If you aren't going to think before you act, then you have to deal with the consequences, and that means getting your values straight." Mahmoud felt put upon, to have to remind his brother of the disgraceful names the fruit seller had called them, and what that meant for the family. He went on, "If any worthless fellow who happens to bear a grudge can impugn the name of this family, then who will respect us? How can we hold our heads up?"

"We could ignore him."

"No, we can't, because others won't; they'll gossip. Then how will we find husbands for our sisters?"

"I see," Hamid acknowledged, but clearly his mind was already on its way out of the room.

Though he had escaped from the lecture as soon as he decently could, Hamid found he could not so easily dismiss his brother's strictures. "Mahmoudbhai is so serious," he grumbled to himself. "If Father had lived, everything would be different." Hamid thought that ever since their father's death, Mahmoud had done nothing but talk about their responsibilities for the family honour, education for Kabir, the youngest in the family, good husbands for the girls. He recognized that his brother was the head of the family now, but wished he'd take life a bit more lightly. After all, he was not quite twenty and deserved to have a little fun, though perhaps that was something Mahmoud had never known.

He ambled over to the window and looked out to where his horse was grazing peacefully, but the sight only reminded him of Mahmoud's lecture. Hurt pride to the fore, he revived an old resentment that Mahmoud never acknowledged his contribution to the family budget, even though his salary was larger than Mahmoud's own. Well, to be fair, he had to admit that if a classmate hadn't spoken to Nawab Rahmatullah for him, he wouldn't have had that job either.

Working for the Nawab was very much to Hamid's liking. Nawab Rahmatullah's jagir, the lands that gave him his income and his title of nawab, was small, but it made him the most important man in the taluq. His house in Khandipur was not much larger than the sprawling ancestral home in which Hamidullah lived, but its mardana was furnished in the western style that had become fashionable in the cities. To the people of Hingaum District it seemed very fine and very grand.

The office, where Hamid functioned as something between glorified office boy and clerk, was just across the courtyard from the residential part of the house. Exuding his customary good humour and affability, Hamid had soon become the pet of the office. The others teased him about the careful way he dressed, his embroidered kurta always ironed with neat creases. They shared their snacks with him and asked office favours of him. He was a familiar figure in the mardana, where he appeared bearing papers requiring the Nawab's signature. He never begrudged the long periods during which the Nawab kept him waiting, for those were periods of private fantasy.

Alone in the mardana, Hamid amused himself by pretending this was actually his home. He imagined wanting a nibble while he waited; he would snap his fingers and the bearer would bring tea and snacks, pakoras, or no, maybe a samosa would be more satisfying. And then it wasn't necessary to imagine. "Ah, good afternoon, bearer. What have we today? Samosas! I was just wishing for one. That will be all, thank you."

Hamid, his tea finished, sprawled in a low chair characteristic of Hingaum District, long legs stretched out in front of him. In this relaxed position he noticed for the first time the stone latticework at the upper floor level that must have been the boundary of the zenana, the women's quarters. A slight movement of the curtain behind it caught his attention: had that been an eye, or did he imagine it? No further movement, though he strained to see. From then on, whenever he went to the house, he contrived to watch that area, but cautiously, for to be caught doing so would have meant the end of his association with the Nawab. Once he thought he saw a bejewelled hand disturb the curtain, but nothing more.

At home one evening, Hamid raised himself on one elbow and settled the bolster more comfortably behind him. His sister Razia, like the others in the zenana, had her own small room opening out onto a private balcony. For each woman in the zenana, the balcony provided privacy, as well as her chance to express her own personality by what she did with it. On hers, Razia had laid out her favourite carpet and bolsters and added potted plants, making it a place of lively colours. When he was not out with his friends, Hamid could often be found there. Although Razia was the second sister of those still at home, four years younger than he, she was a special favourite of his. "Tell me something, Pearl of the Palace," he began.

Razia glanced down at the tiny courtyard where women twittered to one another as they worked, then back into the small room behind the balcony where they sat. "Some palace," she sniffed. Then hastily, for she was afraid that if she hurt his feelings he would leave her and go to the men's part of the house, she added, "but better to be a pearl than a sheni, though I suspect you're one of the few people who could wear a sapphire safely. You're always lucky, it seems."

"Don't call a sapphire sheni. That means evil, but a sapphire can be lucky as well as unlucky. One can always use a bit of luck."

"You wanted to know something."

"Nothing important," he dismissed it with a wave of his hand. "Just gossip. The whispers around the office are that the Nawab Rahmatullah's daughter is the most beautiful woman in Central India. Is that true, do you think?"

"Imagine her for yourself; that's all I could do. Since when do Sunni women visit a Shia zenana?"

At Hamid's protest that ladies talk, and servants from one zenana pass gossip to another, Razia admitted she had heard about the Nawab's daughter Anees. She described her as having skin like burnished copper. Copper was not an unusual colour for Indians, but 'burnished' added a special sheen to it. Her eyes light up a room like a match in the aina khana, Razia went on. An aina khana was a room so completely lined with small pieces of mica that a single match would catch the reflections and light the whole room. That piqued

11

Hamid's imagination, and he filed it in his memory, from where he could take it out from time to time and try to construct the image of a woman whose eyes were so expressive. Before he could pursue that delightful occupation now, however, Razia interrupted with a change of subject, asking what Anees's father, the Nawab, was like.

Describing his boss reminded Hamid of the contradictions he had learned to walk around. On the one hand, the man did not stand on his importance. When the call for noon prayers came, if he happened to be in the office, he didn't rush off to the prayer room, but joined his staff. Of course, his prayer mat was fancier than the others', but Allah, may His name be praised, probably didn't notice things like that. Nor that Sunnis and Shias use different gestures when they pray.

On the other hand, the Nawab was known to be strict. Some called him relentless when he went after something. His staff knew better than to cross him, but they also admitted that he had an odd characteristic: once he got what he wanted, he tended to be compassionate. They sometimes figured the generosity was to celebrate his victory.

"In that case," his listener remarked, "I suspect he pushes his sons and spoils Anees."

"Ah, yes, Anees." Hamid stretched himself lazily and lay back, closing his eyes. "Once as I lay under a tree," he recited softly the traditional beginning of the folk tale: "as I closed my eyes, there suddenly appeared to me a young woman."

2

The men in the office might whisper rumours about the women in the zenana, but rumours did not flow in the opposite direction. Family men had no reason to mention staff to the women. That left Anees, the only daughter of the family and the youngest member of the zenana, to do what she could to satisfy her curiosity about how the others lived. Even that curiosity was not quite respectable, for she was tucked away in purdah.

The purdah system was practised by all classes of Muslims that could afford it and the practice had been adopted also by many Hindus, especially in the north. Women of the working classes had a freedom in the world that their more wealthy sisters could scarcely imagine. The system, with very little variation between households, indeed divided the sexes, for the only men beyond the age of seven who were allowed access to the women's quarters were close relatives: father, husband, brothers, sons. Sons brought their brides home to the family zenana, whereas a daughter was sent out of her paternal home to live with her husband and his family and adopt their ways.

If a woman went to visit another zenana, she first put on a burqa, the head to toe 'personal tent' which camouflaged her appearance. Beyond that, she went in a curtained vehicle; the net eye-piece of her burqa might as well have been made of muslin, for she saw nothing of the streets through which she passed. The world outside the zenana was a foreign country to her. At home, high walls secluded the garden where the ladies took the air, and the entrance to their section was obscured by heavy hangings and guarded by strong and reliable female servants.

Sealed off as it was from the outside world, the zenana was its own small world. Opening off it were the household godowns, the storehouses where supplies were kept. Non-perishables, enough to see the family from harvest to harvest: three kinds of rice, five kinds of lentils, varieties of chillies, spices for all tastes, alongside the achars and chutneys made from them. Then the products that, though long-lasting, would not survive for a whole year: ghee, rice flour, gram flour, brown and white wheat flours. One of the family women handed out supplies to the kitchen staff daily, according to that day's menu. All the cooking for the family was done in the kitchens attached to the zenana, where the women of the family took the responsibility of supervising the various aspects of it, each in her specialty.

Both the ladies and their servants worked at stitching the clothes for the family and embroidering them. Household linen, however, was hemmed by a tailor who sat cross-legged just outside a curtain, under which he pushed each piece as he finished with it. Also arriving on trays pushed under the curtain was jewellery being accumulated for Anees's dowry, or meant to be sent to the sons' brides at wedding time, or for the women already resident in the zenana.

"The jeweller has come." At that cry, all the women of the zenana, servants as well as family, scurried to the spot. Eager hands reached for the pieces—gold and gems and every kind of adornment to reflect the beauty of the young and substitute for it in the old.

"Ooh, what lovely bangles."

"How do you like this pendant, Sister-in-Law?"

"Arre yaar! Are we supposed to be poor, to wear a single stone?"

"Will you get me this gold chain, Amma? See how intricately woven it is."

"Very nice. It has enough strands to be properly heavy. Not like the thin one Hayat Begum wore at Kamal's wedding. Imagine! To shame a husband like that."

Like her brothers, married or single, Anees had her own apartment in one of the wings that made up the zenana of this sprawling house. The rooms were small, but each had a balcony; and it was mainly there, in the air and occasional breezes, that daily life was lived. There, most family members had breakfast when they were ready for it; at lunch time the men were generally off about their business or personal pursuits and the women were served, each on her own balcony, or perhaps socializing on someone else's. The entire family met in the main room of the zenana for dinner. Since mosquitoes arrived with the dusk, the cloth was spread under a vast netting.

Despite the constant pressure of these various activities, there was plenty of time to dream for anyone so inclined, and Anees had always been one of those. Hours passed as she sat strumming her veena or with needlework untouched in her lap. Her imagination, having little to feed on outside the daily routines of the zenana, was generally concerned with her life after the marriage her parents would arrange for her. She wondered what kind of man her father would select. Would he be young, an understudy to his father, until one day he would be summoned to Court to serve His Highness? Or perhaps he had already reached that eminence, the stoutness of his fine figure proclaiming the rich fare with which his table was daily set. In the prime of life, with nothing he needed, nothing left to wish for, he would find himself unexpectedly besotted with love for his new young wife and would pour jewels and silks into her lap.

Sometimes she saw herself, by contrast, as a tragic figure, persecuted by a cruel and relentless mother-in-law, whom she finally transformed by her competence, her patience under suffering, and the succession of grandsons with whom she annually presented her.

Often, practising her music, she sang one of her favourite songs, which began:
What sort of man will my parents find?
Will he be handsome? Will he be kind?
Will he be young and full of fun
Or still hard at work when the day should be done?
Will he do all the things that a girl adores?
Will he love beauty, say, "Especially yours"?

These last few weeks, however, she had ceased asking herself these questions, for her dreams were filled by a tall young man in an embroidered kurta. She had no business to have seen him. It had begun with an altercation with her elder sister-in-law.

"Anees, come away from there. What are you doing standing so long by the purdah screen? You're peeking at the mardana again. You should be ashamed."

Anees straightened the curtain she had twisted to give herself a peephole, carefully aligning the edges against the stone lattice-work. "Not at all, sister-in-law." Her voice was light and lilting, but the shrug of her shoulders spoke of willfulness underneath. "There's nothing wrong with peeking so long as we can't be seen."

"Purdah was not designed just to hide women away. It's meant to separate men and women, and therefore it works two ways. It's disgraceful for you to spy on the mardana."

"The men can come into the zenana whenever they wish and see what we're doing. I mean to spy on the mardana whenever I like. I'd advise you to do it too, Zeenat. You'd be much better off if you kept tabs on that husband of yours."

"How dare you speak of my husband that way!"

Again she shrugged. "He's been my brother for a long time. He had favourites among the dancing girls long before he married you, but you don't even know when they're in the house."

"Really! Anees! A young girl like you to talk such rubbish. Shame on you."

Drawing her pallu over her face as though to demonstrate proper modesty to her young sister-in-law, Zeenat turned and went back to her own balcony. Anees, deliberately defying the rigidly proper woman who was her fun-loving brother's wife, took another peek at the mardana. But the young man down there was now respectfully standing at attention while her father perused the papers he had brought; so, carefully smoothing the edge of the curtain, she went off to find another occupation for herself. Even as she walked away, her head was busy with excuses for passing that spot another day, to keep tabs on this handsome visitor.

Over the next few weeks Khatija, the ayah who had been Anees's wet nurse and who had taken care of her ever since, noticed the change in the girl's demeanour and guessed the reason. Then it became more than a guess. One day, while they were alone in the room, she asked, slowing the strokes with which she brushed the girl's hair to suit the tempo of her conversation, "Do you remember the ancient story you always liked, the one about the young woman on the street who became aware that there was a young man behind her?"

"Of course, Khatija. Tell it to me again," Anees coaxed, wriggling deliciously in anticipation and preparing to enjoy herself.

"Well, the girl became annoyed with his attentions and turned back and spoke to him."

"How bold!"

"Wasn't she! It was allowed in those days. She asked him, 'Why are you following me?' And what do you think he answered.

"He was in love with her because she was so beautiful."

"Exactly. She was in fact beautiful, but still she was not entirely pleased with this flattery. So she said to him, 'Why me? My sister is coming there, a little behind, and she is far more beautiful than I am.' So the young man turned back and the young woman went on her way."

"Was she disappointed?"

"Perhaps a little, but she knew it was no good. In a few moments the young man caught up with her again, all out of breath from hurrying and from his eagerness to speak to her. 'Why did you lie to me?' he demanded. 'You said she was beautiful, but she's old and ugly.'

"'You lied to me first,' the girl replied. 'You said you loved me, but you went running after the first girl you heard about who was more beautiful than I.'"

They laughed together, enjoying not only the story but the unspoken memory of all the other times they had shared it. Khatija took advantage of Anees's good humour to add, "Purdah is to protect young girls from men like that."

"I wish it wouldn't. The girl in the story could protect herself. So could I."

"You know nothing about men. It is better to be protected."

"No. I wish I were poor like you, so I wouldn't have to be shut up here in the zenana."

"Anees, pet, you would do far better to thank Allah for your blessings. Just remember how deceitful the man in the story was.

Besides, there is a young man who follows you down the street, like the girl in the story."

"What are you saying, Khatijabi? You know perfectly well I've never been in a street."

"Of course. Perhaps your shadow has, though, for this young man claims to have fallen in love with you."

Anees bounced up, unmindful of the way her movement had tangled the brush in her hair. "How do you know?"

"He bid me tell you he has written a poem about you."

"Who is he? Tell me!"

"No, that I won't do."

"It doesn't matter; never mind." Anees truly meant this, for her head was so full of the young man she had seen waiting for her father that she didn't for a moment doubt it was he. "But the poem. Tell me that."

"The moon-crowned beauty dare not wear Dhaka muslin."

"What does it mean? Does he mean me?"

"I think he must refer to katan, not Dhaka muslin. What man would know the difference? Katan is a cloth so fine they say it can be destroyed if struck by anything as strong as a moonbeam."

"Then I must be the moon-crowned beauty. How marvellous! No one has ever written a poem about me before."

"Nor shall again, I hope, at least until you are safely married. But even then, husbands are not much given to writing poems about their wives."

"Am I a beauty, Khatija?"

"Oh, child, to me you are more precious than any gem in the Treasury."

"Then, then you know, Khatija, to me this poem is a more precious gift than anything in the Treasury."

"And must be kept as securely locked away, remember. I should never have told you if I didn't think you could keep a secret. It would ruin us both if it were known."

True to her pledge, Anees never referred to this conversation again, nor did it occur to her to inquire how the man had come to make this extraordinary confession to the ayah. Nor would Khatija have told her, for she was ashamed and more than a little afraid of what she knew to be a piece of treachery.

Even if Hamidullah Sahib had not made a sizeable contribution to the dowry of her daughter in the village, she knew she would have succumbed to his blandishments. The dowry was needed for the daughter soon, if a husband was ever to be found for her. And with the father dead, it was a mother's duty to provide it, even though the child was really a stranger to her. Allah in his wisdom had provided a grandmother to look after her, just as he had given Khatija to Anees.

As her reflections brought her back to her young mistress, her face assumed the indulgent smile it always wore when she was thinking of Anees, so that everyone who knew her could read her thoughts.

In spite of her need to amass a dowry, Khatija would never have taken money for a service she had no intention of performing, but she had searched diligently for a way of telling Anees, that might make it a lesson rather than a temptation for the girl. In this she had clearly failed.

She was uncomfortably aware nowadays of what was going on in the young one's mind when she sat with a faraway look, making no progress with her handiwork. And she fussed even more than usual when the thali she had prepared with Anees's favourite delicacies was left with most of the food still on it. Both of them were thankful that Begum Rahmatullah was too preoccupied with preparations for the birth of a first grandchild to take any particular notice of her own daughter. But after that, what?

3

Throughout the morning, the calm of the zenana had give way to bursts of activity, as servants scurried about with jugs of hot water, with piles of clean linen, with cups of tea. As suddenly, silence enveloped them; women sat unmoving, heads cocked for sounds from the room where the senior daughter-in-law laboured to begin the next generation.

"What if it's a girl?" the young sweeper whispered. "Who would tell the Sahib?"

"Be still!" another snapped. "You might be responsible for such a tragedy."

"Nonsense," Khatija said. "There are six sons here. This family is not afraid of girls."

"But would they summon the Hijras if it's not a son?"

The Hijras were important to Hindus and Muslims alike when there was a birth in a family. Their community consisted of people who had been born male but, crushed by the burden of a physiology which felt alien to them, had found the strength, or the courage of despair, to castrate themselves, after which they dressed as women. Living communally, according to explicit traditions and standards of propriety, they earned their living by only one kind of work and that function was theirs exclusively: dancing and singing to bless the newborn. In the mornings, they put their drums on their shoulders and set out one by one to wander on the streets, seeking leads to houses where a birth had taken place.

Families who were poor, or who were greatly disappointed to have been given a girl child, often asked for the blessing immediately, by the single Hijra. People with more to celebrate and the means to do so sent for more dancers and paid in kind—food supplies and clothing, new or second hand, in amounts and quality varying with the prosperity and generosity of the family. For extra rejoicing, they added a few coins.

Before the women could pursue their speculation, a smiling Begum emerged from the room. "Send for my son," she directed. "He has a daughter. Then distribute sweets to everyone. Oh, and when the Hijra comes by, ask for the troupe to come."

"When will that be?"

"Let's see, ten days from now would be good, Insh'Allah (God willing). That will give us plenty of time to prepare the celebration."

"How many Hijras, Begum Sahiba?"

"Arre, I haven't thought of that. Well, seven's an auspicious number, since I have seven children. Yes, let's have seven Hijras."

The ceremony took place in the zenana courtyard, for no woman was in purdah in front of these sexless creatures whom even the Census Bureau did not know how to classify. The women bustled about the courtyard on last-minute errands of real or imagined urgency, while the infant, who was the ostensible cause of all the excitement, slept peacefully in the arms of her ayah. Anees, until then the youngest in the household, had never seen the Hijras and was determined not to miss a moment of the occasion. Accordingly, she established herself at the top of the steps and leaned against a pillar; there she had an unbroken view of all that went on.

When the cry went up that the Hijras had come, word was sent to the mardana, summoning the men, while Khatija went forward to the purdah gate to welcome the troupe. There, at her command, they paused, standing in a little knot while she appeared to count them and examine each face. As she did so, she spoke in a low voice to one of them. "You fool! You stupid fool! Pull your pallu over your face before one of the men recognizes you. Keep your head down and get out of here."

"But," Hamid in a borrowed sari, protested. "But..."

"Just go! I'll keep the others at the gate to hide your departure. My life won't be worth any more than yours, when it's known I let you in."

The spurious Hijra turned and crept away as ordered. But the failure of his scheme was less bitter than it might have been, for he had seen HER; his eyes had actually beheld her. She was a Chola bronze, the most exquisite sculpture in the world, standing there against the pillar; she would be so in his memory for a lifetime. It was almost too kind a fate. He was not sure he could have borne to be in her presence for the whole of the ceremony without somehow betraying himself. God is good.

Of all of them there, Anees was the only other person who noticed that one Hijra less had been admitted than had arrived and knew at once the reason for it. She stood throughout the ceremony with a flush on her cheek and an extraordinary brightness in her eye. If anyone had noticed, they would have attributed it to the excitement and thought nothing of it.

The Hijras' drums picked up their tempo, led by the eldest Hijra, whose thick lips and heavy jowls went unnoticed when one looked at her eyes, enormous in their ring of black kohl. Commanding eyes you couldn't look away from. The drums softened and the eyes directed you to look at the young Hijra, quite beautiful, who seemed absorbed in the words she was singing:

Now there's love on every face
Because you've joined the human race.
Love and joy make a fine alloy
That quirks of fate cannot destroy.
This is the life we wish for you.

The drums grew loud again, the dancing Hijras twirled and bowed, insisting:

Welcome, welcome, welcome. It's lovely to be alive.
Whenever the stars and moon are bright,
You'll be glad you're there in the silver light.
When strangers smile in a friendly way
And their eyes light up as if to say
Welcome, welcome, welcome, it's lovely to be alive.

As soon as the last blessing had been sung, the last reward distributed, the last cup of tea drunk and samosa or jalebi eaten, when everyone retired to their favourite resting place to relax and savour

22

again the satisfaction of a significant occasion well staged, Anees sent for Khatija.

"That was my poet, wasn't it?" she demanded without preliminaries.

"Whatever are you talking about?" Khatija replied without a change of expression, but she could not fool Anees.

"You know exactly what I mean: the eighth Hijra."

"Now you can't count. Everyone knows there were seven Hijras."

"Dancing, yes. But you sent one away first. He came to see me, didn't he? He took that risk for me."

At this Khatija's expression became solemn, even stern. "Now you calm down and listen carefully, Anees. I want you to put that young man out of your head. What you are doing is quite wrong and very unwise."

"Why?"

"He is a most unsuitable young man. Even if he came from a family that your father would accept, which he does not, I would be against him for you."

"But why? Why?"

"Because his actions, especially his action today, show that he is thoughtless, selfish and a gambler. Those are not qualities that make a good husband, and they are certainly not qualities I want to see in the man whom you marry. Now you will please forget him."

"How can you say he's selfish, when he risked his life for a glimpse of me?"

"Because he also risked mine, and if not your life, at least your chances of future happiness. It was a foolhardy thing to do." If Mahmoud had overheard this conversation, he would certainly have admired the accuracy in Khatija's assessment of his brother. She went on, "The only wise thing for you to do is to put him out of your head. I should never have mentioned him to you in the first place."

"But you just said he did risk his life for the love of me. Doesn't that deserve some recognition?"

"You are not the heroine of some romantic fable. You have to do what is proper."

23

"But Khatija, shouldn't he have at least a sign that I know about his daring? Some token to live with, if we are never to see one another, and not even to think of one another any more?" Anees was not used to being denied anything, and when she was forestalled, she made sure it was only momentarily.

It was on the tip of Khatija's tongue to administer a real scolding, but Anees's silent tears moved her more than sobs would have done. "Please, Khatija, just one more time do me this favour. Give him something—give him this." With a quick motion she pulled the sapphire from her finger and held it out. "Please, Khatijabi. If you do just this one more thing for me, I promise I will never mention him again. You asked me to forget him. If I know he has something from me, I promise to try not to think of him any more. I'll be a model of propriety from now on. I'll do everything you want me to. I swear it. Please, Khatijabi."

"I believe you. This is the end of this unhappy business, then." Taking the ring, she tied it into a corner of her sari, saying in a business-like tone, "Now go wash your face and pick up your needlework. Your mother will be wondering why you've accomplished so little lately."

4

It was now two months since Hamid had knocked over the fruit-seller's cart and there had been no subsequent incidents with damage for Mahmoud to repair in his methodical fashion. He was beginning to hope his brother had finally grown into his responsibilities. Fortunately, or unfortunately, he knew nothing about this latest escapade of Hamid's as a Hijra. If he had known, all their lives might have been different. But fate rarely takes account of such omissions, and simply proceeds with the consequences. Mahmoud could hope his brother was beginning to settle down but knew he could not count on it. Hamid's escapades were impulsive, so it was not possible to predict what he might do next.

At least not possible for Mahmoud, who lived by the rules. He believed the job of an eldest son and a head of the family was to protect their honour, support them financially, find good husbands for the sisters and educate the younger boys. You had to constantly think about The Others, which did not leave much room for thinking about yourself. No room, either, for anger, a selfish and demeaning emotion; that's just the way life is. And was for Mahmoud. So when Hamid got into trouble, he didn't even think of scolding him, but tried to train him, to help him learn the lessons from the latest problem.

Occasionally Mahmoud recognized a fleeting wish become a Magistrate, too, but when their father died, he had had to drop out of school to look for a paying position. They were not numerous in their area, but fortunately there was an opening in the tahsil office. The lowest unit of government, the office did the donkeywork of collecting taxes and also keeping records of land and other basic information, with none of the decision-making or the glamour of the higher levels, even the Districts.

Plodding, routine work. Mahmoud was a clerk there. It did not occur to him, as it did occasionally to someone in the District, that access to land records represented power, and that records could be manipulated. If that sort of thing ever occurred in the Hingaum District, it did not appear in Mahmoud's records.

Even Hamid seemed steadier lately. There had been no more disgraceful or upsetting episodes since he demolished the fruit-seller's cart. And he seemed to be taking his job seriously, for he had recently had a small increase in salary. Very comforting. Even while Hamid was donning his sari and assuming an illicit identity, Mahmoud reached for his own farm's red-tape bound file and recorded the value of the government's share of this year's crop. On that basis he could look forward to a satisfying return on their cotton. It had been a good year, with rain and sunshine in the right mixture. Bins in the zenana godown were comfortably full.

That meant he could probably afford to start looking for a husband for Tyaba. She was fifteen. And Razia trailed her by only a year. For them both, it was time.

5

For the weeks following the visit of the Hijras, life in the zenana resumed its peaceful routines, until on the eighteenth day the jeweller arrived, having heard of the birth of a girl. As soon as a daughter was born, prudent families began collecting jewellery for her dowry. The women made the most of such an occasion, engaging in widely ranging discussions before they finally agreed on selections. Although the jeweller came every year, and sometimes more often as special occasions such as weddings or births arose, the excitement was new every time. Smiles, laughter, eager expressions of approval or disapproval of this piece or that filled the air.

Zeenat alone contained her pleasure. She had never forgiven Anees for the remark about her husband's fondness for nautch girls and lost no opportunity to get even. "Amma," she suggested to her mother-in-law, "why don't you give the jeweller that sapphire that Anees sometimes wears in exchange for something more appropriate? It was probably having that bringer-of-bad-luck in the house that accounts for sister-in-law's not having a son."

"Nonsense, Zeenat," her mother-in-law answered with some asperity. "Baby Gulbai is not a piece of bad luck. I will not have her spoken of in that way. Still, perhaps you are right about the sapphire. I'll get Anees a nav ratan. Every woman needs those auspicious stones."

A nav ratan was a single piece, most often worn on the upper arm, containing a specific set of nine stones considered auspicious because of their association with particular planets. Although individual stones might bring good or bad luck, the combination was considered benevolent. Sapphire, associated with Saturn, was believed to bring only bad luck to most people and was often referred to as sheni, evil. It was one of the nine, however, and there its malevolence was thought to be overcome by the others.

Amma went on chatting to no one in particular, though the others quietened down out of respect. "Of course, my own favorite is a cat's eye, but I put a ruby in Anees's tilak because its planet is the sun, and she is the sunshine of my life. With a ruby on her forehead and the nine stones on her arm, she must be protected."

"Quite right. Very wise of you, Amma." The approbation rose like a gentle mist over the assemblage.

Zeenat was not to be done out of her moment. The most irritating thing for her was that Anees paid so little attention to her that she was scarcely aware of the pricks. "The sapphire, Amma?"

"Oh, yes. Where is the child? Ayah, go and bring Anees."

When Anees had seated herself beside her mother and heard the proposal for the exchange, she managed to ask calmly, "Need we, Mother? I like that sapphire; I'd like to keep it."

"Well," her mother hesitated, but then said in tones that allowed for no discussion, "I think we had better. Your father will be making arrangements for your marriage soon, and then we'll need some better jewellery for you. We can't do everything at the last moment. Go and bring it, please."

Anees salaamed quickly and rose to her feet. Some minutes later she was back. "I can't find it. I don't know where it is now."

Her mother frowned. "It must be hereabout somewhere. When did you last wear it?"

"Let me think. It must have been some time ago, I suppose."

"No, it was the day the Hijras were here," Zeenat put in. "I noticed it and thought it very indiscreet to tempt fate on the baby's special day."

"Did you? Then perhaps I did. I don't remember."

"It must be around here someplace," her mother repeated. "Have any of the rest of you seen it?"

"Perhaps the Hijras took it," one of the women suggested, but Zeenat sneered at the possibility, since Anees was wearing it at the time.

"We'll just have to look for it," her mother concluded. "Now get busy, all of you." By the following day it had still not been located and

Nawab Rahmatullah ordered his wife to examine the servants. "Why do you want to meddle in zenana matters?" she complained. "These are my women. You must let me manage them in my own way."

But he was adamant, with the result that everyone who had any access to the zenana at all was lined up in front of her, while she reviewed the facts about the disappearance of the ring and the obvious conclusion that it must have been stolen. Then she instructed them to disperse and reassemble in an hour. At that time, one by one, each would dip her clenched hand into a big pot full of water. Its narrow neck, wide enough only to permit a fist to enter, would preclude anyone's seeing what the hand did inside. If at the end of the parade the ring was found in the pot, that would be the end of the affair. If not, further steps would have to be taken.

The pot contained only water. So Begum Sahiba spoke again to the assembled company. "Allah, who gives us food for our bodies, also looks to the salvation of our souls. Therefore He has arranged that the guilty person, the one who stole this piece of jewellery or who knows about it, will not be able to swallow this food and will therefore convict herself. Please hold out your hands."

Into each outstretched palm she measured a large spoonful of raw rice, then directed them all to eat it. Her sharp eyes watched who hesitated, which hands trembled as they approached the mouth, how the jaws and the throats worked at the dry grains. With a despairing glance at her young mistress, Khatija let out a pitiful wail and sank at her mistress's feet. "Aiyo, Begum Sahiba, forgive your old slave," she gasped between sobs, when she had cleared her tongue of the clinging grains her dry mouth had not been able to cope with.

The Begum's eyes were wide with astonishment; "Khatija! Not you! You don't mean..."

"Aiyee, ji, I stole the accursed sheni."

"But why? Why you?"

"Oh, Begum Sahiba, you have children. You know how hard it is for a mother to deny her own flesh. My child, my only child, must have the clothes and kitchen things for her wedding now; otherwise the family who have spoken for her say they will not wait any longer. Who would marry her then? And how would I support a girl without a husband, when I am old? How could I not help my child, though wrongly?"

"And what became of the ring?" the mother asked coldly.

"Alas, I sold it and have sent the money away."

"Sold it to whom?"

"Only to a man on the street. It was dark; I couldn't see his face."

No one stirred when at this moment Anees flung herself to her knees and touched her mother's feet with her forehead. Tears washing her cheeks, she begged, "Forgive her, Ammijan. Give her the wretched ring! Say it was hers to dispose of as she liked."

"Hush, child, you know nothing about these matters." Her mother spoke sternly, but the tone was gentle, for Khatija's words had found their mark. How, indeed, could she watch this lovely child break her heart over a mere ornament?

The moment was interrupted by Zeenat, who had been standing unmoved by the drama unfolding in front of her. "At least the ayah's story can be checked," she said coldly. "The sahukars (jewellers; also acted as bankers) will know if any money has been sent to the village. Or even whether the ring was offered to one of them."

"Who invited you to speak?" the mother inquired in a voice of ice. "Should we spoil the good name of this house for a few rupees? You'd have our name bandied about the bazaars on the lips of every jewellery merchant who wanted a laugh. Keep your foolish counsel to yourself and let wiser heads handle this matter. You may go to your room."

Zeenat bowed and left; as she did so, she threw Anees a glance which said clearly that the score remained to be evened.

"Hear me, Ammijan," Anees continued her entreaty. "We'll never find another servant so faithful to us as Khatija. We need her. Now that the sheni is out of the house, perhaps the bad luck will go with it. All that's left is for you to forgive her."

"We cannot have a thief in the house, Anees, even if the sheni she stole visits the ill-fortune on herself. Come, get up. It is always sad when a trust is broken, but it must be dealt with." Turning to Khatija, she said, "I have decided. You will return to your village. Go tomorrow morning. Your wages will be sent there regularly, for it is no part of our intention that you should starve. But you are never to come here or have anything to do with this family again."

Khatija stood up, subduing her sobs but her tears were beyond her powers of control. "In the name of Allah the Merciful," she whispered, "may I take leave of Aneesbibi?"

"Since she is responsible for your sentence, it is fitting. Go to her when you have both washed your faces and said your prayers."

When the ayah came into the room, Anees threw herself into her arms. "Oh, Khatijabi, I am so sorry."

"Hush, child. You heard what I said to your mother."

"But I am so sorely punished! What shall I do without you, Khatijabi?"

"You will do your duty and be a credit to me, Insh'Allah," the ayah replied with some of her old asperity. Then her voice softened. "Still, my heart aches, for now they will marry you and I shall not be here to prepare the bride, or to go with you to your husband's home." She wiped away a tear with the corner of her sari.

"When I am married and in my husband's home, I shall certainly send for you."

"Nonsense, my darling. If you have still not learned to obey your mother, how will you ever get along with a mother-in-law? There's fire in you, Anees, and that may be good, though most people think it has no place in a woman's make-up. But you must make sure it's not you who gets burned."

And so they parted. But one person was still not satisfied with the outcome of the affair, even days later. "Mark my words, that sister of yours knows more about this than she's admitting," Zeenat prophesied darkly to her husband, who finally flared up at her.

"Zeenat, will you please stop it! I cannot tell you how angry my father will be if you make any more trouble for Anees. Whatever she may have done, if anything at all, or whatever she may know, she is sufficiently punished by losing Khatija. You see how she is looking these days."

"You'd be suspicious too if you had seen her as often as I have misusing the purdah by peeking."

"Silence! I've heard enough of this subject, I tell you!"

31

But Zeenat was not yet through. Two days later she returned to the attack. "I told you there was more to the story," she asserted to her husband, not even trying to keep the triumph out of her voice. "My woman says her husband saw Khatija talking in the bazaar with one Hamidullah, who is said to be your father's clerk."

Although Rahim rejected his wife's bit of news as gossip, he was troubled by it and finally decided it should be looked into. But he shrank from doing so, for an occasional game of snooker was the limit of his competitive spirit and he abhorred conflict. Accordingly, he dropped a hint to the Captain of the Nawab's Guard to keep an ear out for any such story. Unlike the Nawab's son, the Captain had no scruples at all about confrontation.

6

Mahmoud breathed a deep sigh as he stripped for his evening bath. Ah, home. Through for another day with that wretched tahsil office. Day after day, same thing with the same records. Unless, of course, the Tahsildar tells me to use two lengths of red tape instead of one. Work almost as boring as he is. What a chatterbox. His tongue must have the strength of an elephant, with all the exercise he gives it. I'd quit, if I weren't responsible for this family. Ah, well. No more today.

In the bath, the little melody he hummed became a burble as he ladled another dipper of water over his head. Along with the lather, fatigue and tension sluiced off. He dried himself quickly, then oiled his hair. Very cooling, that. When he had pulled on a crisp, fresh pyjama and kurta—white for the evening, all white with shadow embroidery—he was ready for the six o'clock prayer. Something in a man wants doors, wants to shut out whatever he's just left in his life, so it can't invade the next part. How wise the Holy Prophet was to include evening prayer in the list. I've done my job; the prayer closes that for the night. Now the evening is all mine.

Afterward, filled with peace, he stretched out his legs and picked up a book, noticing as he did so that the servant had set a glass of juice beside it. He never opened the book. A faint strain of music told him that Tyaba, the musical sister, was playing her sarod. She was fifteen; it was time to think of getting her married. Next year at the latest; every year after that she would be considered less marriageable. He hoped he had enough to provide for her properly, though he had to think of Razia, too, in that regard. She would be ready only a year after Tyaba. They had done all right by Nur Jehan, though Father was still alive and earning when she was married. That was a happy marriage; perhaps her husband could help find someone appropriate for the younger sisters. He must write to him.

His thoughts were abruptly interrupted when the door banged open without a knock. Mahmoud stiffened as his younger brother barged into the room with a stranger on either side of him. Their turbans and sashes identified them as belonging to the Nawab Rahmatullah's guard.

"Brother," Hamid quavered, "these two men say that I have stolen a ring from the Nawab."

"Oh?" Not even the Captain of the Guard could have doubted that the surprise in Mahmoud's voice was genuine. "What ring is that?"

Silently Hamid handed him a sapphire. Mahmoud glanced at it only briefly. He didn't dare take too long, as though seeing the ring for the first time (though he was), but had to keep it long enough to think up a story that might clear Hamid. No other possible action crossed his mind; no time to wonder what really had happened. His only reality was the need to protect his brother. There was a saying that a lie told so that good may result is preferable to truth from which harm may come. If that influenced him, he was not conscious of it as he formulated the first lie of his life. When he handed the ring back, the Captain intercepted it.

"Sorry," Mahmoud said evenly, "he couldn't possibly have stolen it, even if he would do such a thing, which I deny. I gave it to him myself." Mahmoud, surprised at the glibness with which the lie slipped from his tongue, wondered whether the others had noticed it. Apparently the Captain had not, for he nodded and made as though to turn away; but then he stopped himself. "May I ask where you got it?"

Mahmoud's hesitation lasted only a beat; then he shrugged. "I bought it from a man in the street. You're missing one?"

"One is missing from the zenana and the Nawab Sahib doesn't take kindly to the loss. How much did you pay for this, by the way?"

Mahmoud felt his stomach turn over. He knew nothing of the value of jewellery, and in any event he hadn't thought it wise to examine the ring too carefully. All he remembered was a moderate-sized stone flanked by small diamonds. What would such a thing be worth, he wondered. "Fifty rupees, as far as I remember."

"You can't mean it. No one would sell a ring like this for only fifty rupees."

"The man told me his father was dying and he had to raise some money quickly to go to him. All he wanted was his train fare and a bit of ready cash. Why should I doubt him?"

"We'll find out," a grim captain promised as he pulled Mahmoud to his feet and marched him off to the jail. Hamid tagged after them, drowning the reality in a flood of protests and declarations of innocence; neither Mahmoud nor the guard spoke. At the gate, Hamid was turned back.

During the week Mahmoud spent in the jail, Hamid brought him food and clean clothes every day, but was repeatedly denied the opportunity to talk to him. The barrister whom he consulted remembered the Old Magistrate, as Mahmoud's father was often called, with respect. Since Mahmoud had never been in trouble before, the barrister assured Hamid that his brother would be let off on the strength of the family's reputation.

At the trial, Mahmoud stood in the dock erect, shoulders square, eyes unwaveringly on the magistrate. Only an occasional tightening of the jaw muscles betrayed anxiety. With a clean-shaven face that just missed being handsome, and dressed in neat, simple pyjama kurta, he looked a respectable young man. Out of place there.

The magistrate never looked at him. Not a glance. For the full five minutes the trial lasted, he kept his eyes on the papers he was fingering. Abruptly, he reached for his gavel and interrupted the proceedings. "Motion denied. Anyone knows that if a sapphire is offered for only fifty rupees, it must be stolen. And to buy stolen goods is an offence against the law, the community, and Nawab Sahib himself. One year simple imprisonment." This time he banged the gavel with finality.

Hamid had expected to take his brother home with him when the trial was over. Hearing the abrupt and dreadful verdict, he buried his face in his hands and wept. When he looked up, Mahmoud was gone, the courtroom empty. Hamid dashed outside, but finding no one there, rushed back to collar the remaining guard. Asked for information as to Mahmoud's whereabouts, he only shrugged, "No way I could know that."

"Khandipur jail?"

"Not likely. That's for pre-trials. No, he'll be on his way to prison somewhere."

Similarly the magistrate, whom Hamidullah waited for and accosted as he emerged from his chambers, looked sternly at the inquirer as he declared, "Young man, once a criminal leaves my court, I have nothing more to do with him."

7

A shaken Mahmoud had been hustled from the courtroom. Returned to the jail, he was taken directly to the Chief Warden, who allowed a slight note of surprise to inflect his voice. "So you're back. Guilty, eh?"

"Not guilty, convicted," the prisoner corrected him.

The guard supplied the information. "One year. Simple."

"Well, so where shall we send him for the year?" The Warden looked at him steadily, taking in the matter-of-fact tone, the posture neither aggressive nor obsequious, the well-modulated voice. "I don't think he's going to cause any trouble. Take him to Benur."

This was more of a kindness than Mahmoud could know, for Benur was the place to which prisoners with good records were transferred for the final period of their sentence. After the harshness of their previous places of incarceration, this was a place of hope. To Mahmoud, who had no reason to know one prison from another, any one of them was a place of doom.

Dipping his pen into the brass inkwell, the Warden wrote, pronouncing each word under his breath as he created it on the paper, "26 October 1879. Kotwal's Jail, Khandipur. Prisoner Sayed Mahmoud is remanded to Benur Prison for one year simple imprisonment, by order of Magistrate Barkat Hussain. Signed, Madan Kumar, Chief Warden." Carefully he folded the paper into an intricate little wad and handed it to the guard, then waved them off.

Without further ceremony, the guard marched Mahmoud out to a waiting tonga and shoved him into it. Not unkindly: the big step up was awkward for a passenger in handcuffs. While he waited for the guard and the driver to get in, Mahmoud looked around again for Hamidullah. In vain. The driver clucked to his pony and flipped the reins, the tonga jerked slightly as it adjusted to the weight of the two rear-facing passengers, and the wheels began to turn.

Mahmoud settled into his seat facing the jail and then, as the tonga turned into the street and the pony hit his stride, the receding scene. Five hours to Benur, they said. Mentally, he could not yet leave Khandipur. His thoughts accompanied his brother home with the news. They followed Hamid through the streets as he walked with increasingly reluctant steps back to the house where the assembled family waited. The shock, the disappointment on their faces as they saw him return alone. Poor Hamid; telling them about the sentence would be the most difficult thing he had ever done.

Mahmoud's own shoulders bent under the blow this would be to his mother. He waited, hoping to see resignation on her features. And the sisters. Perhaps they would feel he had robbed them of any hope of finding proper husbands. Would they be angry with him? Only angry, not pitying, too? Unable to let those dear faces go, he strained to hold on to the last sight of Khandipur as it turned golden through the sun on the dust motes in the air.

By this time the tonga had left the town well behind. As it crested a slight rise to the west, through the rich agricultural lands on which the area's prosperity depended, Mahmoud peered into the distance, hoping to get a glimpse of their small family farm. Try as he might, however, it was only in imagination that he could scan those neat fields and the bouquets of women working there, brightly coloured saris pulled between their legs and tucked into the waistband to keep them out of the way. With a twinge, he hoped Hamid would remember to pay them.

The tonga swerved abruptly to avoid a big pothole; Mahmoud fell against the guard's shoulder, then struggled to right himself as his manacled hands found nothing to grasp. Erect once more, he sat rigidly, anticipating the guard's anger. The guard ignored him. They had sat thus, side by side but each alone, for nearly two hours when the driver stopped at a roadside stand for tea. All three men got out to stretch their limbs.

On the way once again, Mahmoud closed his aching eyes against the dust and glare and tried to relax, to let his body go with the bouncing and jolting. As soon as he shut out the sights that might have distracted him, however, his mind was suffused with the anguish of the past week. Like sliding down a funnel, he could not stop himself from replaying the events. They had begun on the evening of a routine day. There he sat, sipping a glass of fruit juice, when his younger brother had come in accompanied by two strangers.

From that encounter to this moment everything still seemed unreal. The magistrate, who owed his appointment to the Nawab, must have thought it prudent not to enquire too punctiliously into the evidence. The man was clearly prejudiced, obviously uninterested in the circumstances, contemptuously indifferent to Mahmoud's reputation for uprightness. And they call that justice?

Once more the tonga stopped at a tea stall. "Nearly there now," the driver muttered as he watered his pony. "Never mind, old fellow," he went on, patting his animal. "It's a long way, but it means we'll eat for a few days, you and I." Then, to his passengers, "Let's go."

As they resumed the jolting ride, Mahmoud's mind was busy again with the events that had brought him here. How could he have known the flaw in his story? Fifty rupees was a lot of money and he had never had any to spend on jewellery. Whatever ornaments were put away for the girls' marriages had been bought by his mother; he had never looked at them. No way he could have known the value of a ring. All he had meant to do was to protect his brother. That was his duty; love, yes, but duty was paramount. There were certainly no thieves to spoil the family honour, but now he had spoiled it anyway; a family member with a prison record—inconceivable until now.

For what? Hamid couldn't have stolen the ring. Could he? Certainly not, out of the question. But hang it all, why couldn't Hamid have said how he acquired it? How could he let his elder brother go to prison without even attempting an explanation, not to mention an apology? Not that it mattered now. Too late. Prison changed everything.

Prison! His thoughts gave him no respite. How would he ever get through this year? At least it wasn't rigorous imprisonment; men sentenced to that were shackled and made to work on the rock piles. He would never have survived that, for shame as much as for the hardship. Shame enough being tried and sentenced.

He closed his eyes, wearied by the bleakness of his thoughts. Some time later, he opened them again to a very different landscape: a dry and unproductive area, truly a wasteland. Though he saw neither houses nor bazaars, men trudged along the road, sometimes driving a bony water buffalo or lackadaisical goats. He didn't see how people could exist in this dreariness. Presently they passed a high wall, topped by broken glass. With one final lurch, the tonga stopped at an iron gate. Shouts summoned a guard on the inside, who then had to run for keys to unlock the three padlocks and remove the chains that secured it.

Once inside, the gate had barely stopped clanging when the guard ordered Mahmoud to get out and led him down a neatly-raked gravel path, past a series of one-storey buildings with solid doors and only small high windows. Near what must have been the centre of the compound, the guard pushed him through an open door into a small room. The man at the desk, clearly trying to look busy, seemed to be hunting for more papers to shuffle through. Then, perhaps eager to get home for his evening meal, the warden wasted no more time. Sparing only a glance for the order which the guard handed him and none for the man himself, he ordered curtly, "Number nine, solitary block."

Mahmoud protested. "Solitary confinement was not part of my sentence. Only simple imprisonment."

"Everyone starts there," the warden grunted. At his nod, the guard removed the manacles and gave the prisoner a shove towards the exit. Seconds later, he was locked into a small dark cell. Light that filtered through the dirt on a small, high window allowed him to see the only furnishings, a straw mat on the floor and a bucket in the corner. At that moment, the starch that had held him up during his week in the Khandipur jail, the full five minutes of trial time, and the trip to Benur prison dissolved and he collapsed onto the floor in a shuddering heap. Perhaps God knew how long he lay there; certainly Mahmoud did not, nor the uncaring guard.

As awareness of his position came flooding back, misery claimed him. Sitting amid the ruin of his life, he rocked back and forth, feeling only pain, the pain of disgrace, the pain of separation, the pain of disillusion with the brother whom he had loved and trained and envied for his carefree spirit, the pain of being a nobody—no family, no status, no job, no future.

Only on the third day did the despair begin to subside, pushed to the background by an emotion whose expression was new to him, for he had been trained not to show anger. Now that he was alone, anger rose in him like a vomit: he had to spit it out. Hamid! How could he do this to me? Me! I've done so much for him, taken the lectures and the punishments for all his escapades. Why wasn't he man enough to take this one himself! That incompetent magistrate! Destroyed my life as casually as he squashed an ant. The Nawab, who is he to make assumptions he knew nothing about? What does fate have against me, that I'm incarcerated for a crime I didn't commit? What right has this brutish guard to shove me around—me, Sayed Mahmoud, son of a magistrate!

Agitation pulled him to his feet, shouting, "You liars! Frauds! How dare you call me thief? Honourable, that's me. More than you. Any of you. Magistrate included. I never took a bribe in my life. Never gave one, either. No profit for you here, you, you, you bastards!" As he shouted, the door opened and the guard set down the dried-leaf plate onto which his food had been ladled. Mahmoud picked it up just in time to hurl it over the guard's shoulder as the door closed.

Through the door, the guard snarled his reaction, "Rough, eh? More time right here, that's what you'll get for that. More solo-bolo." His coarse laugh rasped along Mahmoud's nerve endings and sobered him.

Relieved also by his outburst, he sat down on the mat to clear his head and to consider what he must do. Clearly, anger was not useful. If he should allow himself to think about his mother and the brothers and sisters for whom he was responsible, he would be consumed by longing, worry, sorrow. All ineffectual, since he could do nothing from here. Or ever, probably. And thinking about what this prison sentence would mean for his job and his future life, that way lay despair. Gradually he worked it out: the only way to survive this year would be to have no feelings at all. No anger, no self-pity, no longing, no hope; just do whatever it might take to get through.

The only light in the cell came from the narrow window high up under the ceiling. By turning his head to look up and over his shoulder, he could just see the patch of sky. He sat staring at it now, steeling himself to feel no response. His prison life had begun.

8

His brother's trial and the confrontation with the family on his return from the court had been almost more than Hamid could bear. Three days he had sat in his room, face to the wall. Three days alone, food refused, company refused, comfort refused. Oh, Mahmoudbhai, forgive me, his anguished thoughts ran. Forgive me. What can I do? How can I say I'm sorry for ruining your life? His mind projected on the wall the images of all those who had been involved in this disaster that had engulfed his family: Anees, his Goddess of Beauty; the Nawab's guard, cold and incredulous; the family, gathered to await his return from the courtroom, each comprehending and adjusting in their own fashion to the verdict that he had to report; his mother's "My son!" under her breath and her silent tears.

The images continued further back, back to the pranks of his childhood. Back to Mahmoud's efforts to protect him from their consequences and to help him understand that they must cease. Well, Mahmoud was right; from now on he must take life more seriously and try to live up to his new responsibilities.

On the fourth day his mother took a hand. "What is this self-indulgence, Hamidullah?" she demanded, bursting into his room without preliminaries. "How can you sit there just staring at the wall all these days?"

Without turning to look at her, Hamidullah asked in a flat tone that sounded curiously unreal, even to himself, "What do you think Mahmoudbhai has to stare at?"

If in her preoccupation she even heard the impertinence, she chose to overlook it. "It's just as well that you remember Mahmoud. In his place, you are now head of the family. Have you forgotten that that gives you responsibilities?" Then with a passion he had not known she possessed, she burst out, "Oh, Hamidbeta, may you be worthy of them!" She flung herself out of the room as unceremoniously as she had entered it.

Shaken by his mother's impassioned plea, Hamid determined to prove he had really learnt from his brother's mentoring. He would take Mahmoud's lessons as the guide to all his conduct. What he could not see was where to begin, and for a time he wallowed in a suspended state. It was the summons from the Nawab Rahmatullah an hour later that bestirred him. When he heard it, the enormity of the family's misfortune swept over him again, knowing that it had cost him his position in the Nawab's office and that an outside income was essential for them.

Loath as he was to meet his employer, he moved without thought to splash a little water on his face and go. An inadvertent movement, however, showed him his haggard face in the mirror. Grabbing his razor, he shook it at his reflection, whispering, "Don't you dare! Don't you show this face outside your room. The world be dammed; this family isn't finished yet."

The Nawab sat at his low desk behind a pile of ledgers from which he looked up immediately when Hamid was announced. His greeting was perfunctory, neither pleasant nor angry. "You understand, Hamidullah," he plunged directly into his message, "that we cannot have you in this office any longer. With your brother's conviction, it is impossible that any of your family should have even the most distant connection here." Hamidullah bowed his head and remained silent. "You will leave at once. If you have any personal belongings in the office, you may collect them on your way out."

Hamid was torn between a need to apologize to his employer and a sense that he must not compound his betrayal of Mahmoud by the implication that his brother was truly guilty as charged. His hesitant stammering was cut short by the Nawab.

"Since you yourself were not implicated in your brother's crime, Hamidullah," he continued, allowing himself to sound avuncular, "I have decided to award you severance pay, ex gratia. Take this envelope, and may you have better luck in the future." With that, Nawab Rahmatullah took up the papers on his desk and Hamid salaamed his departure.

At home, he merely confirmed that he had been dismissed but that the Nawab had provided enough exit pay so that they need not worry until a new source of income had been found. For himself, worry certainly did not describe what was going on in his mind. On opening the envelope, he had found a sum so liberal that it bespoke not only the regard for his own work but also the Nawab's known generosity once his ends had been achieved.

For two more days Hamid stayed at home, but this time not staring at the walls. He was busy scanning the scene. Aware that the Tahsil office would certainly not offer him Mahmoud's now vacant position, he was concerned to evaluate even remote possibilities as options. Paying positions were not numerous in Khandipur.

One circumstance gave him a lead. The family had for generations owned a small farm from which came the rice and lentils that stocked their larder from harvest to harvest. Apart from that, they grew cotton for a cash crop and it was this extra bit of income that provided for education and small luxuries. Hamidullah had never paid much attention to how this was managed. He knew only that the Tahsil office collected the government's share of the crop from the ryots, those sharecropping peasant farmers who did the actual work. After the owner had also claimed his portion, the ryots were free to sell the balance for what they could get.

As a magistrate, their father had had access to the Tahsil records and could extrapolate from the government's share what his own should be. He was known to be a fair landlord: he demanded no more than his share and remitted even that when drought seized the land and baked the life out of it. Accordingly, his people in turn dealt fairly with him. The association had proceeded peacefully over the years, undisturbed when Mahmoud had succeeded to it.

On his first venture out of the house, Hamid went to the Tahsil office. There a clerk, who had been friendly with his brother and who was not averse to receiving a small gift, gave him access to the records not only of his family's farm but also of others in the district. This research confirmed that cotton was the major cash crop of the area but that the growers received very little profit from their labour.

Gradually Hamid formulated a way of using this information. The next few days he made the rounds of the ryots to sound them out about his idea; not only his own ryots but also those whose lands belonged to other local owners or to absentee landlords. His next step was a trip to Nagpur and then to Bombay, to trace the channels through which raw cotton passed and establish contacts with the dealers who sold it to the expanding mills in Ahmedabad, or to the great and hungry textile industry in Manchester.

From this exploratory trip, he returned to the growers he had previously visited and negotiated a pledge to allow him to handle the sales of their cotton crop. It was not easy. Ryots, as always, were suspicious of any person not one of their own and voiced their assumption that he meant to cheat them, as in their experience outsiders, especially money lenders, had always done.

The family reputation with his own ryots helped. "I am not a moneylender," Hamid repeated, wondering how many times he had said this in the past few days. Moneylenders were notorious for the exorbitant rates of interest they charged, so that the amount owed grew from month to month, while the debt passed to the heirs on the death of the borrower. Mesmerized by the urgent needs of the moment, poor people willingly shackled themselves in this way.

Emphasizing the contrast, Hamid declared that, far from lending money, he was offering to buy their crops for a higher price than they could get themselves. The dealers they were accustomed to were not from this district but outsiders. "Why should they care whether your family starves or not?" Hamid challenged. "My family have lived here all our lives and our fathers and grandfathers before us."

One of his listeners nodded and commented to his neighbours on the old Magistrate's incorruptibility. When a young man, a relative newcomer, objected that every official could be bribed, those around him pitched in with their own stories of appreciation for the old Magistrate, comparing him with others less fair than he.

Unperturbed by this murmur, Hamidullah ploughed on. "We, in my family, know that our prosperity depends on the prosperity of you who raise the cash crops here. You, Rajkumar, or you and your sons, Venktappa, and all the others in the district. So here's what I'm proposing. I will buy your entire share of the cotton crop as you harvest it. No more waiting for it to be sold and paid for and the money returned to you at someone else's convenience."

"Entire crop, you say," one ryot objected, "but we also need some for our families to use. We can't pay the price they demand in the market."

"Exactly. You may keep one maund for your own use, for your family to spin and weave for yourselves. But if you keep back any more than those eighty pounds, or if you sell your own maund, then you and I will have done business for the last time. In all the years to come, those who trusted me will laugh at you for passing up such a profitable arrangement."

The Hamidullah charm was persuasive but what really convinced them was his money: not money to look at and yearn for, but to weigh in the hand, to rub between the fingers, to know that the thin time in the weeks before the harvest, when last year's profits were gone and families went hungry waiting for the maturing and sale of this year's crop, that time would be less thin. He paid them now for one third of their crop and at the slightly higher rate he had spoken of. They must notify him when they started their picking and he would pay the balance when the crop was delivered to him.

Hamid was satisfied. It was a start.

9

Satisfied with his first three weeks since Mahmoud's conviction, but still churning within himself, Hamid spent the evening in the zenana. Across the red cement floors of the large common room were scattered bright oriental rugs, some of them so worn their warp showed through the pattern, but with colours still not faded by years of wear. Pillows and bolsters lay always within arm's reach. Variations in their embroidery identified those that had been made by small girls just learning and others that showed the growing skill of the more mature young women. Hangings, embroidered or appliquéd, kept the eyes focused well below the high ceilings, while narrow windows just below those ceilings let out the heat and helped keep the air moving. Depending on their activities of the moment, the occupants either sat cross-legged or stretched out against the bolsters. It was a comfortable, unpretentious room and Hamid thought of it as a refuge where he could be at ease.

All the women wore old cotton saris, their colours nearly washed out. Their hair was done in loose braids allowed to hang down their back. The effect was of a house of mourning. When their mother went to bed, Hamid and the girls started a game of pachisi. It was lackadaisical, as though they were trying with only superficial success to distract themselves from their sorrow. "Must be your turn, Razia." Hamid nudged her gently.

"Is it? Sorry. No, I think it's Tyaba's."

"Right." She threw the dice but before moving her piece, looked up at the others. "Do you remember the time one of our father's cases took him to the mountains and we all went along for a holiday?"

"Oh, yes, and how frightened we were when Mahmoudbhai cut his foot." At the mention of their brother, silence engulfed them. Then all three began talking at once. It was as though they had been embarrassed

47

to mention Mahmoud and uncertain whether doing so might increase their listener's pain, but now that his name had been pronounced, they were freed to speak of him: what it must be like for him, how unfair of the magistrate not to tell them where he was, how they missed him.

Hamid joined in but could not resist reiterating how guilty he felt for his part in Mahmoud's fate. Both Tyaba and Razia assured him they could see nothing to blame him for, at the same time reasserting their faith in the integrity and good intention of bhaiya, elder brother.

In the midst of this sharing of their feelings, Razia held up her hand. "Hush, what was that?" She cocked her head towards the window. This time they all heard the knocking at the door. "Who could it be at this hour?"

Hamid stood up. "The servants have all gone to bed. I'd better go see what it is." Downstairs he unlatched the door and opened it cautiously. "Yes?"

The man standing there was a stranger to him, although his dhoti and the machete he carried proclaimed him a ryot. "Hamidullah Sahib? Forgive me that I bring you bad news."

"Oh? What's that?"

"Narasimha came to our village today. He is munshi for Anwarullah Sahib. You know his lands." A munshi was a clerk, but something more than that, too; he was in a position to manipulate papers and accounts if he so wished and if he was that kind of person. Hamid didn't know Narasimha, but the visitor's mention of bad news in the same breath as the name was a tip-off. "Narasimha has always sold the cotton from Anwarullah Sahib's ryots and a few more," the stranger went on, "and he makes a trifle on it."

"So he was threatening you if you deal with me instead?"

"Jihah (yes, sir). We would like to believe you, but he says you will take our cotton and give us short weight. He has dealt with the brokers so many years, he knows their tricks."

Hamid's reply was a verbal shrug. "His word against mine, as to honesty. So you choose to believe him?"

"Maybe not believe, Sahib. But he has come with his followers. They may be honest friends, though they look like goondas; how can

48

we tell? He says he will force us off the lands if we deal with you. I am newly married. If we lose our lands, how can I support a wife? The others are also worried."

"And so you are afraid of him."

"Jihah. They might even have attacked me if he had known I was coming here to speak to you."

"Then why did you come?" Hamid was intrigued by this young man who was not afraid to admit that he was frightened, yet came.

"If I refuse, won't my mother-in-law be angry with me? She says you will know how to deal with Narasimha. She promises that. Can she promise, Sahib?"

"May I know her good name?"

"She is called Khatija."

At the sound, Hamidullah's face twisted in a grimace, which he mastered and replied quietly, "She can promise. I will be there tomorrow."

The next morning, good as his word, Hamid showed up at the village. Two groups of men stood a little apart from each other but tension was a cord that bound them together. On both sides, some carried their machetes as though called from the fields, some held simple sticks and some were turning rocks over with their feet, keeping contact. From among the strangers, one man detached himself and swaggered over to stand face to face with Hamidullah, too close for courtesy.

"Narasimha," Hamid said.

"Hah." The lack of the respectful ji, sir, was not lost on Hamid.

"I heard you had come."

"Hah."

"Did I understand rightly that you have business with me?"

"Only to tell you to stay out of my business."

"Which is...?"

"To sell the cotton crops from around here. I do that." There was no mistaking the menace in Narasimha's voice. "Do you understand? Others are not welcome to shove their way in."

"I understand you work for Anwarullah Sahib," Hamid ignored the threat and started to shift the battle to ground of his choice. He turned. "Oh, Krishna, can you organize some tea for our guests?" he called to a man in the local camp. Then he turned back to Narasimha. "Come. You and I have some talking to do. Let us ask Khatija, Elder Sister, to give us tea while we occupy her charpoy."

Hamid strode off to a cottage where Khatija was standing in the doorway. Narasimha ran two steps, then apparently aware that this looked as though he were following Hamid, slowed down to a defiantly leisurely pace. When Khatija had poured tea for them and retired, and they were settled on the charpoy that stood outside her cottage, Hamid got down to business. "We can discuss this like reasonable people. We have some things in common, you and I. Neither of us wants to lose face with our men here, and neither of us wants to lose the chance to make money. Am I right, Narasimha?"

"Hah." Although he still used the abrupt syllable without the courteous ji or sahib with it, his tone was less belligerent.

"So to that extent, we share the same aims. Now you, I take it, are accustomed to selling the cotton crop from Anwarullah Sahib's lands."

"And if I am?"

"I want to ask you something. Tell me, this is easy money, isn't it? It doesn't take much effort to sell raw cotton. Am I right?" Hamid's tone was earnest, that of a real novice seeking advice from a pro.

"Does God give us reward without effort? And tedious effort for small reward, too."

"How 'tedious'? You just take the cotton to Bombay, na?"

"Who can afford the trip to Bombay? The Nagpur merchants get the crop from here. And very little they pay, too. Don't delude yourself; nobody gets rich off them." From his tone, Narasimha might as well have spat.

"So it's a lot of work to gain a small profit. But what if you could get that same profit without any effort on your part?"

"Save your breath, newcomer. I have time only for those who talk sense."

"Profit that falls into your lap. You don't even have to reach up and pluck it. Most people just dream of something like that. And next year perhaps even higher income, some small increment, at any rate."

"How?"

"I'll buy the crop out of the field, directly from the ryots, and then pay you as much profit as you got per maund for what you handled last year. In return, you will instruct your people, including Anwarullah's ryots, to deal fairly with me. And see that they do."

"How do I know you will give a proper return?"

Hamidullah laughed. "I don't blame you for being suspicious of me." He suggested that Narasimha inquire from anyone in the village about his family's reputation and pointed out how ready the local ryots were to sign on with him. He went beyond that to admit that he was interested in establishing a long-term business, not just in the first year's profits. That would depend on relationships of mutual trust between him and the ryots as well as the other people he would deal with. So he and Narasimha would have to deal fairly with one another in order for either of them to make a profit.

Narasimha nodded and sat quietly as though thinking this over, but then he came up with another objection. "I couldn't risk it, even if I were interested, which I'm not. If I should agree with you in this way, how could I hold my men? They also would not believe you and would say I'd been hoodwinked."

Hamidullah appeared to think about that for a moment. He looked down, looked into the distance, pulled his earlobe. "I'll tell you what," he exclaimed. From a pocket he produced a stack of one-rupee notes, with which he beat out the emphasis on his words. "Here is fifty rupees. Consider it an advance on this year's sale. You can wave it in their faces and tell them anything you like, so long as you stick to our bargain."

"Achcha. So be it." He reached for the money.

"Thank you, Khatijamma," Hamidullah called into the house as they rose to go. "You have been very helpful."

"Hah," Narasimha grunted. "I agree with what my partner just said."

On the road once more, Hamidullah found that the same charm worked for him as he spoke again with the buyers and exporters, this time negotiating firm agreements. He returned from his trip sufficiently confident of his future to have stationery printed headed, "S. Hamidullah, Cotton Broker".

10

After some days of isolation—Mahmoud had ceased to count—
he was taken from solitary confinement and shoved into another cell.
His first impression, after the narrow confines of his previous one,
was of spaciousness. A window the width of the cell, high in the rear
wall, brightened the room with a streak of sunlight, making the dust
motes shine golden against the dun-coloured walls. "Back to
civilization," he thought before quickly repressing it. Even irony was
unacceptable in his pact with himself.

There were two charpoys. A man sprawled on the string
webbing of one of them looked up as the door clanged shut. Matted
black hair appeared to cushion his head as he lay unmoving; hairs
sprouted from his ears like the veins of an aspen leaf; eyebrows as
thick as caterpillars crawled across his forehead, above eyes that were
the best feature in his heavy face. He appeared to be somewhere in
middle age, his stocky body still powerful. A big water buffalo of a
man, crude, ugly. Only months later did Mahmoud remember that
buffaloes are also valuable.

"Namaste." His voice was rough and he spoke the Hindu
greeting without the usual gesture of respect.

Mahmoud returned it in kind. "Salaam."

Since neither of them could think what to say next, they simply
stared at one another. The other man broke the silence. "So, you are
succeeding in getting out of solitary, I see."

To Mahmoud, the participial phrasing identified the man as a
Tamil, a man from the far South.

"I'm here."

"What for?"

"For a crime I didn't commit."

"Sure. We all saying that, see. Come on, what did you really do?" When he received no answer, he shrugged, then tossed a peanut into the air and caught it in his mouth.

Mahmoud perched on the other charpoy and looked up at the tiny patch of blue that was visible. His thoughts raced out of control. Ya, Allah! How would he ever get through this time? He despised this cellmate, as he despised all the criminals there. He hated being classed as a convict like them. Worse, for he had promised himself not to indulge in feelings, he despised himself for hating them. With an effort, he gained control of himself. Determined not to cave in again, he groped for something to think about.

He looked around the cell, at the window in the rear wall, and back to the one over the door, sliding his eyes quickly over the man sprawled opposite him. But, without realizing where it came from, that gave him an idea and he looked down at his own charpoy. It's, what, it must be about 65 inches long, for a man to sleep on. Looks like another two feet to the wall. That makes, hmm, 89 inches, let's say.

Before he was aware, the bit of sky above his right shoulder had become a slate on which he was figuring the area of the cell. The numbers appeared clearly written, but he could erase or replace them without a rag. Intrigued by this imaginary slate, he made up his mind to remember it.

When their evening meal arrived, Mahmoud edged his neem-leaf plate a little away, unthinkingly maintaining his psychological as well as physical distance. The men ate silently, eyeing one another with surreptitious glances. Mealtime was in any event not a conversational time in most families.

Even without words, however, as they lay on their charpoys at nightfall, the darkness no longer seemed quite so hostile. As in Mahmoud's solitary cell, few sounds penetrated from outside: the distant baying of a jackal, occasionally a dog's bark. Nearby, now, were human sounds: the squeak of the charpoy, the other's breathing, momentary heavy snoring. There was something vaguely comforting in that evidence of another person, even a stranger, near to him. Even so near.

The next morning, Mahmoud's first full day out of solitary, breakfast arrived promptly at six. Unlike the dished-up meal set down for him during his first days, there was now a more personalized service. The guard arrived carrying two buckets, from which, having set out the dried-leaf plates, he ladled out rice and lentils, watery by Mahmoud's standards but edible, and chappaties, those rounds of unleavened bread that were a staple food throughout much of India. No sooner had they finished eating than the cell door again opened. "Work time. Weaving shed for you." The guard jerked a thumb at Mahmoud's cell mate. "This guy'll show you."

All over the prison, cell doors stood open. The men were not escorted to their assigned places, but in the yard guards were conspicuously present. A few men met on the walk and sauntered to their assignments hand in hand in the age-old gesture of friendship. Before they reached their destination, two men going in another direction had patted Mahmoud's companion on the shoulder. In the shed, he walked up to the guard. "Namasteji. New man." With that, he abandoned Mahmoud and sat down at his loom.

The guard led Mahmoud to a loom in the row ahead and one row to the left of his cell-mate's, seated him, pulled a strap up his back. When Mahmoud sat with his hands on his knees, he asked, "Know what to do with this thing? No? Here," to the next man, "you teach him."

The shed was furnished with only the simplest style of loom, known as body loom because, as the weaver sat cross-legged on the floor within a canvas strap which pulled the warp taut, his body substituted for one of the beams of the loom. Mahmoud felt it degraded him from operator to part of the mechanism, resented it, and struggled to suppress that feeling, as all others.

Presently Mahmoud overheard someone whisper, "Who's the nawab?" and his cell-mates's answering growl, "Lay off. I've got him." Mahmoud felt and quickly suppressed a flicker of gratification at being described as a nawab. However sarcastically it had been meant, it also showed that the other prisoners recognized he was different from them. Nawabs were socially superior and often important people. For the rest of the shift, the only speaking was the neighbour-tutor's laconic instructions, issued curtly like orders, and sometimes not even that, but simply a hand reached over to push his into position.

The five-hour stint made for a long morning, but both the mechanism and its operation were simple and Mahmoud was a quick learner. By its end, he was producing cloth—coarse, slubbed, full of patched threads, but clearly cloth. It might even be accepted as a sheet for a prison bed. Tomorrow's would be better. Mahmoud was relieved to have been assigned some activity, for weaving took both strength and endurance. Moreover, to be able to count on seeing other men daily, even in so minimal a social setting, and to have time in a larger environment than the cramped cell, was satisfying. For the first time since his arrival at Benur, his breathing eased a bit.

Back in the cell, both men stretched out on their charpoys. But tired, Mahmoud was not entirely pleased when his cell-mate broke the silence.

"You don't exactly babble, do ya? I'm Ajai. You got a name?"

"Sayed Mahmoud." He sat up. Ajai! a Hindu. If he had been more himself when first shoved into this cell, the "namaste" would have tipped him off. Better watch his step. He determined to volunteer no information.

"You are coming from around here?"

"Khandipur."

Silence.

"You?"

"No special place."

Silence again. Finally Mahmoud could not sustain it any longer. "Have you been here long?"

"I'm being in prison the last five years."

Mahmoud shuddered and looked away. What does one say to a convict? He watched a parade of ants climb the wall and march around the corner, only to exit at the top of the door. For the next few hours the men pecked around one another like a pair of crows, a question here, a comment sometime later, long periods of silent immobility as though there was something to stare at, but neither knew what.

Late in the afternoon Mahmoud again sought his patch of sky, thinking to find it restful. To his surprise, what he now saw there was Hamidullah, his brother, as a six-year old. Hamid had stolen a mango from the fruit-seller's cart and was running down the street, pursued by the peddler's curses. The memory was so vivid that Mahmoud lost the distinction between what he was remembering and his feelings at the present moment. "Hamid did it, and who got punished for it?" he asked himself, unaware that he murmured aloud, "Mujhe (me)."

"Mujhe? What say, bhai?" but Mahmoud made no answer; in fact he was totally unaware of the prison cell, for he was suffering under his mother's reproof. As the eldest, he was supposed to keep the younger ones in line, stop Hamid from doing things that made trouble for them all.

While he still stung from this scolding, another memory appeared, a somewhat older Hamid. This time Mahmoud had taken the initiative to correct him. He had caught Hamid throwing stones at the monkeys in a neighbour's tree and reminded him that monkeys were sacred to Hindus; to live peacefully with their Hindu neighbours, they had to respect the other's beliefs. Hamid's repentance was brief, for he could not resist making a joke about it. Impossible not to join Hamid when he laughed. At the sound Ajai looked up sharply but said nothing.

All right, Mahmoud reminded himself, his thoughts running on, Hamid is inconsiderate but he's also honourable. But would he settle down enough to be responsible, now that he was head of the family? When he began wondering whether he had protected Hamid too much, Mahmoud caught himself, conscious of his determination not to think about all that. He forced himself back to his calculations about the area of the cell.

His mind calmed by mathematical exercises, he was able to return his attention once more to the cell. As they began a conversation, Ajai called his cell-mate Sayed and Mahmoud corrected him, saying that Sayed was simply a kind of title that indicated they were descendants of the Prophet.

Ajai tossed up a peanut and caught it in his mouth. "That so? The Prophet, hey?" He tossed another peanut. "Here, have some."

Mahmoud took a few and put them in his mouth. "Good."

Ajai watched him, a hint of smile softening the corners of his mouth. "You never been in prison before."

"How do you know?"

"Won't I recognize a guy who don't even know how to behave here?"

Ajai explained that the nuts were a treat to be made to last as long as possible by eating one at a time. Mahmoud considered it silly to take a treat in such small quantities it lost most of its flavour but sensed that would not be an acceptable idea to say to Ajai. Sometimes, but not too often, Ajai went on, it was possible to bribe a guard to bring nuts. "Treat, get it? So you are making it last as long as you can, because guards don't do no favours without gettin' somethin' for it." "Bribe." Mahmoud recalled his outburst in his solitary cell that he had never offered anyone a bribe and wondered whether he would be able to hold out here.

That night, Mahmoud had his first dreamless sleep since arriving at Benur. Out of habit, he woke just before dawn and rolled off his charpoy to say the first prayers of the day, then stretched out again without waking Ajai. The arrival of breakfast woke the sleeper and they ate in the usual mealtime silence, then at the guard's orders trudged off to the weaving shed. The morning's work at the loom went more smoothly, and he returned from it less tired than the previous day. Consequently, he did not resent it when Ajai again initiated a conversation. "You know, I been thinking, see. You're seeming like a educated guy. You teach me to speak proper and I'll teach you the ropes here. Bargain?"

"Why do you want to speak 'proper'?"

"So when I get out, maybe I can pass for respectable." Ajai grinned. "Maybe fooling a few people."

"Well, if you want to begin now, you'd say 'fool a few people,' not 'fooling.'"

"Achcha. You're going to school how long?"

"'You went to school.' I graduated from the government school in Khandipur."

"Shows. I knew you're not any ordinary crook."

"Excuse me, Ajai. I am not any kind of a crook, ordinary or not."

Once started on a conversation, these lonely men talked on and on. Ajai warned Mahmoud about the man whom the guard told off to show him about the loom. "He's mean. You cross him, he's likely to slash your loom when you're not looking, then the guard's landing on you for it. Watch out for him."

It crossed Mahmoud's mind to wonder why he should trust Ajai, when he distrusted everyone else in the prison and quite possibly some of the guards. Still, what choice did he have? So the lessons proceeded and over the weeks contributed their bit to a developing relationship. But tutoring and being tutored were not always easy to live with and tension sometimes built on both sides. Ajai got tired of having his ignorance emphasized and Mahmoud sometimes taunted him with it.

Once, after such an exchange, Ajai's clenched fists pushed him up from his seat on the charpoy. "I already said what I mean. Now lay off." He didn't move again but contented himself with glaring at his mate. Both men knew they had somehow to co-exist in this confined space. Trouble between them would bring the wrath of the warden down on their heads, and he was known to be creative in his punishments. Mahmoud threw up his hands, turned and retreated to his patch of blue sky, his slate. These mental excursions helped him return to the cell ready to make peace again.

"Come on, Ajai. Let's travel. What's the furthest you've ever been from here?"

Ajai named a village on the northern border of Tamil Nadu, where he said he had lived as a sprout but was forced out when his pop died and the uncle threw him out. Only nine or ten, not certain about his age, he just wandered around and landed in Puri.

"Puri! What did you do way over there?"

"Dacoit."

"You were a dacoit? You belonged to a gang there?"

"Yup."

"How did you get here then?"

"They was planning to kill the Collector, see. And I'm thinking these foreigners don't like having their people killed. Dacoity's not such a bad life if you got no choice. At least there's mateys. But I didn't think being hanged was part of the deal, not for me, see. I was young, not ready to risk ending it yet."

"If you knew about their plan, how did they let you get away?"

"We was at the railroad station, see, watching for the Collector when he gets off, making sure we're all recognizing him. Then the train starts pulling out again and just as the caboose passes us I'm hopping on and ducking behind the shield there. They don't have no chance to catch up with me."

"Weren't you afraid they'd shoot you?"

"How? Full daylight, lots of people around, see. Besides, I'm out of the way and not so important to them as the Collector."

"What did you do then?"

"Rode the tops of the cars. Turned out it was going to Patna. Over the years I'm wandering this direction."

Mahmoud, trying to imagine the life Ajai was describing, felt certain he could not have been so cool as to hop the train and get away. He was impressed by the number of things Ajai had taken into account in calculating his chance of escape. There was probably a lesson there, though he himself had no thoughts of trying to escape from Benur.

The conversation was interrupted by the key turning in the lock and the guard's voice, "Out! Clean-up time." For an hour every evening the prisoners worked outdoors, sweeping the prison yard, raking the gravel paths around their cell blocks, and generally tidying the place. Some of the men had planted flower beds beside their doors. One seemed to be growing chilli plants, perhaps in the hope of adding more flavour to his food.

That hour was important to Mahmoud and increasingly so as the year wound on. Accustomed to bathing twice a day, thrice during the hot season, this deprivation was one of the most difficult aspects of prison life. The weaving shed became hot, the cell stuffy. Clothes could be changed only every forty-eight hours. Sweaty, dusty, smelly, afraid of catching lice—the old Mahmoud would not have walked on the same side of the street with this one.

Relief came with the chance to stretch and to breathe fresh air after an afternoon in the cells, and it made the nights more bearable.

Besides, when clean-up time was over, half the men were allowed to line up at the pump to bathe and wash the clothes they'd been wearing. "Treats," as Ajai accurately said.

In addition to the fresh air and the exercise, this was a period the inmates enjoyed despite guards at every corner. Talking was officially discouraged but the guards made no objection to brief exchanges so long as the tone was low. They blew the whistle only if the hum became general or someone shouted. This was a chance to see other men, occasionally to exchange a few words, to learn something of the identity of these otherwise anonymous people who shared their constricted world. Alone, Ajai and Mahmoud were two tiny figures adrift on the vast planet; the presence of others with whom they could talk, even briefly, reconnected them to the larger world.

One day Mahmoud felt, rather than identified, a change in the atmosphere. The hot season was well started, with each succeeding day adding its inexorable degrees to the temperature. Heat rash added to Mahmoud's misery, as presumably for all of them. But that didn't seem like enough of an explanation. The men seemed sullen as they performed their cleaning tasks; the only conversations were whispered words that seemed to pass in single file from one man to another. Back in the cell, he accosted a frowning mate. "What's up, Ajai?"

"Don't know. Don't know why I don't know. That's not good."

That was all he could get out of a preoccupied and clearly worried Ajai, for the rest of the day.

The explosion came at clean-up time the next day. As soon as all were out and started on their work, someone at the end of the compound gave a shout. Four men rushed the guard near the baths, and as other guards ran to his aid, men piled onto them. Ajai seized Mahmoud by the arm. "Get back to the cell," he hissed. "Now. Run."

Stunned by the suddenness and strangeness of the attack, it took a minute for Ajai's instructions to sink in; then Mahmoud began to run. But not soon enough. He was only a few steps from the cell when a prisoner he didn't know grabbed him from behind. "Little sneak," the man snarled, arm across Mahmoud's Adam's apple.

"Trying to play the innocent, hey? You're in this too." A jerk of the arm nearly choked him.

Mahmoud tried to pull the arm off but the man kept his grip and Mahmoud's own movements increased the pressure on his throat. A knee landed on his butt. That did it. Mahmoud broke free and began to wrestle, the only adversarial sport he knew, but his opponent used his fists and Mahmoud was no match for him. In seconds he was on the ground, being pummeled and kicked in the head and the ribs. Fortunately, barefoot was part of the prison uniform, so the kicks were not so damaging as they might have been.

Mahmoud had the presence of mind left to roll over to protect his genitals. He reached for his attacker's ankle but before he could get him off balance, Ajai had pulled him off and was beating him up. With the man quickly reduced to a pulp, Ajai bent over him and emphasized his every word with another prod in the ribs. "I told you he's mine. If you ever touch him again, I'll kill you." Then he waded back into the melee.

Mahmoud struggled to his feet, but his head was not working properly and he staggered a few steps, fighting off the nausea that felt almost as bad as his assailant's punches. He was almost grateful when a guard seized him and threw him into his own cell. A few minutes later the key again turned in the lock and Ajai was propelled inside. With the start of the insurrection, even the off-duty guards had quickly mobilized and restored order. Ajai was among the last prisoners to be locked back in their cells.

There came the sound of drumming, a loud and monotonous beat that signaled a forthcoming message from the warden. It ricocheted through Mahmoud's head so he threw up, all down his kurta and onto his charpoy. Pulling off the stinky garment, he mopped up the vomit as best he could, then balled up the kurta and tossed it into a corner.

"All right, all you budmashes," the warden's voice snarled. He went on to vent his spleen with a string of expletives before reviewing the events and their consequences. One guard had been sent to the hospital and the warden advised prisoners who valued their own lives to start praying for him. The four who had started the riot were already on their way back to their maximum security prisons for rigorous imprisonment. Anyone else with a taste for RI, for working on the rock piles, shackled, he went on with heavy sarcasm, need only make the slightest move.

Listening in their cell, where all the air seemed to be sucked up by the warden's voice, Mahmoud hoped this threat might be the final word. Vain hope. The warden had more. Claiming to be more lenient than the men deserved, he sentenced them all to a diet of chappaties and water for a week. For the first night, nothing. Just fast and think about how cooperative they were going to be from now on. "If you don't like that, I'll feed you to the sharks," he concluded. With a nasty laugh at his own humour, the warden set his megaphone inside on the desk, and stalked off.

True to the warden's threat, the next morning at breakfast time each cell received a bucket of brackish water and two chappaties, one for each of the inmates. As the stink in the cell would make a skunk into a rose, Mahmoud used his quota for washing out his kurta. By evening, the chappaties doled out to them had become hard and dry; by the next day they were also mouldy.

At first Ajai and Mahmoud tried to do stretches and other exercises they could accomplish in their cramped quarters, but by the fourth day they simply spent their time lying on their charpoys, unable to muster even the energy to speak to one another. On the last day Mahmoud lay with closed eyes, his laboured breathing becoming more and more shallow. Something triggered Ajai's attention. For a moment he strained to hear. There was no sound of breathing. Mobilizing the strength he had thought was gone, Ajai rolled off his charpoy and over to his cell-mate's. Just as he feared. No rise and fall of the chest. No noisy breath. "Mahm___d," he repeated, over and over, slapping the immobile figure on the cheeks, rubbing up and down the arms with a strong motion, reaching back for his own water cup and sprinkling some on the mask-like face.

"Don't die now, for God's sake. It's the last day. Wake up, baba, it's almost over." Finally Mahmoud's eyelids fluttered, then opened. Ajai was so relieved he almost caved in right there, but he knew he had to keep going. "Come on, you fool, drink this and try to stay awake. Don't you scare me like that again, you hear me?"

Somehow, they managed to sustain the thin thread of life through the night, though Ajai crawled over twice, pushing his cup of water ahead of him, to make Mahmoud drink some. Next morning's breakfast time brought them a thin soup. Instead of their usual assignments, the men were ordered to clean out their cells. After that, most of them again stretched out on their charpoys, but were surprised at noontime when the soup arrived again. Ajai raised questioning eyebrows at the guard, who jerked his thumb over his shoulder and drew his hand across his throat.

"Someone conked out down the line," Ajai explained to Mahmoud. "Warden's making sure he doesn't have to account for too many corpses. Drink up." The evening meal of their normal rice and dal along with a chappati (fresh this time) revived them. The day after that, they resumed their usual routine. Only the increased alertness and scowling expressions of the guards reminded them of their recent riot and its aftermath.

As soon as he was strong enough to bend over without fainting, Mahmoud resumed his five-times-a-day prayers. With no call from a mosque to identify prayer times, he had had to rely on his instincts. Out of habit, he woke before dawn for the first prayer of the day, then lay back on his charpoy until he heard the sounds of the guard down the street beginning to distribute the morning food. Quickly after that, for they were not allowed much time to linger between food and work, then again at noon after returning from the weaving shed, at dusk, and before sleeping, he knelt by his charpoy, rocking back and forth as he murmured the familiar phrases, then touched his forehead to the dirt floor. He was grateful that Ajai maintained a respectful quiet during these devotions.

Awareness of his cell-mate's consideration had gradually melted the reserve between them and something akin to friendship developed. Without that, Mahmoud would not have been moved to ask, "Come on, Ajai. What did you really do to be sent to prison?"

"I stole a ring," Ajai said. Mahmoud smiled. "What's funny about that? I was hungry, meant to sell it for enough to buy a stash of food. If I'd a been able to speak proper, like you've been teaching me, maybe the jeweller wouldn't have known right away that no one like me could own such a stone. I was stupid. I shoulda just stole the food. Now stop laughing!"

"A ring! You were convicted for stealing a ring? So was I! I didn't do it but I might as well have. As for speaking proper, it didn't help a bit. The judge never listened."

"You're telling me, bhai, you're here because of a ring, too?"

"Yes, a sapphire ring."

"I knew the first time I saw you we had something in common. Here, have a nut."

Ajai continued to coach Mahmoud how to toss up nuts to catch in the mouth, criticizing his technique. Starved for entertainment, they developed the game into a competition which gained in intensity. After a time they began to lay bets on their skill. Ajai was the expert, tossing a nut high into the air and catching it. Mahmoud was getting tired of Ajai kidding him about always losing. "Bet you can't do ten without stopping," he wagered, an edge to his voice.

At Ajai's objections he would have to stop long enough to eat one before the next came, Mahmoud insisted that they would have to be swallowed whole in order to eat them without a pause. The first one was easy, followed immediately by another. Still attempting to swallow the third, Ajai failed to throw the fourth straight up and had to leap forward to catch it. Determined not to do that again, he tossed the fifth extra high. It fell fast, straight down into his open mouth— and lodged in his throat. Ajai coughed, beat his chest, gasped laboriously, became first red in the face, then a sickly colour. Panic-stricken, Mahmoud grabbed him about the middle and forced him upside down over his arm, beating him hard on the back. With a retching sound, Ajai disgorged the nut and the next blow forced air into his lungs. He collapsed onto the charpoy.

When he had recovered his breath, he smiled wryly at Mahmoud. "Thanks, bhai, you saved my life."

"You mean I nearly cost you it, with that foolish bet. I wanted to hold you up by the ankles and shake the nut out of you. Next time you choke, make sure there's someone around who's bigger than you."

They sat quietly then; sweat glistened on both faces, not only from the fright just past. The hot season had started early that year and seemed interminable, for the monsoon was late. The glaring sun drained the blue from Mahmoud's little patch of sky, leaving it harsh and brassy. Sweat soaked clothes and bed sheets. Temperatures soared, while appetites and spirits drooped.

At night, in the airless cell, Mahmoud dreamed of the kus-kus grass mats hung over the windows at home, which the servants soaked with water several times a day. The air thus cooled came through with a sweet smell. Flowering trees added colour to the landscape: gul mohur, with its mammoth red blossoms, and jacaranda, blue-laden branches offering colour to the pale sky. Piles of mangoes constantly available made the heat seem almost worth bearing. Here in prison, the only difference from other seasons was that it was harder to endure. Short tempers spread like an epidemic among prisoners and guards alike.

In the weaving shed, Mahmoud raised a damp eyebrow at Ajai and nodded towards a new man. Tall, shaggy, bearded, muscular, the fellow folded into his loom without a glance to either side. Ajai frowned and bent over his loom, the canvas strap across his back wet with sweat. Back in the cell, Mahmoud accosted him. "The heat got you, Ajai? All I did was ask about the new guy."

"Stay away from him, Mahmoud. He's dangerous."

"Now you're a rishi or something? He just came and already you know what he's like."

"If I recognize certain signs, then don't I know about him?" Ajai spat. "Criminal tribe."

"Really bad, hey?"

"Don't talk to him, don't talk about him, don't talk to anyone about anything when he can see you. He'd sooner kill you than correct you if he thinks you're saying something disrespectful about him."

"He must have done something right, to earn a transfer to Benur."

"He's not stupid; he probably knows exactly what he has to do to get out. Don't let it fool you. You never know when he'll become a tiger, see. Personally, I'm preferring the tiger."

"What else can he be, if everyone treats him like one?"

"It's up to you, bhai. You do something stupid, I can't stop you.

The thing is, I'm not having too much more time here. I'd hate to have to break in another new cell-mate."

Alerted by the warning, when it was weaving time Mahmoud watched the newcomer only out of the corner of his eye. Although officially silence was the rule, the men had regularly managed to slip in a greeting or a comment, even to produce an occasional laugh or a bit of song. It was a reasonably friendly place. For any guard on duty that was an advantage, so they overlooked these small infringements. With the arrival of the tribal, however, a pall enveloped the weaving shed. Apparently it was not only Ajai who had recognized the man's character. No more singing. No one looked around, much less smiled or winked at a neighbour.

The new man strode in without a glance at anyone, folded himself into his loom, and looked at nothing but what was under his hands. He slammed the shuttle from side to side with such vigour, or ferocity, that his production soon outstripped that of the other men. They bent over their looms, heads down, not looking at one another, but hands not quite steady wound the shuttle too tight or snapped the threads. Despite the concentration, their output actually declined. Successive guards twitched from foot to foot and hurried out of the building as soon as a replacement arrived.

One morning the tribal stalked in looking at his feet as usual, but instead of plopping into his place, he stood examining his loom. The shuttle had fallen on the floor and the yarn from it had caught in the foot of the man at the next loom as he passed. The tribal eyed the progress of the string until it stopped near the next loom and curled back to the shuttle. Suddenly he pounced; he grabbed the unfortunate weaver by the neck, jerked him to his feet and shook him so his head knocked like a woodpecker, then threw him against the wall. Among the others there was not a motion, not the twitch of a muscle. They all sat with the furry taste of mouldy chappati in their mouths.

Only the guard moved, reached the aggressor as he turned, and punched him in the diaphragm. The tribal's muscles were hard and he scarcely flinched. Instead he jabbed a right fist at the guard's jaw; it was barely parried. They fought ferociously, hitting, ducking, stumbling, punching, breath coming in great gasps. The guard was strong but in the end tired first. The tribal, seemingly invigorated by his opponent's growing fatigue, delivered a wallop that spun the guard around, then felled him with a blow at the base of his skull. Without missing a beat, the attacker bent and picked up the shuttle. He raised it with both hands above his head, pointed end aimed at the ribs of his prostrate opponent.

Ajai sprang. He knocked the shuttle away with such force the tribal staggered backwards. While he was off balance Ajai slugged him so that he fell, then flung himself on top of him. As though galvanized, others leapt up and piled onto him. Bodies squirmed and bounced, rolled and twined. Panting and grunting, they finally managed to pin him down. Even he could no longer struggle under the heap of men on top of him. Everyone joined except Mahmoud, who rushed out to call in additional guards. Meanwhile the weaver victim had attempted to stand, collapsed again, and succeeded in crawling out of the shed.

That afternoon a grim-faced warden announced to the tense inmates that the dangerous convict had been shackled and remanded to a high-security prison. Under consideration was the punishment for prisoner 7702, since fighting was a serious breach of prison rules. 7702—that's Ajai! Mahmoud at once petitioned a guard to take him to the office. The guard didn't bother to look at him, barely deigned to reply. "You got nothing to say to the warden."

"You don't know."

"Wardens don't just chat with prisoners who take a fancy to see them."

"Look, you fool, didn't you see what happened today? Now get off your duff and take me to the office." Mahmoud was too angry to listen to the risk he was taking.

"Ahh, your grandmother's penis!" But he took him.

"Warden, Sahib," Mahmoud pleaded, "it's clear you have not yet been told the full story. Ajai saved the guard's life. He stayed out of it until that goonda knocked the guard down and was about to impale him with the shuttle. That's when Ajai jumped in; he ought to be rewarded, not punished."

"Why should I believe you?"

"Ask the others, Warden Sahib. They all saw it but only Ajai had the courage to act."

"Maybe. But rules are rules. And Ajai was the ring-leader that broke them."

"If you punish Ajai for rescuing the guard, Warden Sahib, you will have to punish me as well, for leaving the weaving shed to summon help."

The warden grunted his dismissal and nothing further was said about punishment, either then or later. With adrenaline pouring through his system, Mahmoud had acted out of instinct, not thinking of honour or fairness but simply certain of what he had to do. Back in the cell, he could not resist asking Ajai how he had had the courage to take on the vicious fellow. Ajai grinned. "You disappoint me, baba. I was beginning to have some hope for you. Couldn't you see that was our guard on the floor? The one who gets the nuts for us? How are we going to manage, if he's done in?"

Never would Mahmoud have imagined he would admire a convicted felon, but there it was.

11

The hot weather was finally over. The monsoon had broken, bringing relief to the suffering inmates at Benur. If they had been at home, they would have danced in the streets or the fields to welcome the first rains. At Benur, the relief was all the greater, shared by the guards. At the first powerful scent of raindrops in the dust, spirits began to revive. When the preliminary showers turned into serious rainfall, the guards opened the cell doors.

Instead of their usual clean-up activity, the men rushed into the downpour, shrieking and laughing like children. For once the guards made no objection to the outbursts. More restrained, but grinning happily, they watched as the men whirled on a spot like dervishes in a trance, beat a tattoo with their bare feet in the puddles, or just stood and let the water stream down their upturned faces.

A good monsoon meant life—life to the crops, life to those who depended on them, life to the world which these men had hopes of rejoining. Within hours, drooping flowers lifted their heads and once again brightened occasional corners of their surroundings. In the month before monsoon ended, clothes would become clammy, cell walls mouldy, some roofs would develop leaks. It didn't matter; that was the price of the blessing. Worth celebrating.

In the weeks following the end of the monsoon, the farmers among the inmates traded comments about the fields they knew would have been ploughed and winter crops sowed. Diwali, the Hindu festival of light, was celebrated with a special meal for everyone. It was one of the two times in the year that meat was served to those who were not vegetarian.

One morning a few days after that, as they sat in their cell finishing the watery rice and dal that was the prison fare at breakfast,

Ajai reminded Mahmoud that his year was nearly over. "You won't have to eat this slop much longer; you'll be outta here. Lucky guy!"

"How about you, Ajai. Isn't your time up soon, too?"

"Coupla months. Watcha gonna…sorry, what are you going to do?"

"No plans."

"Sure. You can go home, take your time about it."

"Home? No, I can't go back to Khandipur."

"They don't want you back? I never had a family, see, and I always wanted one, thought that would be one place I could always go."

"Oh, they'd welcome me, of course. But even they might think about the rumours that would go around: 'The jailbird's back and they've taken him in. Who could trust them now?' That sort of thing. I couldn't put them through that again. Besides, the Tahsildar would never give me back my job. So what would I do there?"

What Mahmoud could not say, even to someone so close as Ajai, was that there was no use going back, no way he could clear his name without implicating his brother. It was to protect Hamid that he was here in prison in the first place. Besides, he could still not imagine what had kept Hamid silent, but had enough confidence in him not to risk exposure. That was a black hole.

"So?"

Mahmoud shook his head slowly. "I'm like you now, a man without a family."

As the end of his year in prison approached, Mahmoud had thought a great deal about his relation with his family. He yearned to see them but what he told Ajai was also accurate. If he could clear his name by going back, it would be worth it, but the only way to do that would be to say he was a liar, he didn't really buy the ring and give it to Hamid. A very dubious way to re-establish his honour, since that would also condemn his brother to take a turn in prison. Two felons in the family were not better than one, surely. But what the alternatives might be, he didn't know. Benur was the only place where he had spent any time except for Khandipur.

Anyway, it was not easy to think of what he might be able to do. He had looked after the family farm, but that was too small to qualify him for managing an estate large enough to hire managerial help. He had been the Tahsildar's munshi, but without a reference from his previous employer, who would hire him now? Very bleak prospect.

"Come on," Mahmoud brought himself back to the moment. "I hear the guard coming down the row. Time to go throw our shuttles."

The following day Ajai was again his bouncy self. "Hey, Mahmoudbhai, I know what you should do when they turn you out of here."

"Glad somebody knows. What?"

"Go to Jehanabad."

"Why Jehanabad, for goodness sake?"

"Stop interrupting and let me tell you. There's a mansabdar owes me a favor, see. He's in the capital, Burhan. Go ask him for a job. He has to give you one when you say I told you to ask him."

Hope had flickered briefly and died as quickly. "It's not me he owes a favour to, Ajai." Mahmoud sat with his hands locked together; that way they couldn't reach out and accept this proffered gift.

"Yeah, it is. He owes me, I owe you, so he owes you. Neat, huh?"

"No, bhai, I can't use up your credit."

"Why not? I can't ever go back to Jehanabad, see. Now, he owes me. If you don't collect, he'll never have to pay, will he? Is that right?"

The hands relaxed just a bit. "Perhaps not, but—"

Ajai sat up straight and flung out both hands, palms up. "Do it, bhai. Who knows? In my next incarnation I might be born a Mussulman; do me good to rack up some credit in advance." A smile belied his shrug.

Mahmoud nodded. "Achcha. I'll think about it." He sat back, assuming this was the end of the conversation. He really did mean to think about it. But Ajai would not be brushed off before he was through.

"Remember, bhai," Ajai hesitated, looking embarrassed. "When you leave here, I'll never see you again." Mahmoud opened his mouth, but Ajai's raised hand forestalled any interruption. "No, don't say anything. I know how these things go. But at least I can think that I was able to do something good for one person in this life, anyway. Return the favour for the only person who's ever been—oh, get on with you. Here, have a peanut."

A fortnight later, as the prison gates again clanged shut, this time leaving Mahmoud on the outside, he stood for a moment gazing in the direction of Khandipur. Had he actually gone there, he would have arrived in time to see the celebrations for Anees's wedding. She was being married to a Nawab from the north, a minor Raja in fact, and the festivities were appropriately grand.

The Rahmatullah household offered sweets to all of Khandipur and dinner on the evening of the Nikah ceremony to whoever lined up at their gate. Even if Hamid had been willing to stand there like a beggar, he could not have forced himself to eat Anees's wedding feast. Instead, he watched the procession from the shadows, then went back to his room to rail and to weep in private. He felt a moment's compunction about Khatija, for whom this should have been the peak experience of her life but who, like Hamid, would partake only in hearsay.

Mahmoud knew nothing of these festivities. Standing near the prison gate, he wondered how the family would really feel if he should walk in now. Happy? Civil of course, but quite likely cold. His mother would probably be glad to see him but he doubted whether she would understand what it would mean for the rest of them. Tyaba and Razia, were they married now? If not, his return would no doubt interfere with finding husbands.

And Hamid, that would be awkward, now that he was accustomed to being the head of the family. Replaced by a head who was an ex-convict. That couldn't be good for any of them. No matter. Since there was no way he could re-establish his own good name without making matters worse for the family, the only honourable thing was to stay away. Home—no such thing for him any more. He must stop thinking as though he had a family.

One more longing look in the direction of Khandipur. "Goodbye, dear ones." Unconsciously, he spoke aloud. "Hamid will look after you now. Forget I exist."

With a deep breath, which he held for a moment before exhaling, he turned and trudged off toward the railroad station. There must be some sort of connection to Burhan.

12

Burhan was the capital city of the princely state of Jehanabad. As in Mahmoud's native state, its population was a mixture of Hindus and Muslims, with minorities of Christians, Sikhs, Buddhists. The Maharajah was Hindu, while the Minister was Muslim. Others in the Cabinet were known as Minister of this or that Department, but the Prime Minister (a title the British discouraged) was always referred to simply as Minister.

While Mahmoud waited for word from Afsur Jung, the man to whom Ajai had sent him, he sat in his small, bare room at the resthouse looking up at the sky. Nothing to do but dream. He would have liked to go out and explore his new city but feared being away if Afsur Jung should send for him.

Not far away, another man also sat dreaming. Not even their dreams connected Mahmoud and the Prime Minister of Jehanabad. Their circumstances could not have been more different. The Minister sat on a white sheet spread over a carpet made in Isfahan of wool from the breast of young sheep, a carpet almost as smooth as silk but springier. The only movement in the room was the slight rise and fall of his chest, just enough so the sunbeam that had made its way through the partly-shuttered window created a shifting pattern on his black neema jama. Its fine silk seemed moulded to his body, which was slight but no longer with the slenderness of youth.

Only those who knew the Minister intimately could have said, looking at his impassive face with its hooded eyes, whether he was concentrating or dreaming. In fact he was doing both. Although he had never been to Afghanistan, the map of that country was complete in his mind. To him the steep mountains, the long valleys, narrow defiles and rocky paths that turned into treacherous torrents after a rainfall higher up—all those scenes of the country were familiar to him. He had taught himself to consider them, not for their beauty but because they were the path of invasion into India. Alexander, Timur, Nadir Shah, the Moghuls—all had taken it to extend their Empire. It was still the path that modern Russians must follow if, as the Paramount Power constantly feared and the Minister hoped, they determined to unseat the British on the sub-continent.

His hope for an invasion from the northwest was a daydream. It salved the wounds when the British bridle was pulled too sharply or the reins held too tight, provided relief from the sour task of getting along with the foreigners for the foreseeable future. Whether it could ever be more than a dream was a question that echoed in the private chambers of his mind. Time again, now, for the severely rational examination that was his habit when assessing whether a situation might be ripe for action.

He reached for a volume at his side, running his finger down the pile until it hesitated at one, then pulled it out. Mountstuart Elphinstone, a good observer and apt to be accurate because he was not afraid to listen to the local people. A nice irony, to place so much reliance on a British observer when calculating the chances of unseating the British or at least shaking their grasp loose a bit. He turned over the pages, scanning rapidly for a particular passage, when a cough in the doorway caused him to look up.

"Excuse me, Your Excellency; the Assistant Resident has called to see you."

Only the Private Secretary, who knew the Minister's every expression from twenty years of working together, could recognize the measure of his distaste as he replied, "Then I suppose I must see him." He rose and stepped with unhurried tread across the room, down a corridor lined on one wall with miniature paintings and on the other with windows onto an interior courtyard, and into his dressing room. There, his valet wordlessly produced a turban, black with a narrow gold thread, flat and round in the style his family had always worn.

At the door he paused to step into leather slippers, as soft and supple as the hands of the servant who pressed his feet at night.

Respectably shod, he continued into the next courtyard, toward the Angrezi Khana, as the English Room was known to his household. He regarded walking into it as the equivalent of going outside his deori, and he would no more have thought of entering it without shoes than of stepping into the street barefoot. To British people, the issue of wearing or not wearing shoes indoors carried implications of status, and he would not for anything appear to be acknowledging inferiority.

Quite different for him was the habit of going without shoes within the rest of his home, or in stockinged feet in cold weather, a simple matter of cleanliness and local custom.

A moment's pause near the fountain to admire the roses which had bloomed this morning; an English flower, but he was fond of them, perfect at every stage. Unfortunately not like their diplomats, particularly this Assistant Resident. Some day the man would be transferred, God willing. Until then he must be suffered. With a deep breath suspiciously like a sigh, he turned toward the rooms he had recently had built especially for the reception of Western visitors. Dirty fellows they were, tracking the dust of the streets indoors on their great clumping boots. Even the Resident, vain of his appearance, disdained to remove his shoes.

But the new rooms had solved the problem: the British were happy not only because they could now keep their shoes on but also because they flattered themselves on their growing influence, at this evidence of what they were pleased to call "the spread of civilization." Behind his impassive mask he could smile at their self-deception, for they would never penetrate beyond these rooms and see that life continued its traditional course in the rest of the deori.

Entering, he salaamed the visitor, who got quickly to his feet from the chair where he had been sprawling. "Good morning, Your Excellency."

13

On Mahmoud's first contact with the man to whom Ajai had sent him, Afsur Jung had slipped him a small bunch of folded notes with the comment that if a job were found, he would need to look presentable, a credit to his sponsor. His first act on leaving the man was to go to the bazaar and buy himself two kurtas and two churdidar pyjamas; the churidar's bracelets of wrinkles around the ankles were very fashionable.

Finding a place to stay posed no great problem now that he was solvent again. He located a room to rent which contained all that he really needed: a table, one chair, a rickety wash stand in one corner, a small sigiri on which he could at least make coffee, a charpoy. He looked with distaste at the thin pad on the charpoy. After prison, he would have been able to sleep on anything, but struggling to regain his self-respect, he thought he required more than a pad that was no thicker than a woven cover. Rolling it up and tucking it under his arm, he set out to find a mattress-maker to improve it.

The directions from a stranger proved correct; from some paces away he spotted a worker beating a pile of kapok. The string on his bowed wand caught the fibres and broke them loose from the solidified mass, leaving them fluffed. He knew the process, for his mother had sent for the mattress man once or twice a year to have the family mattresses fluffed and cleaned. Mahmoud wanted that done to his: the ticking would be unstitched, the kapok pulled out and beaten, then stuffed back into the newly washed and dried ticking and re-stitched. At the end, the mattress would have doubled its depth and would smell sweetly of the sun and the bushes on which it had been stretched to dry. He felt better, just anticipating it.

While his mattress was being worked on, Mahmoud walked off in search of a coffee maker, a small lower pot he would fill with water and set on the sigiri. There the flame would heat the water and force it into the upper pot, where the coffee powder was. Moved off the heat, strong coffee would trickle back into the lower pot, where it would remain until wanted.

Next he needed a tumbler which could be filled about a third with the decoction and then filled with hot milk. That meant he also needed a small pan to heat the milk. All of those new possessions were brass, lined with tin to be safe. Mahmoud smiled, thinking how their bright surfaces would light up the little room. Last of all, he bought a bed sheet and wondered whether it too had been made in a prison like Benur.

Afsur Jung had raised no question about the transfer of obligation but said that he needed a bit of time to find a situation for him. He explained that he did not personally know Major Naughton, Secretary of His Highness's Military Department, but had been of some small service to someone who was known to the Major. Or possibly that man would know another who was close to the Major. On that basis he promised to see that Mahmoud was recommended for a position in the Military Department. Mahmoud smiled inwardly at the number of chits that were being called on in order to provide him with a job.

The system clearly worked. Within a few days, Mahmoud received word that he should report immediately to the Military Department; he was to be munshi (clerk) to Major Naughton. As he waited for the Major to appear, Mahmoud surveyed his surroundings and concluded that one government office was like another. This simply replicated the Tahsil office in Khandipur. Cupboards lined the walls; the doors hanging open revealed piles and piles of folders, all bound with red tape. The table and chair that were the only other furniture were not quite decrepit but showed no signs of having been taken care of.

When he was shown into the Major's office and caught a first glimpse of his new employer, a slight tightening of his insides, a tension such as he experienced when he froze and waited to see if a cobra would strike, warned Mahmoud to be careful. The Major was only marginally taller than Mahmoud himself, broad-shouldered and showing the beginnings of a paunch, with thinning hair that had either been blonde and was darkening or had been brown and was being bleached by the Indian sun. The pencil mustache was too thin to resolve the colour question but gave the face a kind of perpetual grimace. Not a face one took to easily.

Though he spoke the local language with a slight British accent, the Major was fluent enough to suggest he had been in the country for some years. His clothes were informal, twill trousers and open-neck shirt, no jacket, but in spite of that he was clearly not a man with whom to let down the barriers. Perhaps it was the military bearing that reminded Mahmoud of the prison guards.

Mahmoud was aware that he also was being sized up, as the Major took his seat behind the desk and looked him over in silence. Aside from the stare, neither a smile nor a nod acknowledged him. "You can read and write, I presume?" were the Major's first words.

"Certainly, Sahib."

"Major Sahib."

"Certainly, Major Sahib. I am adept in our local language. I have had no occasion to learn yours." Fortunately, out of all the multiplicity of languages in India, that spoken in Burhan was close enough to Mahmoud's mother tongue to pose no problems. In the days while he waited for word from Afsur Jung, he had taken pains to learn the local script, so he felt quite confident in describing himself as adept.

"No matter. Our business is all in the local lingo. You will fair copy the letters and invoices I give you. When I say fair, that's exactly what I mean. No sloppy characters one has to puzzle out."

"No, Major Sahib."

"All right. Here's your first assignment." He stood and picked up a slim sheaf of papers from his desk, motioned Mahmoud into the outer office and pointed to a small table on which the only objects were an inkwell and a thin stack of fresh paper. Dropping the papers on the table, he ordered, "Get busy," and strode back to his own office.

The assignment was not difficult, merely to make a fair copy of letters that came in the Major's own scrawl. He worked more slowly than he needed, both to make certain he did not commit any errors on this, his first day, but also so that he would not appear to be loafing if the Major should come through the room again. Better to seem overloaded than idle. As he finished each letter, he read it back against the original, verifying his reading of it. Obviously the Major spoke the local language better than he wrote it, for Mahmoud found several errors, but he would have to know his employer pretty well before he would risk correcting him.

After a fortnight, he did venture a comment when he came across an error that could make a substantial difference to the meaning of the rest of the letter. "Begging Major Sahib's pardon," he began when Naughton stopped by his desk, "I am sure the Major Sahib knows what a difference one small stroke on this character makes to the whole meaning. Perhaps some distraction occurred just then. Is it correct this way, or should I add the stroke across it?"

"It's quite obvious the stroke belongs there," Naughton said. "Don't let such things pass. That's what you're here for."

Emboldened, Mahmoud began to make the corrections but was meticulous about adding a note calling attention to the change. One day he went too far. "When you speak, this word is correct," he told his boss, "but it seems to have been written phonetically, perhaps in a moment's absent-mindedness. When it is written this way it means something very different."

The Major snatched the paper out of Mahmoud's hand. "Since when did you consider yourself a teacher? Stick to your job or I'll fine you for wasting time."

"Yes, Major Sahib," Mahmoud bowed and went back to his desk. But the next time the letter came to him, he was reassured to see that it included his suggestion.

This was as close as Mahmoud could remember to taking initiative on a job, and he found he enjoyed it. Exercised his brain a little. Perhaps life could consist of something besides taking orders, though he didn't quite see how. There would be a very clear line beyond which the Major would not tolerate criticisms, no matter how tactfully presented. Then a possibility opened up, though not in a way Mahmoud would have chosen.

When the Major realized the breadth of his new munshi's abilities, he set him to do additional things. Although the title remained the same, the assignments gradually began to involve greatly enlarged responsibility, presently including duties as accountant as well. In that capacity Mahmoud had to deal with all the orders, invoices, and accounts of the Military Department which, after he had fair copied, he had to enter in successions of ledgers and then make the accounts balance.

Six weeks into his new duties, it dawned on Mahmoud that the reason he had to struggle so to make the various records correspond was that Major Naughton was defrauding His Highness by passing bills that were forged or falsified and embezzling the resulting funds. He's a termite, Mahmoud thought; he eats away the heart of the accounts, but nothing shows on the outside. Till one day the whole structure will collapse. On his head. Suddenly he realized on whose head it was likely to collapse. If he was there, then wouldn't he be blamed for the crime? He felt he couldn't get out of there fast enough.

"Absolutely not," the Major said when Mahmoud spoke to him about leaving. "I won't hear of your resigning. You just got here and I went through all the trouble of breaking you in. Now you stay and justify the effort I put into training you."

"I am grateful for the opportunity, Major Sahib, but I do not feel I can do this kind of work properly. Not to the standard it deserves."

"Rubbish. You're very ungrateful. If you need to have your little ego inflated, I'll tell you you're too valuable to the department to leave. Now get back to work."

Afsur Jung, appealed to, said, "My dear chap, don't you realize what an awkward position you would place me in by leaving so soon after I exerted myself to get the post for you? The height of ingratitude, that's what it is. I advise you to stay on and do your best."

Uncertain whether the man might still retain a hold on Ajai and not wanting to call further attention to himself in the Department, Mahmoud felt trapped into continuing. The important thing was to figure out a way to protect himself. During the next few days his mind was busy working out a scheme. To fight a termite, be a termite. Day by day, whenever he dared, he made copies of forged bills. At first, every time the Major spoke to him, he held his breath, afraid the secret had been discovered.

"Our new chap's timid as a gal in purdah," Naughton reported to his assistant, Harry Corder. "Hardly dares look at me when I give him orders."

"Just as well," Corder replied. "Let's hope he stays so passive."

However, Mahmoud was gradually becoming more bold; as time passed, he even managed to secrete a few incriminating documents in Major Naughton's own hand. That was not an easy step. Mahmoud knew that to take something that did not belong to him, even a piece of paper with no intrinsic value, was stealing. No honourable person steals. But embezzlement was an even more serious crime, and not to steal the paper might well land the charge of embezzlement on his head. There was nothing honourable about going to prison. Back and forth he went, honour vs. self-preservation.

Then one day he took one of Naughton's invoices, the first one, home with him and hid it among the clothes in his tin trunk. To deflect suspicion from himself, he worked hard. Outside of work he lived like a monk, afraid of developing relationships that might entangle him, afraid of inadvertently giving away some hint that would betray him. The waiter at the little shop where he took his meals, the dhobi who once a week took his soiled clothes to the river to beat on the rocks and return them the next day, a little more faded each time but smelling of sunshine, the landlord who nodded good evening and occasionally exchanged a non-committal word—these were his social contacts.

In the evenings he missed Ajai and had moments when it would have felt good even to see their guard. Once, in a deep well of loneliness, he thought he would probably have more company if he were sitting naked on top of a mountain. But no, the gods would cry foul, where's your sacred thread?

Even the mountain top seemed less a fantasy than the days in Khandipur. A mere dream. A time when he had friends at the office, and when he left work he went back to a home filled with bustle and purpose, laughter and people he could count on. The memory of Hamid's capers acquired the patina of distance, seeming less burdensome and more fun than they had at the time.

After living for more than a year as he had determined to do in Burhan, outwardly a hermit, inwardly on edge, Mahmoud reached the end of his tether. Working for the Major was too much like being in prison again. No respect, no interest, no sense of purpose in his life, not even Ajai to toss peanuts with, and no end to his sentence. Unless the Major opened a trap door. Mahmoud assured himself he would not be on it.

One evening, he went to the telegraph office and filled in a form he addressed to himself. "Father dying. Come at once. Mother," he wrote. This he handed to the operator, together with a large rupee note. "Will you stamp this for me, please, as though it had just arrived?" The operator stared at him for a minute, then pocketed the rupees and stamped the telegram as requested. He handed it back with a wink. Mahmoud nodded and put it in his pocket.

At the office the next morning, he applied for compassionate leave of absence to return to Khandipur, saying that his father was dying, and produced the confirmatory telegram. This the Major granted with the stipulation of a few days' delay to complete a report. The delay took no account of how near death the putative father might be, but Mahmoud did not dare push his lie too far.

In the office on his final day there, Mahmoud threw his head back and stared out the window. The angle was scarcely necessary now, for the window was reasonably large and low. Still, it had become habitual from that other time when the small patch of blue up near the ceiling of his cell had been so precious a reminder that the world outside did actually exist and pursued its accustomed way and would no doubt continue to do so when he was again a part of it. He was sitting in that position and adding up the column of figures projected on the sky when Major Naughton came in.

"What's the matter, Mahmoud, don't we give you enough work to keep you occupied here? Or is it just that you don't believe in giving His Highness a day's work in return for your wages?"

"No, Sahib. I mean, yes, of course, Major Sahib. I was doing a sum in my head when you came in."

"No doubt an abacus would be faster; that's why one is provided to you. See that you keep at it. I've been waiting since yesterday for the copy of the letter to the Commandant of the Third Lancers. All that stuff has to be cleared out before you can go, you know."

"Yes, Major Sahib. At once."

Naughton spied some slips on Mahmoud's desk and seized them. "How did you get these? What are they doing on your desk?"

"I was just trying to get yesterday's accounts to balance, Major Sahib, so I could leave them in good order. When I had trouble reconciling the totals this morning, I thought perhaps those were the missing vouchers." He was choosing his words carefully and hoped, correctly, it seemed, that Naughton was too busy flying off the handle to notice.

"I do the thinking around here, is that clear? You're paid to fair copy letters and do the accounts when I give you the facts to work with. Not before. Savvy?"

"I understand."

"And no more ferreting around after vouchers and invoices I haven't signed yet. When they're approved and signed, I'll give them to you and that's soon enough for you to begin to worry about them."

"Excuse me, Major Sahib. Now about that letter to the Third Lancers."

"Get on with it," Naughton ordered and turning on his heel withdrew into his own office, closing the door behind him. There he went straight on through to the office of his assistant, Harry Corder. Allowing his bulky frame to pleat into a low chair, he concentrated on balancing his boots on a corner of the table while remarking casually, "I'm afraid our friend out there is growing curious. I caught him with these."

Corder held out his hand for the vouchers, riffled through them, and whistled. "If he's already seen these, we'd better let them go as they are. Pity. Such a waste."

"Maybe I can have a word with Chiminlal anyway. Tell him we've made a mistake and will rectify it on the next invoice."

"I've been afraid this would happen sometime," Corder gloomed. "We should have let him go when he wanted to resign."

"Damn, Harry, you know we agreed then that we couldn't do without him yet. He's too useful to us. Our scapegoat if we need one," Naughton added.

"Actually, I let you talk me into that, Philip, because I'd had it up to here with entering those bloody things myself. His prison record did make him seem like a safe bet, of course."

"Exactly. If anyone questions us, whose word would they be likely to believe? A nigger jailbird or a couple of officers and gentlemen, late of Her Majesty's service? Perhaps it's a good thing he's going on leave tomorrow. He'll have forgotten these figures by the time he comes back."

"Leave? You're letting him get out of your reach?" The assistant was incredulous.

"Had to. The bugger brought a telegram that his father is dying. You can't hold a man under those conditions. But he'll be back. That's certain, because I'm keeping back two months of his pay, just to guarantee it."

"For all I care, he can have his wish and quit, just as soon as I have one more lakh (100,000) tucked away. I can taste it, I'm so close."

"Sometimes I rather envy you, Harry. The trouble with me is that I never set a clear goal the way you did. More greedy, maybe. Anyway it means that now I lack your agreeable sense of progress."

Corder clasped his hands behind his head and slid his bulk more comfortably down in his chair, while his eyes assumed a far-away look. His brother had written about a place he had a line on down in Cornwall: park, orchard, trout stream, a few acres for kitchen garden—not too big. Corder thought it might suit him very well and had been dreaming of what he would do with it.

His first need, once the place was secured, would be a wife. Maybe some school teacher who'd like to exchange a classroom full of children for a nursery full. He had no doubt he would find someone who would have him: after twenty years in India, any white woman would look good to him. "She needn't be so young, either," Corder went on, explaining his plans. "In fact if she's not, she'll be so grateful to me for releasing her from spinsterhood that she'll be wife, mother, khansama, nautch girl, drinking companion—the lot, and still count herself lucky."

"You might manage it, at that, by Jove! At least you know what you want." Naughton got up and paced restlessly to the window, the click of his boots on the stone floor the only clean sound in the room. "I only know what I don't want. I'm so damn sick of these flies, and dried-up rivers, and nothing to see through the window but brown earth, brown plants, brown people. I could do with a bit of real life.

Sometimes I think I'll go mad if I don't get Home on leave—the music halls, the pubs, yes, the girls, too. God, how I miss them!"

It was Naughton's turn to own up to his dreams: nothing short of London, perhaps a flat in Bayswater.

"Good," Corder approved. "I'll stay with you when I come up to town, and when your city friends know all your trophies and are tired of your stories of how you got them, you can come to Cornwall and we'll go fishing together."

"Sounds good," Naughton agreed in a more cheerful tone. "And unless Mr. Munshi out there sets the cat among the pigeons, another couple of years should see us Home."

"God! I can't wait!"

Two days later Naughton was back in Corder's office, this time dithering with anxiety. "What can he want?" he exclaimed aloud for the twentieth time.

"Calm down, old chap. This isn't the first time the Minister's sent for you."

"Not at all, but the difference—the big difference—is that this is the first time he's said to bring the books with me."

"Caused quite a fluttering in the dovecote, hasn't he," Corder observed with a laugh that sounded hollow even to himself. Naughton, still churning, missed the tone and whirled on him. "What the bloody hell are you so calm about? You're in this as much as I am, you know. What're you going to say when the Minister asks about all those forged bills and commissions that went into our pockets? 'Major Naughton told me to do it?' Not much of a defence, is it?"

"You're forgetting the sacrificial lamb."

"Sorry, Harry. I've been so jumpy I've barely slept. Why doesn't the Minister say to come on over, instead of leaving us three days to stew about it?"

"Probably because he thinks we're honest but inefficient, so he's very kindly giving us three days to get our books in order. Come on. Let's take a look-see."

"I'll tell you one thing I've been efficient about. At least I had my wits about me when that summons came from the palace. I sent a telegraphic signal to Dennison to hold up Sayed Mahmoud when he came through Dinpur."

"Jolly good. How did you manage that?"

"Truth, my boy. Always the best policy. Told him Sayed Mahmoud might be wanted here in connection with irregularities in the accounts and to hold him for further word. He can wait till we see what the Minister says."

14

What the Minister had to say was far from comfortable for Naughton, as he sweated out the interview the next morning. Seated at a table in the Angrezi Khana with the Military Department books spread out before him, the Minister picked out detail after detail to query.

"And this? What is this payment to Chiminlal?"

Naughton squinted at the figures. "That's for winter uniforms for the Lancers, Your Excellency." This morning was proving every bit as difficult as he had feared it might be. He could have cursed his luck in having so acute a boss. The Minister was not only quick but his mind seemed to be a complete filing case of facts about the state and actions taken by his government, down to the most minute detail. Dennison had complained that even the appointment of a new station master at Dinpur had had to have His Excellency's approval. Fortunately Dennison had not required confirmation of the order before complying with his friend's request to detain Sayed Mahmoud there.

The Major's mind was abruptly brought back to the moment by His Excellency's next question. "The estimate we approved was one-third lower than this. How did it get to be this figure?"

Naughton's voice assumed its smoothest tone. "That fool of a munshi made a mistake on an earlier payment, Your Excellency, and then he sent it out without waiting until I had had a chance to check the figures. I had a word with Chiminlal and we agreed simply to reconcile the difference in the next payment."

Naughton half expected to have to identify the original error and was busy making mental calculations when the Minister nodded and closed the books. Naughton breathed a silent sigh of relief; his brain was nearly numb with the effort of keeping straight in his head the explanations he had been giving out all morning and the resultant columns of imaginary figures he had had to keep up to date.

The Minister moved away from the table to a comfortable chair, in which he sat well back, ankles neatly crossed, ramrod spine not deigning to acknowledge the support available just behind it. Still he looked at ease. Damn chameleon, Naughton thought irreverently; fits in anywhere. Normally he liked the Minister and even admired his astuteness, but relief now made him resentful and fatigue turned it to pettiness.

"Major," His Excellency began, "I need your help and must rely on you to keep what I am asking you to do completely confidential."

"You have my word, Your Excellency," Naughton murmured, but the Minister did not wait for the assurance. Whatever the Major thought he was doing, the Minister had satisfied himself that the books had been cooked (he permitted himself a moment's enjoyment of this British slang expression, so descriptive, and his conviction that Naughton himself would have used it in this situation). He had no doubt at all that it was the Major's doing. In fact, this morning's confirmation of his suspicions about the embezzlement gave him what he was looking for, as it provided him an extra hold over the Military Secretary. He would need that for the plan he had in mind, for which he trusted no one.

"I require additional funds for the Secret Account for a purpose I do not wish to explain to anyone else and certainly not to the Resident, who occasionally demands financial reports from us. Do you understand?"

"Perfectly, Your Excellency."

"The Secret Account, as you no doubt know, though we have never spoken of it, is a legally acceptable account to cover intelligence operations. I have in mind a slight extension of those operations, still legal, but certain not to please the Residency people. It seems to me from this examination of your books that you could conceal five lakhs in them during the course of the next few months. Am I correct in that assumption?"

"I could try, Your Excellency. I should have to practise a bit to find the best way, of course; still, I have no doubt that in a short time

I could devise a system that would manage to lose that much money so thoroughly that accountants could not easily find it."

"I expected you would say that. Shall I consider it agreed?"

"You may count on it, Your Excellency. And may I say that I am sensible of the honour when you repose so much confidence in me?"

The Minister smiled, leaving Naughton to wonder whether the words he spoke were non-committal or threatening: "I am not in the habit of acting rashly. Good morning, Major."

The Minister might have been surprised, but in view of his closing words perhaps he might not have been after all, by the behavior of his Military Secretary on reaching his own office. "Well, Harry," Naughton exclaimed, throwing open the door to his assistant's office, "the track was muddy but we're home dry!" He proceeded to recount the morning, not in the least underplaying the efforts it had caused him.

"I don't believe it!" Harry Corder snickered. "I can't believe it," he repeated, chuckling, then rolled from side to side in his chair in such a cachinnation he could barely speak. "You! And me! That you and I should be ordered to cook the books. Oh, it's too delicious!"

"And the icing on the cake," Naughton reminded him when they had caught their breath, "is that now we're free of the little munshi. Any irregularities that might be discovered from now on can be blamed on the Minister's orders."

Corder began to hum.

"Oh, life's become rosy for me," he extemporized.

"A gigantical cup of hot tea.

From the threat of bar, sinister,

Saved by the Minister,

Oh, Fate has behaved handsomely."

He bowed to the Major, who stood and curtsied; then the two of them galloped around the room to the tune of their own voices bellowing in all sincerity, "Yes, fate has behaved handsomely!"

15

The "little munshi" in whose departure the two Englishmen rejoiced was also happy at the parting of their ways, though he had less reason to celebrate. He had spent a miserable week in Dinpur. When the train halted at the station, he got down to stretch his legs and breathe some clean air. Immediately the station master approached. "Excuse me, Sahib. You are one Sayed Mahmoud?"

"I am."

"Come this way. Talukdar send for you."

In the station itself a tall man with a manner to match said, "Sayed Mahmoud? You are to remain in Dinpur until further notice." Asserting that it was an official order, though it stopped short of constituting arrest, the Talukdar forbade Mahmoud to continue his journey and warned him that he would be watched. Any attempt to slip off on his own would be severely dealt with. Mahmoud's demand to know the reason evoked the information that he might be required to return to Burhan to explain irregularities in his accounts.

Appalled at this reversal of what he had considered his escape, Mahmoud walked the streets, paced the parks, ordered innumerable cups of tea he was too restless to drink. He sought comfort in the thought of the papers in his possession that would incriminate the Major. The reassurance was brief, however: if his luggage was searched he could be charged with the theft of them. In this fashion he worried his way through a week. Then, without explanation, the Talukdar said he was free to leave. He did not even stop to wonder what had made the Major change his mind about holding him.

His only thought on leaving Burhan was to get away, but once over the border and out of the reach of the Major or the jurisdiction of Jehanabad, Mahmoud had to decide where to go. The yearning to see his mother, Hamid, and the sisters at home made him weak; but whatever his problems, he was still the eldest son and responsible for their welfare. So Khandipur was out of the question. He could not go and stay with his married sister, Nur Jehan, because as her eldest brother he owed her protection and not the other way around.

The clouds in his brain thinned a little when he remembered that Nur Jehan had a much older widowed sister-in-law in Lucknow, who eked out a living for herself and her children by doing shadow embroidery. Now that was a different proposition entirely. Mahmoud had, naturally, never met the widow, since she was in purdah, but he clearly remembered her late husband. Habib Hussein had brought his family to Khandipur for his brother's wedding to Nur Jehan. Mahmoud had known something about him, since they had investigated the whole family before agreeing to marry Nur Jehan into it.

Habib Hussein possessed a reputation as a respected member of the Lucknow community and a revered teacher. The school he founded was the most prestigious in the city. Patient and understanding, he had become known for never expelling a student but for working successfully even with boys whose families despaired of them. Accordingly, his school received ever broader support. In person, Mahmoud found him a pleasant man, full of interesting tidbits of information which he supplied at unexpected moments.

Nevertheless, something about him had made Mahmoud glad that his sister was marrying the brother, not this schoolmaster. Despite his obvious integrity, Habib Hussein seemed soft. Mahmoud suspected Habib was too trusting, naively ready to rely on the good in everyone. Or perhaps he lived so exclusively among like-minded people that he failed to recognize the darker sides of life.

Important as honour and civility were to Mahmoud, he began to question whether it was possible to place too much reliance on them. That was a failure Mahmoud himself was prone to in those days, but the questions seemed prescient in view of the man's dreadful fate. Mahmoud wondered whether that story would make it more or less likely that the widow would take him as a paying guest.

❂

Habib Hussein, the headmaster, was looking for the new maths book for Standard 4. He had asked Krishna Rao, the Standard 5 instructor, whether examining that book might give them some new ideas for the next level also, but learned that only the previous day Rafi, the Standard 4 maths instructor, had said the books were not in yet.

"Did you look?"

"No. They're for his class, so I assumed he would know."

"I'm sure they're here," the headmaster said. "In fact, I think I saw them yesterday. I'll look when I get a moment and let you know if I find them."

Several hours later, in the storeroom, Habib required only a minute to spot the new maths books piled into a box in a rather haphazard fashion. He extracted a copy for himself and one for Krishna Rao but then decided to straighten the piles so that the remaining copies would not get damaged. In doing so he found the cause of the disorder: a small box that unbalanced the books on top of it. He picked it up and turned it over and over, looking for an indication of whose it might be and how it came to be there.

Finding no hint on the outside, he opened it—and gasped. Coiled inside was a necklace of emeralds and diamonds worth, at a guess, a small fortune. With a glance around to make sure no one else was in the room, he snapped the box shut and slipped it into the pocket of his kurta.

Back in his office, hands clasped behind his back, he paced the floor. Minutes—miles?—later, he summoned Rafi. "Why did you tell Krishna Rao yesterday that the new maths books had not arrived?"

"I didn't think they had."

"Yet here is your signature on the receipt."

"Oh, oh, yes; that's right. I was so busy the day they arrived that it slipped my mind."

"And even an inquiry by a colleague did not recall it for you?" Habib was not easily put off.

"Evidently not."

"You are sure that is the only reason?"

"Of course. What other reason would I have for putting Krishna Rao off?"

"Perhaps this had something to do with it." Habib laid the box on the desk between them without taking his eyes from Rafi's face. He thought he saw the teacher's jaw tighten but Rafi's denial came smoothly.

"I have no idea what that is."

"Then you say it's not yours? You didn't hide it in the box of maths books?"

"No, of course not."

"If it's not yours, then you have no objection to my keeping it—or disposing of it."

Rafi sat with head down so that Habib could scarcely see his expression. After what seemed minutes, he looked up, his face distorted by an emotion Habib could not decipher. Anguish? Terror?

"Don't do that, Headmaster Sahib. I beg you. It will be gone by morning. You need never have known about it."

"Did you steal this necklace, Rafi?" Rafi shook his head slowly. "Then what are you doing with it?"

"They said if I didn't hide it for them, they'd kill me."

"Who said so?" Habib's tone demanded a reply.

"The dacoits."

"Which dacoits? Name them."

Again Rafi seemed to struggle with himself but, instead of answering, merely shook his head.

"You don't intend to answer that. I see." Habib made to get up from his chair, seemed to think better of it, sat down again. "Well, Rafi, because you're a good teacher, I'll offer you this bargain. If you will tell me who they are, I'll see that they are prosecuted." Habib thought he heard a quick intake of breath from Rafi. "I'll do everything I can to protect you; that's a promise."

"Oh, Sahib, I dare not tell."

"Then there's only one other way, Rafi. Here is what you must do. You will take this box with the necklace to the police. Go now. Simply turn it over to them. You may tell them anything you like about how you came to have it. They can try to find the thieves without involving you. If you do not do that, I will go to them myself in the morning. I'm giving you this chance to regain your honour, rather than turn you in now."

"Don't make me do that, Headmaster Sahib. I beg you. It will cost me my life. Please forget you've seen it."

Habib stared fixedly at Rafi. With a quivering breath, the teacher straightened his spine and detached himself from the chair joint by joint. Then, picking up the box from the desk, he slunk out of the room.

Not many men would have told their wives about this situation but Habib had always paid Selma the compliment of believing her instincts sound and her insights valuable. That evening, he described the situation to her in detail, expressing anguish at the thought of possibly destroying the life of a gifted teacher but at the same time determined to uphold the standards he believed essential for the school and the community. She agreed with his estimate of what he must do but urged caution. "It's not like disciplining an unruly pupil. After all, what do you know about dacoits?"

"Not much, my dear. Except that they stick together and protect each other."

"Perhaps Rafi was right to be afraid of them. Do be careful tomorrow."

They went to bed somewhat later than usual. Habib fell asleep in his habitual, disciplined fashion; on her side of the bed, Selma tossed and turned for a while longer. She must have fallen asleep, however, for she was awakened by a hand over her face. Her head was snapped to one side as a gag was shoved into her mouth and tightened around her neck. At the same time, her husband's groan ended in a shriek and a warm sticky substance spread along her side. Bucking, squirming, fighting the hands that were holding her down, she managed to roll over far enough to see Habib. His face was almost unrecognizable in the grimace that twisted it.

Two masked men stood over him; one held a knife that was dark and dripping. She squeezed her eyes shut, but forced them open just as the man plunged the knife again between her husband's ribs. His heart's blood covered her. Frozen in shock, she watched them stand for a moment surveying their work; then one of them said, "Good. He's done for." Without displaying a trace of emotion, the man wiped the knife on Habib's clothing. Another opened the window and stepped through; the hands released her and that man followed the others. They were gone.

Selma rolled over and touched Habib's face with her forehead. It was still warm, but the glazed eyes verified the dacoit's verdict. Habib had died, had bled to death, and his blood was all over her. After a struggle with her bonds, she finally got her hands loose and untied the gag. Just in time; in another moment she would have choked on her vomit.

❂

Mahmoud shuddered at the memory; so honourable a man deserved a better end. The shiver shook off the past as well, and brought him back to his plight of the moment. The thought of Selma had given him an idea. She was close enough to family to be approachable, but distant enough so that he could with propriety ask to become a paying guest in her home. Perhaps she would welcome the income. It would do until he found work, at any rate, and perhaps work might be available in Lucknow. It would be worth exploring. Accordingly he turned his face northward.

At Lucknow, he hazarded a direction and set out on foot. Upon reaching the section of the town where he believed the widow lived, he inquired of a rickshawallah, "Can you tell me where to find the house of Habib Hussein?"

"Habib Hussein, the teacher?"

"The same."

"You're about three years too late. He is no more."

"Just so. Yet I have business with his family."

"Please sit. I can take you."

At the house, Mahmoud caught hold of one of the widow's children playing in the street to go in to his mother with a message. It was apparently effective, for he was admitted to the house, to a room that was pleasant and clean, though shabby. The youngster brought him a glass of cooling sherbet, which he sipped appreciatively. Presently the widow came forward to meet him, heavily veiled. It did not take long to complete the usual round of greetings and compliments and to exhaust their small stock of news about mutual relatives.

Cautiously, Mahmoud broached the topic that had brought him to her house, walking round and round it like an animal turning circles to make up its nest before lying down.

The widow was most hesitant. "What you ask is very difficult," she began. Her sentences were interspersed with long pauses as she searched for the right thoughts and the words with which to clothe them. "My late husband's relatives might be very distressed by such an arrangement."

She explained that, though her in-laws did not help her ("Perhaps I am too cruel a reminder of the manner of his passing"), they might know of her situation. If they heard she had taken a man into the house, they might consider it scandalous enough to adversely affect her son's future or the girls' chances of making good marriages.

Still, even the most respected teacher did not earn much money, so when she was left with the three children, her only skill by which to support them was her shadow embroidery. Though hers was considered among the best, it was not possible for a single needle to support a family, especially since, as the children became older, their needs increased.

Mahmoud barely listened to the words; her pleasantly modulated voice was well-suited to the music of Urdu, and that language was spoken in its purest form in Lucknow. The reception accorded to this unexpected visitor and the reasons for her hesitation were genteel. It would be comforting to live once again in a household managed by a woman. He took her final comment as his lead.

"So some supplementary income might be welcome."

"Yes, that's true. Even more than welcome, it would be a great relief. Besides, you saw my son. He will soon be of an age to need the guidance of a man. I had thought of sending him to my brother, but if this should work out perhaps I could keep him with me for a while longer."

So it was arranged. Mahmoud moved into the room she set apart for him, gave her a sum of money from his savings, and told her to let him know when that was exhausted. After a few days' rest, he set about looking for work, but in a city where he had neither friend nor relative in a position to ask favours for him, opportunities were elusive. By the end of two months he thought he had seen the inside of every office in Lucknow but nowhere found employment.

Then began the rounds of shops and the less inviting workplaces. Izzat, he thought, respect and dignity, are for those who can afford them.

Still the living was pleasant, the food to his taste, and the widow, after weeks of merely formal contact, was gradually becoming more sociable. Their loneliness was eased as Selma occasionally invited Mahmoud into her sitting room in the evening, when the children were in bed and the light too faint for embroidery. The proprieties were carefully observed, for she veiled herself and kept an old serving woman sitting in a corner of the room.

As their friendship grew, the topics of their conversation broadened. Mahmoud, recalling Habib's estimate of his wife's ability, began to feel it had been accurate. He found himself looking forward to the evening invitations.

Nevertheless, it was a worrisome time. As work eluded him, his small fund of savings dwindled away, especially since Major Naughton had kept back his last two months of salary. As the weeks passed, he began to wonder a bit anxiously whether he had made a wise move in committing himself to Lucknow. Then fate revealed her hand.

16

There came to the door one evening a messenger with word that the Minister from Jehanabad was in Lucknow and bade Sayed Mahmoud to call on him. Mahmoud tilted his head in his habitual gesture, considering the possibility of refusing or of devising some way to elude the messenger and disappear into the night. He dismissed the thought as quickly as it came, for if the Minister could find him in Lucknow he could find him wherever he might go.

With a bow, Mahmoud acknowledged, "His Excellency's wish is my great pleasure to fulfill. Unfortunately, since his slave does not move in such exalted circles, I am ignorant where he has put up."

"It hardly signifies," the messenger assured him, "since my own instructions are to guide you there." Then, as Mahmoud eyed him dubiously, he added, "Don't be misled by my lack of uniform. I was expressly instructed to dress in a way to make me inconspicuous." His manner suggested that the very idea was laughable. At the same time, he assured his reluctant listener, "You may be confident I will conduct you safely to your interview and back here again."

Since he had after all very little choice, Mahmoud agreed, his courage bolstered by the thought of the documents which he had tucked away among his possessions. They were his defence in case Major Naughton was making trouble for him. But why that should involve the Minister himself caused him no little anxiety. The only route to an answer, however, lay in following the messenger. As he excused himself to go and change into clothes that were more appropriate for the audience, Mahmoud hoped that his movements were less jerky than they felt, betraying his tension. With a tug at the lock on his tin trunk, a tug for luck, he set out into the night with his guide.

The walk soothed him, for the streets, though still thronged, seemed muted, as though the night had already begun to exert a gently tranquillising influence. The crowd thinned as they left the bazaar behind and entered an area of high walls surrounding what must have been large compounds. The houses, set far back, were not visible from the street. His guide showed no disposition to chat; by the time they stepped through a low postern gate, Mahmoud knew no more about this encounter than when they had set out, but his composure had returned.

The messenger was evidently known to the guards, for they saluted and let the pair pass without a challenge. Since this was a private house, they left their shoes at the door, then turned down a long corridor. The marble floors were cool under their feet despite the heat outside. The door to an inner room was opened by a chaprassi in white, the wide red band of office decorated with the heavy brass seal of his master. The messenger enunciated quietly, "Sayed Mahmoud, Your Excellency," nudged him forward, and disappeared.

Mahmoud's hand barely missed grazing the floor as he made his salaam ritual six times, murmuring, "Salaam aleikum."

"Valeikum salaam," the seated figure replied simply. The room was too large to be generally illuminated by the oil lamps set in the wall niches, but the Minister's face was in clear view and Mahmoud was aware that the spot to which His Excellency motioned him put him in the light as well.

Other than that gesture, the Minister neither smiled nor frowned, but sat regarding his visitor gravely, with a look which seemed to penetrate Mahmoud's carefully achieved calm. Mahmoud felt the challenge but refused to be discomfited, forcing his feet not to give way to traitorous shuffling, and his expression to remain impassive.

Finally the Minister spoke. "Sayed Mahmoud, why did you not return to us in Jehanabad when your leave was up?"

"I sent my resignation in proper form."

"You have not told me why."

"Forgive me, Huzoor. It was for family reasons."

"Yet you have not visited your family. Nor would you, I suppose, under the circumstances. And it is no doubt to your credit that you do not visit the consequences of your record on them."

It flashed across Mahmoud's consciousness that the Minister knew a great deal more about him than there was any reason to expect, but so far he could make nothing of the fact.

"Perhaps," the Minister resumed his matter-of-fact observations, "you were afraid because of the irregularities in the Military Accounts on which you worked."

"I am afraid of nothing, Your Excellency, because I have done nothing wrong."

"Still, the irregularities are there."

"They are not my irregularities, Your Excellency."

"Well spoken. But assertion is far from proof."

"Proof can be supplied."

"For your sake, I trust it will be forthcoming at the proper time."

Pressing for an indication of "proper time," Mahmoud learned that charges had not yet been filed against him and that the Minister apparently was offering him a way of escaping them. "I have been thinking," he said, "there might be a way you could establish your good faith, a way that might make it unnecessary ever to open the question of the Military Accounts." Just as he had established a hold over the Major before entrusting him with the task of secreting confidential funds, so the Minister played with Mahmoud until he felt secure in trusting him with the mission.

Mahmoud looked steadily at the Minister. The latter shifted his gaze to the window, appearing to stare beyond the night blackness into the far distance. "I have need of a man who can carry a message to the Khan Sahib in Kabul," he said softly. Then his gaze moved again and seemed to bore into Mahmoud's thoughts, perceiving or perhaps assuming the turbulence. After allowing Mahmoud a few moments' reflection, he resumed, "It would not be a comfortable journey or even necessarily a safe one. The British actively discourage communication between Afghanistan and India. It would be rewarded accordingly."

The opportunity to earn an income was certainly attractive. The past year and a half had taught Mahmoud to regard the future as an unknown and to evaluate its various contingencies. He spoke out of that experience now, unaware of how close his reply came to a commitment. "If it is so risky, a man cannot simply go there. Some excuse for travelling would be required."

"That has occurred to me. But it needs to be an excuse the messenger can carry off, if necessary. Have you a suggestion?"

"Perhaps...I wonder...it's just a thought but it might be worth a try...perhaps a man who goes to become the disciple of a holy man would be able to reach the destination."

"Does that mean you agree?" the Minister inquired sharply.

It was Mahmoud's turn to gaze into the blackness outside, eyes upward, as though contemplating the mountains. "If I do not agree to go?" he asked.

"I am sure the Military Secretary would regret having to spend time on a trial."

"I do not fear such a trial, for I know my innocence."

"But, perhaps, you fear such a commission as I offer?"

"Yes. I mean no. I do not wish to go. But still, I do not fear it." The Minister's taunt had caught him. At the same time, this seemed like an opportunity to extend his horizons, to be on his own in new ways and new places, possibly to learn something that would make him employable at a job more interesting than that of munshi. "So, all right, I will do my best, Your Excellency."

"Good. Then I may tell you that the Akhund of Swat is a friend. If you can get to his court, he will see that you reach Kabul. Until then, you must make your own way."

"In that case, Excellency, I shall require some justification for travelling."

"You just suggested the character of a holy man."

"Unfortunately, Excellency, as I'm sure you know even though it seems to have escaped your attention for the moment, Islamic holy men are not like their Hindu counterparts who simply wander as they please and exist by begging. The Koran lays on every man an obligation to earn his living."

"So what do you propose?" The asperity of the Minister's tone warned Mahmoud to justify his impertinence.

"It needs to be something unusual, I suppose; something which will explain my request to see the Khan, if necessary. A simple worker, a weaver, even a craftsman would not do. An artist might be admitted."

"True, but do you have the talent which might be needed along the way to justify the pose?"

"Alas, no. A jeweller can always command the attention of a ruler, but to carry precious gems would be to attract the attention of dacoits and other criminals. Besides, I know nothing about them."

"That was your downfall once, and I don't imagine you learned to appraise jewels in prison."

"Exactly. But it must be something important people desire, or, or, that piques their curiosity. Something novel. Now, I wonder...I have heard there is a newer fashion which is said to fascinate many of the rich; it is known as pocket watches. I have heard there is a style called repeater—marvellous, if it's true, such a small instrument to chime the hour. That would be certain to please a ruler. Especially with a jewel embedded in the key. I could carry a stock of pocket watches to interest Your Excellency's powerful friends."

"Extravagance is a habit quickly acquired, I see," the Minister commented, causing Mahmoud to hold his breath until he added, "Very well. I shall have pocket watches made ready for you, for the Khan and the Akhund. A small supply; you may need a few extras for bargaining or other purposes we cannot now foresee. You will also receive money for your expenses. Whatever is not spent is yours to keep. Beyond that, you will be recompensed only on your return."

"And if I do gain an audience with the Khan Sahib, what then?"

"You are to tell him you bring a message from me which is for his ears alone. No one who may help you on the way should be given an inkling of it, or of where you are headed."

"And the message?"

"The message is, 'If the wind blows from the northwest, will you tie down your tent flaps against it? Or will you use its strength? We keep a watch on the weather.' Repeat it."

Mahmoud did so.

"Good."

"But what am I to say when the Khan asks me why you hate the British?"

For a moment, the Minister's black eyes flashed but he as quickly controlled the reaction and said suavely, "Since you are keen enough to ask the question, you are no doubt astute enough also to answer it according to the circumstances of the moment. If the Khan gives you an answer, come back here to Lucknow and send word to me that a great Sufi has a message from the beyond for me. I will make arrangements to get your message."

"I could as well deliver it to Burhan."

"Let us understand one another, Sayed Mahmoud. Your instructions are never to return to Jehanabad. Not ever. You must bear in mind how very confidential your mission is, not only the contents of it but also the fact. I have had to make special arrangements to finance it and cannot risk questions being asked. You should take care not under any circumstances to appear again in Burhan. There, the question of the Military Accounts might be raised."

"I understand, Your Excellency. I will come back to Lucknow only."

"Payment for the service will be made to you here, but no one must know where your money comes from."

"Very well, Your Excellency."

"How soon can you start?"

For the first time, Mahmoud smiled. "As soon as the watches are ready, Your Excellency."

"Good. Affairs are slower here because I am not in my own place. Let us say ten days from now. All further arrangements will be made with the man who brought you here."

Mahmoud bowed. "Will Your Excellency allow your servant one question?"

The Minister was also greatly relaxed. "Two."

"Why me? Why have you chosen someone whom you hardly know, who does not even belong to your state?"

"As for the first part of your questions, you underrate me, Sayed Mahmoud. It hasn't really escaped your notice, has it, that I know a great deal about you? You have a record to live down, it is true, but you do not panic or give the game away under pressure; you think on your feet; and you are a convincing liar." At this last, Mahmoud opened his mouth to protest but quickly restrained himself. The Minister continued as though he had not noticed the impulse and its correction. "All good qualifications for this assignment. Are we all set?"

"You offered me two, Your Excellency. My second is more of a condition than a question. I have agreed with a respectable widow to pay rent to her for my meals and lodging. It is not right that she should be deprived of this income. She should be paid Rs. 500 on the day I depart and the same sum, annually if necessary, until I am back in my rooms there."

The Minister regarded Mahmoud for a long moment before saying quietly, "It shall be done."

"Then, Your Excellency, I take your leave. Allah, the All-Knowing, will watch over both of us until I return."

Making his royal salaams, Mahmoud backed out of the room. At the door, he was stopped by the Minister's voice. "Sayed Mahmoud, one more reason for selecting you: you are a hard bargainer." As he closed the door, Mahmoud thought he heard the Minister laugh.

17

Back again in Jehanabad, the Minister duly sent a demi-official letter reporting to the Resident his return from a satisfactory pilgrimage to the famous shrine in Lucknow. Within the hour, a uniformed chaprassi arrived at the deori to deliver a note written on heavy paper and bearing the seal of the Residency. "The Resident would be pleased," it read, "if the Minister would breakfast with him tomorrow morning at eleven."

Despite the courtesy of the invitation, the Minister knew from long acquaintance that it constituted a command and would involve official business. It was by such niceties that the Paramount Power clothed their assumption of authority to direct and manipulate the princely states. All of the Minister's considerable diplomatic skill was required in order to circumvent that assumption, and even then not always successfully.

That morning the Minister dressed with his usual care. A simple pyjama and kurta, to maintain the fiction of an informal social occasion, of heavy silk richly embroidered, as appropriate for his status. The outer courtyard swarmed with several hundred men who opened a way and salaamed politely when the Minister emerged. His appearance was the signal for the big gates to be swung open and the first ranks surged out, following the pennant bearers. These men were from his private army, whose numbers he had cut back as an example for the other nobles to follow.

As he mounted his elephant, the rest of the men fell in around or behind him; the regular army would have marched in parade columns. The irregulars had no uniforms, only a sash denoting their Master, and they filled the narrow street in a jostling, laughing crowd. The hawkers with their ready-to-cook snacks and the peddlers with their push-carts piled high with fruits or vegetables pulled their equipment alongside the walls out of the way. Beggars, children, women in burqas, men festooned with weapons of all sorts, most of them ancient—all that crowd that normally made the street so lively— now either pressed against the walls to watch the spectacle or slipped into the nearest shop to avoid the crush.

The first of the retainers arrived at the Residency far enough in advance so that the gates were already open when the Minister's elephant reached them. Unlike the Minister's deori, where the gardens existed within the succession of enclosed courtyards, the Residency sat in a ten-acre garden. What in England would have been green lawn, however, was here in this arid land burned brown. Carefully tended shrubs and flowers in big earthen pots provided colour while conserving water.

In the midst of this expanse was a Palladian mansion approached by a long flight of stairs, which also bore potted plants. The columns and arches at the top were surmounted by a cornice with intricately carved figures. The overall effect was appropriately imposing as a setting for the Viceroy's political representative.

Dismounting, the Minister was met on the lowest step by the Second Secretary and on the top one by the Assistant Resident, new, the Minister was surprised to see, young and pleasant looking. Possibly too young, he reflected briefly; a seasoned political agent calculated carefully what he could carry off and was therefore at least somewhat predictable, but a young one was often impulsive. He must be studied. Not even the most fleeting shadow on his composed features betrayed these thoughts. The young man introduced himself as Ian McAllum and led the Minister indoors.

Down the long corridors they passed numerous servants in Anglicized uniforms, some bustling about an errand, others simply being available for a summons. All bowed deeply and salaamed the Minister. Then through an anteroom and into the high-ceilinged room where the Resident had been sitting. Hearing the footsteps, he rose. Tall, long face made longer by its small goatee, the Guardsman he had once been was reflected in his erect bearing, despite the jowls beginning to sag and the substantial paunch that stretched his coat.

Dressed more appropriately for London than for this hot climate, he managed to dab at his perspiring face and tuck the handkerchief back up his coat sleeve before his guest appeared. As they entered, he took three steps to the edge of the carpet, where he greeted his visitor.

The proprieties having thus been satisfied, the Assistant retired and the two men stepped alone into the dining room. It was a formal room, large enough to accommodate a dinner party of at least sixty people, with buffets showing off the silver, and serving tables at intervals. For this more intimate occasion, the two were served at a smaller table set in front of a window, through which they looked out on the garden. White table linen, starched napkins which crackled when unfolded, and full sets of silverware seemed to belie the implied informality of the occasion.

During breakfast they rehearsed the acceptable interchanges: inquiries about the health of His Highness and of the Queen Empress; whether the Minister's trip had been comfortable; whether the Resident's new garden was growing properly. These verbal minuets were as much a part of their social skills as was their other behaviour. The Resident, unable to fault the Minister's impeccable table manners, concluded his guest had been coached by an Englishman and silently hoped he would pass on the custom to his countrymen, those disgusting barbarians who took up their food with their fingers.

At the close of the meal, the pair moved to severely straight armchairs set in the bay window, a good spot for a private conversation. The oleander hedge facing it was still in bloom. A bearer placed a final cup of tea at each one's elbow and retired. Only then did the Resident lead the conversation around to questions concerning the state. "It has come to my attention," he began, "that the quarterly financial report is now long past due."

Certain that this was not the main business of the day, the Minister remained silent, leaving the burden of continuing on the Resident.

"I recognize, of course, the difficulties of gathering information from the Districts, but even making allowance for that, the delay is now excessive." Still no reply from his guest, so the Resident persevered. "But because I respect your good faith, I do not wish to report this matter to Calcutta."

"I understand," the Minister murmured.

"There is another point to consider. As it may attract the Viceroy's attention, I thought it wise to bring it to Your Excellency's notice first."

The Minister raised one eyebrow.

"There are persistent rumours in the city that the Jehanabad army is being greatly enlarged. You know that violates the agreement that the Viceroy advised you of last year."

"I am sure the Resident Sahib knows how to understand street rumours."

"Are you saying the rumours are untrue?"

The Minister responded with a barely perceptible bow.

"And can you assure me that the army stands at precisely the same strength now as at this time last year?"

"Very nearly. There has been only a very slight increase."

"You know that is not allowed."

"May I point out that the Resident Sahib himself urged me to reduce the size of the irregular armies in the State. I have used several means of approach to persuade the nobles to do so, each from his own troops. But we cannot have armed men roaming the countryside with no means of support. So a few have been absorbed into the regular army, only the few who could not be otherwise taken care of."

"That is reasonable. But I hope that 'few' is a literal report. The Viceroy would be very displeased with any significant increase in the absolute numbers. Now about that financial report. May I expect it in a fortnight's time?"

"I will expedite it, Resident Sahib. There will be only one substantial difference from the previous quarter, and that is a modest increase in the military budget."

"In view of your reference just now to 'only a few,' I find that surprising."

"In order to absorb as many of the irregulars as essential for public safety, it was necessary to retire those of the regulars who were willing to be released or were approaching the end of their term of service. Severance pay accounts for a good deal of the increase."

"Is that it, then?"

"Not quite. At the urging of His Highness's Military Secretary—Major Naughton—we have issued new uniforms to all the troops. It is some years now since they received their last outfits. Moreover, during the last growing season we experienced a severe drought as you know."

"Only too well," the Resident nodded.

"That has greatly increased the price of food, which carries a double penalty: it increases not only the costs of the regular messes, but also the dearness allowance paid to support the families."

"Very well, Your Excellency, I shall examine these accounts with interest. When they are completed, Mr. McAllum will come to you to receive them, in case there should be anything you might wish to explain."

By signaling for the sprinkling of rosewater and the passing of paan, the digestive in its shiny green betel leaf, the Resident indicated the end of the interview.

The Minister returned to his own deori with the satisfied impression that the conversation had gone well. Still, it was worth mulling over to be certain he had not missed any cue. It had certainly not been difficult to deflect possible future questions about the military budget. The Resident tried to threaten him with the parting thrust about 'examining the accounts' but appeared to swallow the explanations. Time for a word with Major Naughton to make sure that the money for the Secret Account was securely camouflaged. Sayed Mahmood should be well on his way by now; nothing must prevent the delivery of that message.

His thoughts continued in the same vein as he dismounted the elephant and headed to his dressing room. It was not an unreasonable message. The Tsar had always threatened the Queen's hegemony in India. The British call it the Great Game; typical of their arrogance. But the Russians might really mount an invasion. If they did, they would never be able to hold Afghanistan; anyone who had read history at all knew that. No one, not even the Mughals, had. A boy there receives a gun as his first toy and every youth wears his acquaintance with his tribe's territory as casually as his own cloak. In such a country, outsiders have no chance.

The ministerial head, now bare of its heavy turban, wagged slowly. If it ever came to that, he reminded himself, His Highness would require some help understanding that his Minister did not want the Russians to replace the British here. What he hoped for was a moratorium. If the Russians were allowed to cross those mountains, they could worry the British in North India enough to distract their attention from the 'safer' South, where Jehanabad was a leading state. He could use that time to plug some of the holes the British slipped through into the affairs of the State.

Foreigners were like the water hyacinths; you plant one for your pleasure and before you can realize the enjoyment, it has spread so it chokes the streams.

18

Even as the Minister sparred with the Resident, Sayed Mahmoud was on a train huff-chuffing its way across the Gangetic plain towards Delhi. He had taken a third-class ticket in order to be in the character of a simple countryman, one unlikely to be carrying anything that might be of interest to thieves. Unaccustomed to luxury in the years just past, he was not dismayed by the bare wooden benches that lined the carriages.

He had arrived at the station well ahead of train time, knowing the crush that would compete for space. As soon as the gates opened, Mahmoud sprinted to his bogey. There, by dint of his early arrival and judicious use of elbows, he managed to secure a corner seat. Like most country people, he travelled with his belongings tied up in a bundle. To get it out of the way and also make it inconspicuous in the unlikely possibility there might be a thief on board, he shoved it under the seat and tucked it back as far as it would go. It contained two sets of clothing for warm weather and one for cool as well as two shawls against the possibility of being caught by colder weather in the mountains. Not very likely: July now, and back in Lucknow before the end of the year, he calculated.

Hidden in the midst of the clothing, tightly wrapped in a smaller parcel so as not to arouse curiosity in case it should be seen, was the expense money the Minister had provided, together with the small stock of watches. In addition to the more elegant ones intended as gifts for the Akhund and the Khan, the plainer ones would be useful for barter or bribes, as needed. Since every person of any importance was protected by chaprassis at the gate and secretaries or munshis in the office, it was important also to have baksheesh readily available. With this in mind he had changed some of his gold for rupees and smaller coins before he set out.

In a second small bundle was tied the food he had brought for the first part of the journey: a packet of kedgeree, the combination of rice and lentils which provided concentrated nourishment, several forms of snacks, a small jar of pickles with which to flavour the food he might buy along the way.

Satisfied with his efforts, Mahmoud settled back to survey the crowded car. Workmen with their tools, families with numerous bundles including large supplies of food which would be shared with neighbours at intervals, farmers travelling with chickens tied by their legs into bunches, heads buried under their wings, a bit like the infants women hid under their saris as they nursed them: the passenger list was like the census of a village.

When the train started, the rhythm of the sound and movement lulled him. Tucking his feet up, he slept and woke, dozed and roused himself to lethargic wakefulness, enough to gesture to the tea wallahs on each station platform for a cup of their brew, hot, sweet and milky. After some hours he stood up to stretch. "Oho," the passenger sitting across from him said. "Look who's decided to join the company. We thought you didn't like the sight of us, keeping your eyes closed the whole way."

Mahmoud grinned.

"Now you're awake," a heavy-set woman said, "you might as well have something to eat. Take this rice."

"No, no," another protested. "You must start with a chapatti. Have this."

On all sides the friendly passengers pressed food on him. Thinking he should reciprocate with some of his snacks, Mahmoud leaned down to reach his bundle, only to find that the rocking of the car had moved the food package behind the larger one. When he pulled it slightly forward to reach behind it, the man next to him, perhaps thinking to be helpful, picked it up, then mimed collapsing under the weight. "Arre, what do you carry in here? Gold?" he exclaimed.

"Ingots," Mahmoud replied with a smile and reached for his bundle. "Never travel without them." Though his fellow passengers laughed at his joke, he made up his mind no longer to risk carrying his precious stock in a bundle that anyone might seize. In Delhi he would find a tailor to make other arrangements for it.

When the station at Delhi was called, he got up, stretched his cramped limbs, and started to brush off the soot that had blackened his clothes. "Keep your dirt to yourself," a voice at his elbow snarled, "we have our own to deal with."

Taking the measure of the burly Sikh who had spoken, he attempted a pleasantry: "No need to get upset, brother. There's plenty of the stuff to go around." But he did not object when the man, who had boarded at the last stop, slid into his corner seat. Standing for a few moments would restore the circulation in his legs before they would have to carry him across the station and goodness knows how far away from it until he found lodging.

He had determined to spend a few days in this ancient city, to visit the great Jama Masjid, saunter down the famous street called Chandni Chowk, to see what they were selling, what was popular in this part of the world, and possibly to find a watchmaker who would be receptive to his questions. That would lend legitimacy to his delay. He tied his modest bundles together and carried them in one hand, slipping a finger under the knot. A householder bringing home the results of his shopping might have carried it like that.

Stepping out of the station, he paused to look around and was enchanted to recognize on the skyline the white-domed minarets of Jama Masjid. The streets were crowded with the familiar assortment: people walking, pushing loaded carts, cooking snacks to hawk, pi dogs and elephants, goats, cows, tongas and jutkas and wagons.

New to him were camels, some pulling heavy loads, looking down superciliously on the rest of the traffic, and knowing they would deliver the goods as well as their sleeping master to the right address; others swayed under the loaded saddlebags that seemed to double their girth. Many of them had come across the Rajasthan desert, some even from Karachi, carrying carpets and other treasures from Persia and Afghanistan.

Launching himself into the sea of humanity, Mahmoud struck a direction and continued on it until it shortly intersected a main street, which had to be Chandni Chowk. The buildings were not ancient, for they had been burnt to the ground or razed when Nadir Shah's troops ransacked the city in 1724, and again in the uprising of 1857 that the British called the Mutiny. Many were scarcely older than Mahmoud himself; their stone or stucco exteriors were undistinguished, with homes above and shops below. The very ordinariness of it put him at ease.

Children played in the streets. With a sudden lightness of heart, Mahmoud hopscotched through a rice-flour diagram, much to the amusement of the little girls who had laid it out. But when he smiled at them, they ran away giggling. Further on, a group of boys played kabaddi. Mahmoud picked up a stick someone had dropped and joined in. At the end of the round, they gathered around him. "Who are you?"

"Just a man who used to be a boy like you."

"But you're not from here. Where did you play kabaddi?"

"In the town where I grew up."

"And did strange men come and play with you?"

"There weren't many strangers in our little town. Not like here—just look at the crowds in this street."

One of the youngsters spat. "What do you expect? Only women stay indoors. C'mon. Let's play."

Mahmoud continued down the avenue. In the back of his mind was a faint concern that even a child had spotted him so quickly as an outsider, but the host of new impressions crowded it out. He had expected to find on Chandni Chowk only the shops of silversmiths, or at least of jewellers. Surely those were the things appropriate to the Moonlight Bazaar.

To his surprise, the street was crowded with all sorts of activities: men frying vegetable pakoras or sweet jalebis or stirring up mutton curries, mild to his southern palate but mouth-wateringly aromatic, nevertheless. Sword sharpeners whirling their grindstones put an edge on daggers or kitchen knives indiscriminately. Forgers shaped tools or water pots. People everywhere, stepping around the goats and cattle, elbowing their way forward when they were blocked from entering a shop, or standing in the middle of the street and impeding traffic in both directions while they greeted acquaintances and exchanged gossip with them.

One such group, somewhat larger and more vocal than others, completely obstructed movement on the street while they carried on their social rituals of "wishing" one another. (The expression covered the whole range of formality to informality in greeting and taking leave of friends or acquaintances, whether in paying formal calls or in chance encounters.) The group proceeded to a leisurely exchange of news along with good-natured raillery.

As Mahmoud stood listening, idly waiting for them to disperse so he could get through, a pedestrian coming from the other side shouted self-importantly, "Out of my way. Clear the street!" These imperious orders issued from a tall, broad-shouldered man who was probably in his mid- or upper-forties. His erect posture and embroidered vest barely disguised the paunch that strained his silk kurta. Clearly a minor official of some sort, accustomed to insisting on his authority.

"Look who's giving these orders!" a man on the edge of the group sneered. Mahmoud wondered idly whether the fellow was hoping to improve his position by this quick defence of the group.

"Have you eyes?" the challenger responded. "Can't you see I serve the Commissioner Sahib?"

"This is an Indian street. Foreigners, even the Commissioner, do not give the orders here. So you will wait there until your manners improve."

At this the men accompanying the stranger stepped between him and the crowd. "Have some respect," one of them threatened, "or my chappal on your heads will open a path." At this, men on both sides began shouting insults: budmash! swine! haramzada! son of a whore! go back and lick the foreigner's boots.

With every shout the crowd seemed to multiply on both sides and the shoving and jostling became more menacing. A stone whizzed past Mahmoud's ear; before he could duck, another struck him painfully in the shoulder while a third almost simultaneously tore a jagged path along his hair line. Less afraid of these injuries than of the possibility that police in the British service might show up and catch him in their net, Mahmoud slipped back through the throng. "Arre, you!" a voice behind him shouted. Was it directed at him? He quickened his step, but the voice shouted again, "Wait, you!"

Panic pushed Mahmoud into running blindly, anywhere—but where? Just go! Is he closer? Mustn't look back, might stumble. Can't run much longer. Where to hide? Here. No, there. There, just ahead, just there, a jewellery shop! As he ducked in, he had barely time to notice from the corner of his eye a pocket watch prominently displayed in the front case. The owner was already on his feet. Before Mahmoud's pursuer could follow him inside, the owner had pulled down the iron shutter that closed his shop and, with only a slight struggle, made the hasps meet sufficiently to accept the padlock. Then he turned and greeted his visitor calmly. "Salaam, brother."

"Valeikum salaam," Mahmoud replied with formal courtesy.

"So you've already had enough of the excitement. Were you with the group that started it?"

Mahmoud forced his breathing into a more normal pattern before replying. "A bystander only and no friend to either party. It's true I felt threatened by a stranger who seemed to pursue me. I can't imagine what he wanted."

"You're clearly not from here. That's enough to raise official suspicions, even if you haven't done anything. Wait here a moment. I'll bring some water to wash away the blood and we'll see what damage you've suffered."

Mahmoud sank to the floor and waited with his head on his fist. His sudden weakness was as much from relief at his escape as from the loss of blood, which was flowing freely in the manner of scalp wounds. The owner reappeared from a back room carrying a wet cloth with which he mopped Mahmoud's temple. "Nothing serious," he reported cheerfully, "though the scab will add nothing to your beauty."

"Are Delhiwallas always so obstreperous with one another?"

"Sometimes it happens. You're new here, are you? What brings you to our city?"

Mahmoud studied his rescuer. Even had he not noticed the name Kamaluddin stenciled on the account book at his side, the crocheted cap the man wore would have identified him as a Muslim. Safe. "In truth, brother, why should I lie? I had no plan for Delhi. I am on my way north and thought only to stop over here for a few days."

"North? You know the British control the Punjab and don't welcome strangers there. Or do you mean to seek them out in Simla?"

"Neither one. I have a fancy to study with a famous holy man. It's to him I'm turning my face."

"A Mussulman who is a holy man in the North. You must refer to the Akhund of Swat."

"None other. The most advanced Sufi of our time. I have long yearned for his guidance."

"Then you must be a Sufi yourself, and no beginner, to hope that the Akhund would accept you as a pupil."

Mahmoud bowed his head modestly; no need to admit how much of a beginner he was.

Kamaluddin continued. "Don't you know that the British are even more suspicious of people going to Swat than to the Punjab? Men have been hanged for it. Just for going there."

"So I have heard."

"This sounds like madness. There must be learned Sufis in safer places. Why not study with a pir in Allahabad or even Lucknow?"

"I feel called to study with the Akhund."

"You will not find the going easy. The English don't trust Indians; every one of them who sees you will suspect you of being a spy, and that's a capital crime. They say it takes very little evidence to convict, even if you haven't done anything."

"Allah ho Akbar. God is Great," Mahmoud replied, head down. The Minister's warning that the British 'actively discourage' travel between India and Afghanistan was proving to be a major understatement.

Kamaluddin had another idea, but Mahmoud maintained his silence largely for lack of an adequate answer. "Too bad you don't know some Englishman you could travel with, maybe as his interpreter or something. Ah, well, if you must go, I suppose you must. Let me suggest to you, come home with me for a few days until your wounds are healed. Your way will be smoother if people don't see the blood and suspect you of mischief. My home is yours so long as you need it."

Mahmoud took a moment to reply, letting his inner tensions go, one by one; still he felt a faint uneasiness at accepting an offer which put him under an obligation he was not likely ever to repay. As his body rocked to and fro in rhythm with his thoughts, his glance chanced to light on the pocket watch in the showcase. "You are interested in Sufism, brother?"

"I would learn from you," his host acknowledged.

"Then I shall teach you the elements of Sufism and you shall teach me some elementary things about the mechanism of this watch I see here. We shall each be the other's tutor."

"Good."

"But I should warn you. You will have a harder time to teach me than I you."

"How so?"

"I know nothing at all about watches. Only seen a few and got curious. But you have already set your foot on the path of Sufism."

"You misunderstood me. I know nothing about Sufism."

"Exactly. Sufism deals with two opposites in life: mysticism, which we shall not touch on, and love. Love expresses itself in actions of caring for other people, as you took me in just now, though you knew me not at all."

"One must help people who need it. That is our duty."

"There you are. Duty is a Sufi concept. Our great Saint, Nizamuddin, said, 'I swear by God, that He holds dear those who love Him for the sake of human beings and also those who love human beings for the sake of God.'"

At the end of another ten days, Mahmoud's bruises had healed and his hair now adequately covered the small remaining scar. More importantly in his view, he could now adjust the timing of a watch and do simple repairs. What he did not recognize was the ease he had begun to feel in the presence of strangers and the ingeniousness with which he invented personal history or explanations when they seemed to be required, while minimizing the outright lies.

Mahmoud-the-emissary had already moved a considerable way from the literal-minded Mahmoud-the-Talukdar's-munshi. It was time to move on.

His host, for his part, was also satisfied with his bargain. "I thank you for this introduction to Sufism. I now understand better the implications of duty, and that includes learning more." Then, moving briskly to the practical, he advised, "You can take the train as far as Batala. Stop there with a jeweller called Haji Ali Akbar. Tell him you come from me. He will take you in and will know to whom to commend you next."

"You have been most kind. We shall meet again, Insh'Allah."

"May Allah go with you."

19

Leaving Delhi, confident that he was not being observed, Mahmoud treated himself to a second-class ticket. This time he stayed awake and paid more attention to the countryside through which he was passing. On his return journey, he might need to be familiar with the territory. He was also prodded to alertness by a renewed sense of the urgency of his mission, as though staying awake could make up for what he now thought of as his two-week holiday in Delhi.

At Ambala the line turned almost due north and at each station the breeze coming through the opened windows of the carriage felt cooler. It was a welcome change, for the bodies crowded onto the wooden seats inevitably made the air within seem hot. The Sikhs, whose country this was, were big, sturdy men and women, rawboned, muscular, not people to be daunted by physical challenges. Acutely conscious of his own slight build and clean-shaven face, self-conscious about his bulky country turban when he eyed the locals' neatly-wound headdress, and nervously aware of their curious stares, he heartily wished himself out of the Punjab.

He wished so even more vehemently as he became aware of a middle-aged Sikh sitting across the aisle from him who seemed to be watching him. The luxuriant black beard was neatly rolled in a net, while the mustache hid a grim mouth. The very lack of any expression other than the fixed gaze increased the menace of the face. Mahmoud looked away, looked down, looked in the other direction, but no matter where he looked, he felt the man's eyes on him.

As people moved around the carriage or got off and were replaced by new passengers, Mahmoud edged his way down the bench to the other end of the bogey. The eyes followed him. He began to imagine how comforting it would be if some hugely obese person should sit down beside him, someone big enough to shield him from those malevolent eyes.

Mahmoud experienced a momentary relief as the train pulled in to Ludhiana, for the man who had so tormented him got up and picked up his bundle; he was getting off. But the relief was premature; hope was immediately dashed as the man approached him and now said firmly, "Let's go. You'll get off here and come with me."

"You must have mistaken me for someone else," Mahmoud replied, trying to sound matter-of-fact. "I continue on from here."

"Not yet, you won't. You'll come with me," the man repeated, flashing a police badge. "The Collector Sahib likes to talk to any strangers in our part of the country."

This was what he had been repeatedly warned about: although it was now two decades since the uprising of 1857, the British still regarded any incursion into the Punjab as suspicious. Strangers could be picked up for questioning and investigation on any pretext whatsoever, or without any. Even convicted, as Kamaluddin had warned.

Since compliance was his only option, Mahmoud picked up his bundles and preceded the policeman off the train. From the station they walked in silence to the Collector's office, actually a bungalow in a big, shady compound. There Mahmoud's escort merely nodded to the guard at the gate, who admitted them without comment. The desk clerk looked up from his book and tore off a corner of paper to mark his place before nodding at the policeman who swaggered in.

"Collector in?"

The clerk yawned, stretched, then shook his head. "No."

"Where is he?"

"Riding circuit, of course."

"So when's he back in station?"

"Day after tomorrow, provided he's on schedule."

"You'll have to keep this chap till then," the policeman responded. "And be sure you put down that I was the one who brought him in. Alone. I don't intend to share the bounty with anyone."

The clerk nodded without comment.

"He's yours, then," the policeman said, and strode out.

The clerk made a face behind the retreating back, then eyed Mahmoud for a moment. "Come," he said and led the way to the back part of the house. There he showed Mahmoud into a small room, sparsely furnished with a charpoy tipped up against a wall, a washstand with a pitcher of water, and a bucket. But clean. Its single window was barred in the usual style with straight iron pipes.

"I'll have to lock the door," the man said, in more of a chatty tone than he had deigned to use with the policeman, "but I'll see that you get food this evening. Don't worry about that. You're not from around here, that's clear. South would be my guess."

During the pause while he set the charpoy onto its four legs, Mahmoud closed his inner gates against any temptation to respond to this friendly tone with information. But the clerk went on as though his prisoner had attempted an interruption, "No, don't tell me. When the Collector asks, I'd rather be able to say I don't know anything about you. Unfortunately, he's not very hospitable to outsiders like you."

"We'll have to see what happens, then," Mahmoud said, thankful to the student for sparing him one more lie. "Do you run this place by yourself?"

"When the Collector's out, the guard and I are on our own."

"Don't you have many prisoners like me?"

"Not often. Though that guy who brought you in, he's a bounty hound. He'd bring someone every day if he could find 'em. Suspects everybody he sees. Personally, I have more faith in my fellow man." The clerk interrupted his monologue to step out of the room without bothering to lock the door behind him and returned a moment later with a pillow under one arm and a razai over the other. He plumped it a bit, then spread it on the charpoy and added the pillow.

"I'm a student," he resumed, "so this job suits me fine, because there's so little to do I have plenty of time to do my homework. I guess I better go send the guard for your food, though. I'm off in an hour."

"You have to wait till your relief arrives?"

"What relief? You're locked in. Guard's out front. You'll have to entertain yourself till I come back in the morning."

Relieved at not being questioned before he had time to take stock, Mahmoud sank onto the charpoy. Aware also that this was merely a reprieve, he set to work immediately to think out his situation. The best he could expect, if he was cleared of spying, was that the Collector would have him escorted out of the Punjab, back southward most certainly, possibly even as far as Delhi. That was the wrong direction; he would have to think of a way to establish his innocent presence, to allow him to resume his journey without surveillance.

At worst, he would be imprisoned. Surely they couldn't hang him, since they could prove no illegal activity or spying charges. Still, there were better things to do with his life than go back to prison. And the first one of them was to get to Kabul.

It was fortunate, in any case, that his room was at the back of the bungalow and there were no other occupants. The guard seemed to content himself with watching the gate; at least, by midnight Mahmoud had heard no steps around the building. He examined the bars at the window with fingers and with what sight was possible from the faint moonlight. It was clearly an old building, possibly not in the best of repair. He began to twirl a bar, muffling the sound by wrapping its base with his turban, then worked it back and forth methodically, so that the rough end of the iron bar acted as a rasp on the wood. Back and forth, back and forth. From time to time he stopped to shake out the rumal and brush the sawdust away.

Finally he had ground the iron deep enough into the sill so that he was able to slide the top edge of the bar out of the wood and remove it. Then more rasping, and another bar out. He stood and stretched, moving his shoulder its full range, shaking his fingers to loosen the cramp. To the bars again. Just before dawn, he removed still another bar and realized if he made himself small he could squeeze through the opening.

While he worked he had surveyed the trees that were visible from his window and chosen one whose branches would give him access to the compound wall. Now he exhaled deeply and pushed his body through the space he had created, reached back for his bundle, then quickly flattened against the house until he was sure there was no one in sight. A fleeting thought for the nice student who had given him dinner, a hope this escape would not cause trouble for him. Only an instant Mahmoud stood there; time was precious, with daylight developing fast. He raced across the intervening space and scaled the tree, stretched to reach the top of the wall, then dropped his meager possessions over and jumped down.

He landed with a thud on a small unevenness that rolled him over and almost in the same motion rolled back to get his feet under him. Before he could stand up, a policeman on early duty came around the corner. Seeing the squatting figure, he seized him by the collar. As Mahmoud felt himself being pulled upright he straightened his clothes and brushed the grass off his shoulders as though reaching for the hand holding him.

"What're you doing here at this hour?" a rough voice demanded.

"Just relieving myself," Mahmoud replied. "What do you think a man does against a wall at this hour?"

The policeman laughed and gave him a friendly shove. "Get on with you, then."

As casually as he could manage, Mahmoud hooked a finger under the knot of his bundle and walked off in what he hoped was the direction of the road out of town. Managing to find a northward leading road, he lurked in the cornfield bordering it until he spotted a bullock cart with a swaying figure at the front. A farmer, obviously, confident that his bullocks knew their route. Perhaps he would welcome a companion. Mahmoud stepped into the road and grasped the bridle of the near animal, steering it to the side. The sudden bumpiness woke the driver.

"Take a rider?"

Nodding, the man gestured to the space beside him. Mahmoud clambered up, talking the while. To involve the farmer at once in a conversation was safer than risking questions, at least until they were well away from the town. In fact, the man proved to be a voluble talker and the passenger could genuinely commiserate about the uncertainties of agriculture as a way of life, be both sympathetic and knowledgeable about the hazards of drought, locusts, shortages of fertilizer and cash. The steady clop-clop of the bullocks' hooves and the creaking of the wooden wheels were no more than background sounds which could not impede the flow of the conversation. Surprised at how quickly they had reached the next town, Mahmoud dropped off, confident that his new friend would not betray him. The train to Batala came through within the hour and Mahmoud boarded it without incidents.

In Batala, the guard to whom he surrendered his ticket at the gate did not even glance up. Mahmoud steeled himself to walk confidently into the city, according to his Delhi friend's directions to Haji Ali Akbar's shop. This time his walk was uneventful. A pause to verify the name over the shop also provided a moment to survey the inside. Smaller than Kamaluddin's, its constricted space barely allowed two or three customers to sit with the owner. Fortunately, there were none at the moment. A small assortment of gold ornaments was on display; no doubt the valuable items were kept safely in the back.

In the usual fashion, the owner sat cross-legged on a white sheet; white hair, white kurta—there was nothing to distract a possible buyer from the beauty of the gold work or dazzling colour of gems, should the proprietor choose to produce them. A low desk in front of him bore the account books, but they were not the focus of attention now. Instead the man, whom Mahmoud assumed was Haji Ali Akbar, sat gazing down the street, alert for customers. When he caught Mahmoud's eye, he made a gesture of invitation.

Mahmoud ventured in and introduced himself. The Haji, though polite, was less cordial than the Delhi host. His first reaction was to wave his assistant to the back room and then to gesture Mahmoud to a seat. His straggly beard bobbed and swayed as he probed for information which would confirm that the stranger had actually been sent in the way he claimed.

"Ah, yes, Kamaluddin. Who did you say introduced you to him?"

"No one, but it was fortunate for me that when I happened into his shop, we struck up first a conversation and then a friendship. I spent nearly two weeks with him."

"Two weeks. Indeed. I have not seen him for some years. Is his shop still in the same place?"

The formal tone worried Mahmoud. Was this truly the man Kamaluddin had meant him to contact? Could it be that the Haji had switched loyalties since Kamaluddin had last seen him? If so, would he now betray both of them to the British? It was not easy to keep his mind on the questions.

"Same place I couldn't say, since I myself was new to Delhi. It's in Chandni Chowk, a short walk from the Commissioner's compound."

"So you stayed for two weeks. You must have gone to Friday prayers at the Jama Masjid."

"I went there several times. A very, very fine experience. But for Friday prayers I went with my host to the mosque he prefers. A beautiful small one in his neighbourhood."

"Yes, his favorite." The Haji permitted himself a smile. "You must excuse me for questioning you. In this place we need to be cautious; the British may easily take it into their heads that we're harboring spies. Tell me, you're not going on Haj?" To Mahmoud's negative assurance he sighed. "A pity. My wife is most cordial to Hajis. Ah, well, we shall tell her you're a pilgrim, which I suppose you are, going to the Akhund. But you must be very careful. The British do not look kindly on strangers entering the Punjab. Afghanistan is even worse."

"So I've heard." This was better. The man was Kamaluddin's friend after all. Safe. "Have you any advice for me to help negotiate it?"

"Yes, I have some advice. Take plenty of money and plenty of guns. Yes, guns. They are a most acceptable gift, and one of the best barter items. My man can buy them for you here, if you like. I am trusted in the bazaar, where your presence would only raise questions."

So it came about that Mahmoud, who had never held a gun in his life, found himself loaded with them: a brace of rifles, the best, in case he should need an additional gift for the Khan, and several ordinary carbines for trading purposes. They made a bulky package in their burlap wrapping, awkward but manageable. Mahmoud worried a bit about their being so recognizable. Still, to disguise their shape would make them too unwieldy to take on the horse which must now become his means of conveyance.

The horse was not only a familiar conveyance, but a safer one, since he could avoid cities and other areas where travellers were likely to encounter police and informers. The Haji also traded a watch for gold coins at an acceptable rate, negotiated the purchase of a horse for him, and deputed a trustworthy man to act as bearer, guide, and guarantor.

On their way this man, Abdul Ghani, began to teach Mahmoud the rudiments of the Pushtu language, which he would need as soon as they reached the borders of Swat and then Afghanistan. "Local lingo," as the Major would say. Indian ears, even of villagers with no schooling, were tuned to changes of language every few hundred miles or less. Like others of his countrymen, Mahmoud spoke several languages and had no trouble picking up a new one. Before the first day was out he was conversing in it, uninhibited by mistakes and un-self-conscious when he needed to ask for help.

Laughing, stumbling, scanning for directions in which to increase Mahmoud's linguistic skills, the two exchanged stories about their childhoods, explored the differing folkways of their regions, sang songs, both folk and religious, and in these and other ways laid the foundations of a friendship. Thus occupied, the days passed quickly.

Past the Sikhs' holy city of Amritsar with its golden temple, they reached Lahore without incident. It seemed wiser to seek lodging on the outskirts than to venture into the heart of the city; in doing so, they committed their first blunder. Tired, they put their trust in the first man who approached them, when they should have had their guard up. As they hesitated at the corner where a street, narrow and unpaved but clearly a city street, intersected their road, a man accosted them. "You not know Lahore. I help. Me Lahori, know city very well."

That he spotted them immediately as strangers confirmed them in the determination not to risk going into the city and should have alerted them, like insects with antennae out quivering in anticipation of danger. But greasy clothes hanging limply from a thin body, matted hair and crude speech elicited their sympathy. Without consultation, Mahmoud decided to employ him. "Do you know some place we can stay near here?"

"Come." He led them to an unprepossessing small hotel, not too clean but with an available room. "You need supplies, yes? You tell, I buy you."

"If we write a list of what we need, could you read it?"

"Not read. You say. I by-heart it very fast."

"Never mind; I'll go with him," Abdul Ghani volunteered. "You stay here with our things. Rest a bit." Mahmoud was not averse to the suggestion. With the others away, he heaped in the corner the belongings they would not need for the night and laid out the shawls and packs they would sleep on. He did a few stretching exercises to limber up after a day in the saddle, then sat down and yawned luxuriously.

Thirty minutes later the guide showed up again. "We found room in better hotel, Sahib. Come."

"How better?"

"Much better. More comfy, very good cook. All fine, same price."

"What have you done with Abdul Ghani?"

"Your friend wait there for you."

"And the horses?"

"Not necessary move them. Not so far."

Mahmoud began stowing their possessions back in the saddle bags, intending to give them to the guide to carry, but without waiting he picked up the package of burlap-wrapped guns and shouldered it. "Here, I'll take that," Mahmoud protested.

"Nay, Sahib, this very heavy. You strangers my country, I must help, be useful you."

As they walked, the guide increased his pace and was presently hurrying ahead; Mahmoud realized that the aim was to lose him. As he ran to catch up, saddlebags bouncing against his thighs, he wondered how he could establish his claim to the package if it should come to an altercation in the street. He was saved from that necessity by the memory of a ruse that reached far back into his childhood: picking up a stone as he ran, he quickly unfurled his turban and tied the rock into a corner of it.

He held this improvised weapon in his hand waiting for the right moment. It seemed propitious when the guide turned into a side street where there were fortunately few people. Mahmoud, praying that he could still aim as accurately as his ten-year old self, hurled the rock forward with a low motion, so that the cloth wrapped itself several times around the guide's ankle. He staggered. A quick tug on the end of the rumal sent him sprawling, the breath knocked out of him. The package bounced into the gutter. Without wasting a glance at the man, Mahmoud seized the burlap and, retrieving his rumal complete with rock, made his rapid way back to where he had started.

In the room a puzzled Abdul Ghani demanded, "Where did you disappear? What are you doing lugging all our stuff through the streets? What's happened?"

"Tell you later. First, does that guide know you're back here?"

"I don't suppose so. I lost him."

"How?"

"I was buying supplies in the bazaar. When I turned around he'd disappeared. So I finished and found my way back here. What's going on?"

"He pulled a ruse and tried to steal the rifles. I knocked him out and rushed back here with them."

"Good. Turned out all right."

"Maybe, but he just might think of a way of getting even with us. What if he figures that if he reported us to the British, they'd give him a reward? Might even be more profitable than selling our guns."

"Oh! Good thinking! We better get out of here right now. But where to?"

Mahmoud really had no idea. "Maybe we have to camp out."

Abdul Ghani was not in favour of that. "Not wise. It's already dark. And near the city, robbers and thugs are more dangerous than the animals."

That they always loaded their horses the same way was a time-saver now, and it needed only an extra minute to squeeze the renewed supplies into the saddle bags. They circled the city, judging their location by the cooking fires near the small houses or the oil lamps hung from the rafters of the shops in the bazaars. Although it was important not to let the tranquillity of the scene lull them into carelessness, even the sharp lookout they kept did not suggest that anyone was paying attention to them, nor that there were any officials in the area. It was late when they found quarters in a small inn on the northern edge. There, they took care to barricade the door but slept undisturbed and set out again early in the morning.

At Rasulnagar, the Chenab River could be crossed only by ferry. They were among the first passengers aboard and established themselves in the comfortable centre of the craft. The comfort was brief as more and more people, with and without mounts, crowded aboard. "Oh, ho, ferryman," Abdul Ghani protested. "What are you trying to do, packing us in like this? Enough! Let us push off!"

"Nay, sahib, I am a poor man. How can I refuse passengers with money to pay their fares?"

"Is it your ferry, then?" those on the banks challenged Abdul Ghani, "or are you a Maharajah, to have the transport all to yourself? Come on, ferryman. We also need to cross. Let's get on with it."

"Do you want a swim, then?" Abdul Ghani persisted, but the ferryman continued to grab the outstretched coins and the waiting passengers pushed their way on board.

Tempers were still rising as the ferry pushed off. Resentment rose to anger as the horses became restless in the crush and people standing near them felt threatened by the hooves. Using elbows as well as voices, they jostled Mahmoud and Abdul Ghani out of their comfortable places and pushed them towards the railing. Though it seemed rude and unfair when it happened, it turned out to be a blessing. About mid-river, the guide nudged his companion. "Look at the water line," he whispered. "The ferry is sinking. Let's mount, just in case."

Now others also began to notice the problem. Mothers set small children on their hips, while fathers commanded older ones to stay near. "What's happening?" voices demanded with increasing insistence. People began elbowing their way to the upstream edge. Their weight tilted the boat so that it took on water and in the developing panic a man was pushed into the river. With a roar another jumped after him. Since there was no space for the horses to manage a leap over the railing, Mahmoud got down and kicked and strained at it until he had broken out enough to get their mounts through.

Meanwhile Abdul Ghani had his hands full controlling the horses as well as the crowd that was trying to stop them. In fact the hooves of the frightened animals were even more effective than the man in keeping the attackers at bay. Threats and curses, however, were clearly audible above the screams of the women and children. "Stop them! They're wrecking the boat."

"Drown if you wish; leave us the ferry!"

Some voices called on Yama, the Hindu god of the underworld, to deal with the pair; some simply called them abusive names or threatened personal violence. A self-important passenger took up the cry. "You foreigners think you can do anything you like in our territory. We'll see about that. Just wait!" There it was again: even with such slight acquaintance, they were recognized as outsiders.

Finally Mahmoud succeeded in kicking the obstructive rail overboard and flung himself on his mount. The animals needed no urging into the water and gamely swam the remaining distance to the shore. During those moments of reprieve, Mahmoud had thought about their immediate steps. Since they had been called foreigners, it would be only reasonable to get out of there quickly, but could they rush off and leave all those passengers to drown?

They climbed up on the far bank and, without a word, the two of them began to hitch the horses to the hempen rope by which the ferry was connected to both shores. With combined strength, they managed to pull it far enough along so the passengers could disembark with nothing more serious than wet ankles. Despite their assistance, the distraught ferryman kept shouting imprecations at them and threatening to make them pay damages for wrecking his boat.

Before the first passengers reached dry land, the two had remounted and raced northward. By the end of the day, shouting with pleasure at their luck, they splashed across the Jhelum River, which, although swift, was low enough to be forded comfortably. On the opposite bank they made camp. String from their packs was quickly fashioned into fishing lines. By dusk, a mere blink that warned of approaching night, they had feasted on grilled fish with rice and dal, spiced with the last of the widow's pickles. With the fire banked high enough to discourage predators, they said their last prayers of the day, spread their shawls on the ground and slept.

The next day their path began to climb. The altitude was not enough to affect the men but necessitated more frequent rests for the horses. Mahmoud chafed at the slower pace, but Abdul Ghani was unruffled. And indeed, after doing their calculations which indicated another week on the way, Mahmoud was more willing to accept his companion's philosophical "What's one more day?"

20

Traversing uplands and foothills, keeping the mountains on one side, Mahmoud and Abdul Ghani figured they would reach Mardan in just under a week. The city was at the southern end of Swat, before the steep ascents and rocky defiles really began, but deep enough into Swat territory to confirm much they had heard about it.

The Swat valley was wide, fertile, hot. The sun polished the leaves on the teak trees, caught in the rough bark and hung there, riffled through the grasses, intensifying their colours, green, golden, purplish brown. The land would be like that as far as Mardan, the first city they might reach. After that, they would have several days' climb into the high country, hoping to find the Akhund at his Retreat there.

It was a comfortable trip emotionally, as there had been no British in Swat since their second disastrous defeat in Afghanistan in 1879. There were, in fact, only British spies and local informers in Afghanistan itself.

Swat Valley was farmed by sturdy people. Their long faces and big noses seemed somehow incongruous with their mild manners. Mahmoud was curious about them. In response, Abdul Ghani described them as proud, hard working, hospitable. "Don't challenge them, though," he added. "They become insolent and that can grow into a fight if you let it."

The warning came in good time. Just after midday, a man working in a field near their route hailed them. "Salaam aleikum, strangers. Welcome to our valley."

"Valeikum salaam. It's a privilege to ride through such a beautiful area."

"Nay, but riding is thirsty work, even through beautiful countryside. Come sit under my trees for a breath and my wife will pour you some tea."

With a quick glance at each other they agreed, fearful that refusal of hospitality might be taken as an insult. Summoned by a shout, the woman appeared, the end of her dupatta flung across her face but not otherwise veiled. "Tea," her husband commanded. She nodded and disappeared, presently returned bearing a tray. Abdul Ghani and their host faced one another, sitting in the traditional erect, cross-legged position. Mahmoud, more ready to relax, leaned against the tree trunk and stretched his legs out, carefully aiming them away from the other two. The last thing he wanted was to be seen as discourteous.

Two cups of hot tea, heavily sugared, renewed his energy and he was able to ask questions about the local agriculture which established him also as a farmer. This allowed their host to brag about his farm and its current crops, comparing them favorably with farms in India, about which he clearly knew nothing. Remembering Abdul Ghani's warning, Mahmoud did not attempt to correct him and simply confined himself to admiring what he had seen so far in Swat. After conversing for a decent interval, they got up to take their leave.

"Oh, but you can't go yet. You must take food with us," their host protested.

Mahmoud's adventures so far had taught him some of the difference between tact, as Abdul Ghani counseled, and the giving and receiving of orders, as he had done with his father and then the Tahsildar, or instructing others, as with Hamid. Now he exercised his new approach. "We are grateful to your good self, but as travellers we must be on our way, rested and refreshed by your hospitality."

"No, no, it is not our custom to let strangers go without appropriate hospitality. Your path will still be there, even if you wait and have a proper meal."

"Please excuse us, host sahib. We are sure you understand well the pressure of duty."

"Then you must take your food with you." Tying a string on the neck of a goat feeding nearby, he pressed the other end into Mahmoud's hand and waved them off.

As they rode along leading their "dinner," Mahmoud wondered aloud what they could do with this animal. They couldn't just turn him loose, at least not until they were far enough away from his home so he wouldn't show up there again. They might have to return by the same route, and such an insult would not be forgotten. "A pity we couldn't have stayed. Fresh mutton would have tasted good."

"Agreed, but there are leopards in these hills. I don't fancy sleeping next to a stake-out."

"Arre, bhai, let's stop really early tonight. We can roast this goat. There's a pinch of spices left in my pack we can flavour it with. Let's have the feast our host wanted to give us."

And so they did. Abdul Ghani, who was versed in the halal prayers, slaughtered the goat while Mahmoud gathered the wood and arranged stones in a generous circle for a big campfire. Then he cut two sturdy forked sticks and planted their straight stems firmly in the ground at the edge of the circle. Across them, he laid another strong stick, straight this time, on which to impale the meat for roasting.

Once that was done, they gathered up all the waste parts and carried them a little ways from the campsite. There they scratched a shallow pit for them, which they covered over with the scraped out soil and added the bits of branches stripped from the roasting sticks, topping it all with some rocks. If a predator should find the scraps, it would not be until after the men had left the area. That done, they could relax and sit around the fire telling stories in Pushtu and singing until time to eat, then to bank the fires, say their prayers, and sleep.

When they finally reached Mardan, they spent the evening sitting with the other travellers over a hookah, the water pipe which, with its myriad of designs and decorations, was common all over the subcontinent. As the tube passed from hand to hand, Mahmoud and Abdul Ghani listened to the convivial chatter, sifting it for any information that would help them formulate their plans for the next few days. So it was quite accidentally that they learned a piece of news that saved them several days' arduous climb into the Swat high country: the Akhund was in Mardan itself. Word was that a local landowner had vacated his house for the distinguished guest. "Next to the mosque," was the most definite instruction they could glean.

Eager to establish a meeting lest he move on before they could contact him, they set out to find the Akhund early the next morning.

Mahmoud prepared for this meeting carefully. As merchants it was Kamaluddin's and Haji Ali Akbar's job to meet the public freely. The Akhund, on the other hand, would no doubt be protected by layers of servants. This would therefore be the first time he would need the cover of the watches the Minister had supplied him. He extracted one from the deep secret pocket, wrapped it in a white handkerchief, and stowed it in the pocket of his kurta. He felt a little nervous about how to approach the intervening servants, but decided he could only wait and see what their reaction was.

At the Akhund's gate, they accosted the guard. "Arre, bhai, you serve the Akhund Sahib, na? Since you are here, then he also is in Mardan."

"And if he is, what's that to you?"

"I crave an audience with him."

"You! Do you think just anyone who takes a fancy to see him can be admitted to the presence?"

"But I am not just anyone. I am a jeweller with an ingenious new device that would interest him."

"Shows how ignorant you are, thinking His Holiness would buy jewellery. It's gems of wisdom that occupy his attention."

"My gem is not without its own wisdom."

"I've told you he's busy. Now stop wasting my time. Go!"

"But—"

"Go! Go!"

Before the guard could lay hands on Mahmoud, Abdul Ghani stepped between them and quietly slipped some coins into his hand.

"Well, I can't stop you. But don't assume the Secretary will be as good natured as I am."

As the guard looked the other way, the two bent low and slipped through the postern gate. The courtyard was neat but simple, while the furnishings inside the house were austere. They found the Secretary easily enough and handed him some coins which, learning his lesson from Abdul Ghani, Mahmoud had hastily wrapped in a piece of paper. "This is our application for an audience with His Holiness."

The Secretary weighed the coins in his hand. "You'll have to wait; he's meditating just now and can't be disturbed."

While they waited, Mahmoud asked Abdul Ghani to remain in the reception area when they were invited inside. With the Minister's strict instructions not to let anyone know the purpose of his mission, or who had instigated it, he was always careful to speak of it only in the most guarded terms when he had to ask for help. Now, since the Minister himself had said he could confide in the Akhund, Mahmoud would reveal for the first time who had sent him and that his purpose was to contact the Khan. For that he needed complete privacy.

Half an hour later, Mahmoud was ushered into a sizeable, but sparsely-furnished room. At one side a low desk bore a few papers. Across from it and under the window, mats for sitting; no pictures, no objects offered distractions. Almost immediately, the Akhund strode in, his long, sleeveless gown sweeping the floor, and gestured to his guest to be seated on the mat.

"Ah, yes, the Minister of Jehanabad," he nodded when Mahmoud had completed his introduction. "From time to time over the years, he and I have exchanged courtesies, even favours," here he permitted himself a twinkle, "though I have never had the pleasure of meeting him in person."

"Still, he esteems your friendship."

"He sends me a jeweller to show a new device, my servants say. It must be a very unusual device, to come from him in this fashion."

"A device and a message. Please accept this pocket watch with His Excellency's compliments and best wishes."

The Akhund spent several minutes examining the gift with obvious pleasure, even holding it to his ear. At length he laid it down. "It speaks of time and eternity. Now, what can I do for you here?"

When he learned the object of Mahmoud's visit, he sat for a moment, silently tapping his chin with his forefinger. "You realize, I assume, that this mission is not without considerable risk. The British are very intolerant of intruders into Afghanistan. Still, they themselves are not very welcome there, either, although their spies are numerous. A greater danger is from the local people. Each tribe guards its territory jealously."

"So I understand. Have you some guidance for me, Your Holiness?"

"Not immediately. We need to secure instructions for the final stage of your trip."

"Secure instructions? From whom, if not from you, Sahibji?"

"From the Khan. That's your destination, isn't it?"

"Oh, you'll send a telegraphic signal to the Khan, then?"

"Unfortunately, those conveniences have not reached either these mountains, or the Afghan ones. No, I cannot rely on man's inventions," he smiled and indicated the watch, "in spite of their ingeniousness."

"So, what will you do, if I may ask?"

"It need not concern you, as it involves steps known only to the most advanced Sufis. That is why you have come to me, isn't it? I shall visit with the Khan tonight. If you will be so good as to come back tomorrow morning I shall have some word for you about your onward journey."

Mahmoud, despite having a little knowledge of Sufism, was only slightly less mystified than Abdul Ghani would have been. "Visit the Khan!" he could not repress the exclamation. "Surely that takes some days of travel."

The Akhund only smiled. "A beginner Sufi without knowledge needs only instruction, but one without faith is a contradiction."

"May I watch this journey you propose to take tonight?"

His Holiness shook his head. "To see a Sufi leave his body is very dangerous; it almost certainly means death for the practitioner and quite likely also for the observer. So we shall meet in the morning. In the meantime, let me remind you not to neglect your prayers."

With that Mahmoud had to be content, but the news he received the next day was sufficient reward for his unsatisfied curiosity.

"The Khan will receive you," the Akhund told Mahmoud, "but you must send your companion home from here. You will need to take one of my men as guide and escort. Although the way lies through the territory of two tribes and skirts a third, one man will be enough, since he will be known to come from me." He paused for a deep breath and a searching look at his visitor. "You will meet with no hostility, though the Khan had a rather puzzling message for you to be careful on the fourth and fifth days, for they will be somewhat perilous for you. Beyond that he did not specify. How much time do you need before you start?"

"Two days, in order to rest a bit and renew our supplies. Can your man also help us do that? Then we shall set out in our separate directions."

Mahmoud and Abdul Ghani each felt a tug when the moment of parting arrived, for they had been companions for a very long distance, both geographical and emotional. "A safe journey," they wished one another. "We shall meet again, Insh'Allah." Having said so, they mounted their horses and turned their faces to opposite points of the compass.

21

Aslam Sharif, the Akhund's man, fit Abdul Ghani's description of Swat men: hard working, hospitable, and proud. He was not inclined to accept Mahmoud as an equal until he had shown that he did not regard himself as a superior. Once over that hurdle, Sharif turned out to be a pleasant enough companion, active and efficient in setting up their simple camping arrangements in the evenings. Still, Mahmoud missed the sense of kinship he had established with Abdul Ghani on so many levels.

The new guide had no need to feel that kind of isolation, for from time to time they met local Afghans, sometimes singly but more often in groups. Invariably they hailed Sharif and stopped for a brief gossip, speaking more quickly than Mahmoud could follow or in a dialect he could not recognize. He felt an inward shiver at what it would be like if these men should become their enemies. If it were ever necessary to fight, it would clearly be better to fight along with them than against them. The thought made him thankful for the Khan's assurance that they would meet no hostility from the tribes.

The first few days passed with slow but steady progress up the heights, through the pass, down the narrow descent where the horses picked their way cautiously, as though aware that a misstep would tumble them into a gorge a thousand feet below. Mahmoud kept his eyes on the path, tried not to look down. "Do you remember," he asked his companion, "the story of the young Babur? When he lost an engagement to the Afghans and they were pressing him hard, he leapt his horse off a cliff, swam the river in which they landed, and lived to conquer Delhi."

"Yes. Must have happened in a spot like this."

"Not a comforting thought. I'll be glad when we're through this part." He was thankful for the Khan's prediction they wouldn't meet any hostility on the way but had forgotten the dark side of the prophecy.

The fourth day out recalled it forcibly to mind. They had agreed to start that day hunting for game to augment their dwindling supplies. Tethering their horses, they set off. Two small hares would provide dinner for that night, but they persevered, hoping to bag something more substantial. As the sun rose higher and higher, Mahmoud grew impatient, regarding the day as wasted; they were making no progress towards Kabul. He knew almost nothing about handling a gun and had neither the understanding nor the patience of a true hunter, so his share of these efforts was as a lookout. Even at that, Sharif was more competent than he.

"Look," the guide whispered, pointing to a ram upwind of them whose head and neck had just appeared from behind a boulder. "Just what we want."

Intent on his grazing, the animal turned his head away from them and Mahmoud said, disappointed, "Too bad. You can't hit him from here and by the time we get to where he is he'll be somewhere else."

"No, no, bhai. Don't worry. I can bounce a shot off the next rock so it will get him in the neck."

He took aim, the gun roared, but before the mountains could pick up the echo, Mahmoud staggered and fell back against a boulder. "Ya, Allah, what have you done!" he bellowed.

Eyes popping, Sharif stared at the blood streaming down Mahmoud's leg. "Sorry, Sahib. So sorry. Not my fault."

"Fault, schmalt! You've ruined me!"

"Not I! The animal moved. I adjusted my aim. A small rough spot in the rock, that's all. Deflected the shot, that's what," Sharif gibbered.

"Stop this jabbering, you fool, and get the bullet out of my leg! I'm standing in blood."

Action calmed Sharif. Pulling his hunting knife from his girdle, he propped the leg on his knee and set to work, all the time keeping up a running commentary on Mahmoud's shouted imprecations. "Tut, tut, you'll never make a mountain man if you make such a noise over a small accident. I've seen men have a leg amputated with less fuss. Ah, here's your bullet. It just nicked the bone; it didn't break it. You're lucky."

"You're the one who's lucky, Aslam Sharif. If the leg were broken, you would have had to carry me on your back to Kabul." Exhausted, he sank back while Sharif bound up the wound with strips torn from his rumal.

"There. I suppose that's it for today. You won't be wanting to ride just now. I'd best bring the horses forward and tether them near us. Then I'll set up camp and cook the hares we bagged. You'll want your food, anyway."

The next day the wound was fiery red, hot and painful, and Mahmoud was burning up.

Concern made Sharif diffident. "Sahib," he suggested, "there is a man only about an hour's ride away. Just an ignorant villager, but he knows which leaves and roots are good for fever. Wounds, too. We could go consult him."

"Can't ride," Mahmoud panted. "How control horse...only...one leg? No use." He turned his head to look at the campsite. "Better bring here. Come, prop me up. Gun. Water. Right. Now go. Be quick, no longer than you must."

By the time Sharif returned with the hakim, they found the patient delirious with fever. "Must make haste," the hakim said; "I brought many right supplies, praise Allah. You please bathe his face with cold water. Important we bring the fever down. I prepare the medicines for that."

For two days and nights they took turns watching by Mahmoud, who was sometimes conscious and sometimes clearly out of his head. The hakim spent most of his waking hours with his mortar and pestle, grinding a paste from herbs and leaves, twigs and seeds of various kinds and even some sort of nut, none of which Sharif recognized. Some of this he made into poultices which he applied to the wound, changing them frequently. Others he diluted with water and coaxed the patient to drink when he was awake, or dribbled over his tongue when he was not.

Between times, he roamed the area looking for new supplies. At frequent intervals they tried to get a little water between the parched lips, or alternately to soothe Mahmoud and protect the wound when he became restless. Time measured out the hours by the spoonful, but the guide chafed for a dipper full.

On the third day, Mahmoud shook all over like a sail that has just been turned into the wind, after which he fell deeply asleep. Sharif was greatly alarmed, but whether more for himself or for his patient it was impossible to tell. "Oh, hakimbhai, we have killed him!" he wailed.

The hakim patted his shoulder. "No, contrary. We won. One hour or two you feel his skin—cool again. Till then, sit by him. Make to drink water if he wakes. Keep on his forehead a wet cloth. I go my village for fresh supplies. Back by evening."

Indeed it turned out as predicted. "Infection is conquered; now we must help leg heal also."

"Help me...sit up. What day is it?"

"You sick three days."

"So weak so fast."

"Never mind. Herbs," he held up a small leaf-wrapped packet, "to build your strength. And Sharif, here, made good broth; put pep back in you."

For three more days, Mahmoud alternately slept and chafed at the delay. Then the hakim declared himself satisfied. "Let him rest one, two more days," he directed. "Then maybe could to travel, but shorter days only, remember."

Mahmoud was well enough to agree and to pay the hakim handsomely for his services. But the leg, though recovering, continued so painful that mounting his horse was difficult and he could ride for only a few hours before needing relief. Even after several days on the move, riding required all his concentration. It was perhaps while shifting in the saddle that he jerked the reins unthinkingly. The horse veered suddenly, slipped on a rock that overturned under him, and skidded wildly for a moment before he fell. The fall was away from Mahmoud's injured leg, and he had time to slip out of the stirrups, so that he rolled away as the animal came down heavily.

"Allah the Merciful! Allah the Merciful!" Sharif intoned as he jumped down and rushed over; "Say you're not hurt."

"At least I'm alive. Let me check. My leg...no, I can move it, just." He grimaced with the effort. "It's bleeding again. No, it's not. That dripped from my nose. Must have landed on it. And my shoulder is sore." He swung his elbow, testing the full range of motion from the shoulder, then stretched to check his back. "I guess I'll do. Listen to my horse. See to him."

Unable to get up, the animal lay neighing pitifully, its foreleg clearly broken. Mahmoud, rocking back and forth with the pain both of his injuries, and of the loss of his mount, covered his face while Sharif shot it.

The loss of the horse meant a much slower pace, for Mahmoud rode on the remaining mount and could move only as fast as Sharif could walk. Once or twice a day he rested while the guide hunted game for their food. It was during one of those forays of Sharif's that Mahmoud, dozing on the ground, was awakened by a kick and found himself surrounded by a half dozen Afghans.

"Get up!" he was ordered.

Mahmoud struggled to his feet but when prodded to move, he faltered and would have fallen had one of the Afghans not caught him. A quick argument among his captors, and he was picked up like a sack of grain and flung, face down, across one of their horses. With every one of the animal's steps his leg bounced painfully; nor had he any idea how long the journey took, since he lost consciousness several times. He knew simply that about the time he felt he couldn't stand much more of this, he was hauled off the animal and deposited on the floor of a hut, then heard a key turn in the lock.

The hut was small, unfurnished, and only dimly lit by a tiny window. Its floor of tamped earth was reasonably clean, but the hut smelled of stale food and sweat. Only after he had rested a bit and collected himself did he notice another figure in the room silently regarding him. "Salaam," Mahmoud ventured. The other merely nodded. Mahmoud wondered what this fellow had done to become a prisoner, or was he, like Mahmoud himself, possibly just a source of income for their captors. Giving them both time to adjust to one another's presence, Mahmoud lay back and busied himself with figuring his odds.

144

If Aslam Sharif found him in time, all would be well. If not, would his captors be satisfied with ransom? Or would it mean his life? It would, if this tribe were in league with the British. He made another attempt to learn something from his cellmate.

"You been here long?"

"Some days." From the man's easy Pushtu, Mahmoud realized he was Afghan, but probably from a different tribe; not a prisoner of war or he would have been dealt with summarily. So perhaps someone worth ransoming. Mahmoud found the idea vaguely comforting.

"You don't look like you're starving."

"They feed you, as long as they think it'd be profitable."

"Is that why they want us, then?'

No response. They sat for a while, busy with their separate thoughts. Then, "You're not from around here. What brings you?" his fellow captive inquired.

"Hoping for trade. And you?"

"Same, perhaps."

Mahmoud noted the perhaps. Worth a try. Afghans could be no less aware than the British that Russia had its eye on their country, but whether as a step into India, as invaders since Genghis Khan had used it, to unseat the British there, or as a step toward a warm-water outlet on the Indian ocean, or just to satisfy an empire's insatiable appetite for expansion, no one knew. Mahmoud launched his kite. "If the Russians should come here, would they set the two of us free or keep us captive? What do you think?"

"Won't come."

"What makes you so sure?"

The other laughed. "For what? Every time Russian army moves two miles, British bring their forces half way across the continent. Very cheap for the Russians."

Mahmoud nodded. Bad news for the Minister. Perhaps it won't matter what the Khan replies. As though out of conversational ideas, the two sat in silence again. Mahmoud was aware of the growing darkness in the hut and reconciled himself to spending the night. At least the protection of the building and the presence of another body would mitigate the night temperature. Before he had settled down, however, the key turned in the lock and a man set down two leaf plates and doled out kedgeree and naan. Enough nourishment to keep a man alive, though not enough to keep him in fighting trim. Very careful calculation.

Darkness passed into day outside the hut, but Mahmoud's thoughts were still in a moonless night. Life at that moment seemed to consist only of questions to which there was no obvious answer. Where was Aslam Sharif? Mahmoud rejected the possibility that Sharif was a traitor, selling him to the locals, since he was accountable to the Akhund. Perhaps he was less knowledgeable or less acceptable to the Afghans than reputed. Since those fellows had also no doubt grabbed his possessions, Mahmoud wondered whether they would accept the rifles as ransom. The package was unmistakable, so there was no way to deny having them; not much use as ransom, however, since they already had them. So what more would they demand? Gold, probably, but he couldn't be sure he had enough to buy his life. Anyway, how could he appear to the Khan, with no gift?

Of course, these men might be followers of the Khan. If he told them he was expected by the Khan, they might send him on his way, even help him. It was tempting, until he recalled he was strictly forbidden to tell anyone whatsoever about his mission.

On the third day, Mahmoud thought he heard voices outside the hut. Sharif's voice? Or illusion, someone who sounds like him? The conversation dragged on without moving away from the hut. So perhaps it did have something to do with the occupants. Finally, a key in the door. An Afghan figure pulled Mahmoud to his feet, hoisted him to his shoulder and dumped him outside. There indeed stood Aslam Sharif.

"Just where have you been?" Mahmoud asked furiously.

"Looking for you. Successfully, it appears. Now if you'll just give these gentlemen a bit of gold, we'll be off. I've already loaded our gear onto my horse."

"Gold! Why should I pay these robbers anything? If necessary, you should pay them yourself. You're supposed to protect me from this kind of thing."

"Comes from your clumsiness with your horse. While I was off hunting food for you, how could they know you were with me?"

"You've cost me three days of travel. How are you going to make up for that?"

"Can't make it up by standing here talking. Come now, just a bit of baksheesh and we're off."

"For what, again?"

"Let's say, a thank you for their hospitality."

Defeated, Mahmoud extracted the smallest sum he could manage without revealing the hoard in his hidden pocket. The men were obviously not pleased but made no effort to stop them when Sharif helped Mahmoud onto the horse and they set off again.

Kabul was still a long way off. Mahmoud chafed at their slow pace but knew he could do no better. They reached Kabul six days later. As they approached the city, Sharif dallied, created diversions, frequently declared a halt for some excuse or another.

"Sharif, I wish I had a stick to whack you with. Why do we dawdle in this irritating fashion?"

"Waiting, Sahib. For night time."

"Why, for goodness sake? We can see the city from here. Let's just get there and be done with it."

"Sahib, I can pass for an Afghan, but you don't look like one. Can't walk alone. In the city, people will ask questions, follow us. They see me take you to Khushal Gaffar's compound, they'll start rumours he's harbouring a spy."

"Who's Khushal Gaffar supposed to be?"

"Disciple of the Akhund. Lives very near to the palace. Very convenient. So better to be careful."

Darkness came at last and, despite the late hour of their arrival, their host bade them welcome. He gave them a room with a separate entrance which he begged them to consider theirs for as long as they might require it. Food arrived on trays twice a day. Fruits—apples, melons, and grapes, cooled in the mountain streams—were in season. Mahmoud spent large parts of each day lying with his leg elevated, but forced himself every day to stand or walk a little longer, supported by the cane his host had thoughtfully presented. Gradually his strength returned.

22

Mahmoud let most of a week pass in this kind of convalescence, for he was determined not to be dependent on any assistance when he presented himself to the Khan. At the end of that time he felt able to initiate contact. Since, after the impulsive firing, he no longer trusted Sharif's discretion or, especially, his good sense, he went by himself. Abdul Ghani had been more of a companion than simply a guide. He had accompanied Mahmoud to the point of the interview and taught him how to tip the various levels of gatekeepers, but Sharif had not gained that close a relationship, so he did not raise questions when Mahmoud announced that he would be off to pay a call on the Khan. Sharif could accompany him only as far as the palace gate.

It had become almost habitual for Mahmoud to present a few coins to the chowkidar at the gate, but once inside he seemed to be expected, for each functionary passed him to another without challenge. The courtyard was uncluttered and spacious, large enough to be a mustering point for the guards and even some part of the Khan's army. The palace itself, with two-foot stone walls, stone floors bare in the corridors, shields and swords the only decoration on the walls, made Mahmoud think of a fortress.

Almost more quickly than he had prepared himself for, he was announced and limped into the presence of the Khan. A dozen men stood or lounged about the room, while the ruler sat alone on a silk carpet; one man squatted at its edge, nodding as the Khan gesticulated. The carpet, finely knotted in a bold pattern of brilliant reds and blues blended by a soft beige was an appropriate setting for a powerful leader. Mahmoud wondered for a moment whether this was really the Khan, however, for the man wore only the baggy cotton pyjama and loose kurta of the mountain men. Whether in homespun or brocades, however, important persons merited six deep salaams; Mahmoud took two steps forward and began them: "Asalaam aleikum."

"Valeikum salaam," the Khan interrupted the series. Shoving aside the gun which lay at his knee, he gestured to a place on the carpet. "Come sit here near me and tell me about your journey. You come from Jehanabad, I understand."

"I do, Your Excellency, but my journey actually began in Lucknow, whence I set out to reach the Akhund of Swat. I need not bore you with the recital from there on, for you are already familiar with it."

The Khan motioned to the wounded leg. "So this is the danger I foretold to the Akhund, but couldn't clearly see. Tell me about it."

Mahmoud recounted the episode, emphasizing the skill and devotion of the hakim from the eastern village.

"Aslam Sharif is a fool," the Khan pronounced. "Any of my Pathans could have made that shot. Still, do not be too hard on him, or on the Akhund for sending him with you. He has made the trip many times and is well known and accepted by many tribes; he knew precisely where to go to find the hakim for you, after all. Well, enough of that. The Akhund gave me to understand that you bring a message for me."

Here was the second indication within minutes that the Khan was accustomed to cut to the chase. That would keep those around him on their toes, alert for any subtle signals that might guide them. It was not lost on Mahmoud. "I do, Your Excellency, one whose extreme confidentiality was impressed upon me again and again."

The Khan motioned to his attendants to leave the room, but as they were complying he called one back. "You come sit with us, Farooq. We may need your diplomacy." As he turned back to Mahmoud, he must have seen how hesitant the envoy looked at being faced with an additional person, for he put his hand on Farooq's shoulder. "You see, Farooq is my thoughtful one. He's so busy looking at all sides of a question that he doesn't have time to be impulsive. Keeps me cautious."

The conversation continued over cups of tea the Khan himself poured in a seemingly endless stream from a copper samovar decorated with silver in patterns which Mahmoud admired out of the corner of his eye but could not identify.

"Achcha, Sayed Mahmoud. Tell us about things in Jehanabad. How is His Highness's health, may Allah protect him?"

"When I left there, he was in good health."

"And His Excellency, the Minister? The same, I trust."

Mahmoud was thankful that at frequent moments during the journey he had been preparing himself for this question. He had expected the Khan might ask not only about the Minister but about Mahmoud's own relationship to him. Now he was armed with a reply that was the truth, though perhaps spread a little thin. "He is in good health, Khan Sahib, and vigorous. His reputation, perhaps spread by those close to him and so in a position to know, is that he reflects deeply on matters that concern the State. Like your Farooq Sahib here, he considers his actions carefully."

"Good, good."

"My Minister is a well-wisher of the Khan Sahib, whom he holds in high esteem." Mahmoud hoped to make the occasion as impressive as possible, and as gratifying to the Khan, without making the Minister sound like a petitioner. Extracting the special watch from his pocket, he placed it on a white handkerchief and laid it before the ruler. "To express his regard," he continued, "he has instructed his slave to present this token to the Khan Sahib. It may already be a familiar item here and even in the Khan Sahib's possession. In any case he hopes this particular repeater watch will be acceptable. The amethyst in the key is meant to suggest that the relation between the two leaders of their people is precious."

The Khan picked up the watch and examined it closely; with a quizzical glance at Mahmoud, he pried open the back cover and fitted the key. When he had turned it a few times and heard the chimes, he laughed. "Achchacha! Very good!"

Mahmoud congratulated himself for having thought of it while it was still a novelty in the mountains. He was also thankful that the Minister had given him a generous supply of them. When he was sure of the Khan's satisfaction, he turned to Farooq and held out on his folded handkerchief a simpler version of the watch. "Had my Minister known how you are lodged in your Khan Sahib's heart, he would have sent this specifically for you. Please accept it as though it came directly from him." At this, Mahmoud thought he detected a faint sign of approval from the Khan.

He turned back to the leader. "My Minister wishes you to have a special pair of rifles, as well. I myself bought them in Batala with help from a local well-wisher." He refrained from giving himself credit for the idea. "I did not think it prudent to bring them on this visit until I was known by your servants. I shall bring them in the evening."

"Not wise," the Khan replied. "I will send a man for them when the time is propitious."

"My Minister has also sent you a question. Is the time auspicious for repeating it?"

"Ask away."

"He asks, 'If the wind blows from the northwest, will you tie down your tent flaps against it? Or will you use its strength? We keep a watch on the weather.'"

The Khan listened gravely. He sat for several minutes in silence, scratching his short beard thoughtfully. Then, with a glance at Farooq, he spoke. "So you stay with Khushal Gaffar. A very reliable man. Are you comfortable enough there?"

"He is most hospitable, generous in anticipating our needs. And Aslam Sharif takes good care of me; he's as good a butler as a guide."

"Food all right?"

"Delicious and plentiful."

"As it should be, Insh'Allah. Well, Mr. Emissary-in-Disguise, I have kept you long enough. You understand I cannot reply to your esteemed Minister by myself. I must consult my advisers. I shall hold their hands while I take their pulse and look deeply into their eyes, and in the end I shall know whether they are giving their genuine opinion. Eh, Farooq?" His hearty laugh filled the room. "I shall send you word in due course."

Mahmoud found himself liking the man; it was not hard to see how he had earned his following. He wondered whether it was disloyal to compare him to his own Minister. The Minister was widely regarded in Jehanabad with not a little awe and even a good deal of affection, but no one had so much as hinted that he might have a sense of humour. Dignified, distant, and upright described him.

The Khan, on the other hand, was clearly a field man. Not for him the theatrical gesture of galloping his horse off the cliff and making his way alone into enemy territory to start over again on his quest for empire. He would choose his companions carefully and keep them around him to share his defeats, if any, his almost certain triumphs, his quandaries and his decisions. And they would accompany him on any adventure. No wonder the Minister, so opposite in almost every respect except honour, knew from his place on the plains that this man of the mountains could be trusted.

23

The brightly coloured flowers in Khushal Gaffar's gardens raised Mahmoud's spirits, and the alternation of sun and shade assured his comfort as he limped about or sat resting on conveniently placed benches. Despite this luxury, the garden walls began to look increasingly like the walls of Benur prison, and his confinement within them a more comfortable version of the two captivities already met on this journey. Restless, he forgot Aslam Sharif's caution in entering the city only under cover of darkness because of Mahmoud's obvious foreignness. Sure that Sharif would insist on coming along, and desiring some independence, Mahmoud slipped through their private gate without a word to his guide and set out to test his leg by exploring the city.

His host's residence was in Bala Hissar, the citadel which rose sharply out of the bowl formed by the surrounding mountains. Instead of turning in the direction of the Khan's palace, this time Mahmoud turned away from it, towards the bazaar. On the way he passed a spot from which he could look down the escarpment to the town and cantonment below. Peculiar place to locate the troops, he thought; even a rank civilian knows that an army has to hold the heights. The barracks appeared both solid and vulnerable, built many years ago by the British out of either arrogance or carelessness, apparently. No wonder the Minister had so little regard for them.

Still, Kabul was a pleasing sight. In the distance, the river; in the foreground, gardens and fountains; and in this green valley, great orchards with their sparkles of yellow and red fruit among the greenery of leaves. Most of them, apricots, figs, apples, walnuts, grapes, were new to Mahmoud, so different from the fruits of the plains where he had grown up. Just as the patterns of the rugs the

Afghan women knotted, or of their woven kilims, differed from the cotton durries of Khandipur. "So beautiful," he thought, "but to enjoy all this, a stranger must prove himself by negotiating so many hazards along the way. Fortunately, I survived them. My country is more welcoming."

Turning back, he continued his stroll toward the bazaar. The narrow streets were similar to those he had traversed on his journey here: barbers shaved customers and cleaned their ears; cobblers mended chappals and the sturdier local boots; even dentists openly displayed the pliers and other tools of their trade. As he stopped at a push cart to buy some grapes, nestled in wood shavings to protect them for the journey from the vineyards, Mahmoud reflected that these people looked more like Sikhs than the people among whom he had grown up. Tall, big beards balancing their big noses, big turbans dwarfing all the rest or tightly woven hats clapped on their heads. He wondered whether the choice was significant.

The men wore hugely baggy pyjamas and kurtas cut wide and with loose sleeves, all roomy enough to hide things inside: snacks, contraband, smuggled items, weapons. Mahmoud's were nearly the opposite, close fitting and neat. He was accustomed to wearing churdidars, whose tight fit above the bracelet of wrinkles at the ankle revealed the shapeliness of the leg, and straight-cut kurtas over that. What made him feel naked, however, was not the shape of his clothes but his lack of arms. Every man in the streets carried a rifle, often of the old muzzle-loading type, slung from his shoulder, and many also had a dagger in the belt.

As he moseyed along, stopping when a gap in the buildings offered a long view, he became aware that he was followed. He crossed the street; a quick glance out of the corner of his eye confirmed that not one but two burly men were not only also crossing but gaining on him. To run would attract attention, the worst thing. So he stepped out as smartly as his limp allowed, with a purposeful expression on his face. Before he had taken more than a few steps, the pair caught up with him and each grasped an arm. "Come," one murmured in his ear. Mahmoud kept walking, ignoring them. The fingers on his arms tightened. "Come with us," the voice repeated.

Mahmoud stopped. "I am going to the bazaar," he began in a firm voice, but his captors interrupted him.

"Do not make a scene in public or you will be in real trouble. This is not an auspicious time for going to the bazaar."

He had no choice except to conceal his panic. A few steps more and they turned into an alley so narrow that the sun could never pierce the shadows cast by the buildings on either side. Past four entrances down the dark lane, then up a flight of wooden stairs and back along the balcony to a door at the end. There one of the men produced a huge brass key and with much rattling and shaking managed to undo the lock.

They stepped into a large room, sparsely furnished but apparently inhabited, for a suit of men's clothing hung from a nail in the wall and in a bucket of water in one corner floated a dipper for drinking. In another corner lay a pile of heavy kapok-filled quilts: two for sleeping on, two for sleeping under. On the floor was a sheepskin.

At a gesture from one of the men, Mahmoud sank down on the sheepskin. His game leg ached from the exercise of walking, more exercise in the past two hours than at any time since his injury. His lips formed a tight streak across his face; he would not give his captors the satisfaction of questioning them. If the silence were to be broken, it would have to be at their initiative. The less he said, the less they could learn from him.

That escape was impossible was clear: one of the men sat between him and the door, the other near the window. It puzzled him that they made no menacing gestures; the atmosphere was one of waiting. The only movement in the room came from the man near the window, who occasionally got up and peered through the slats of the closed shutters. Mahmoud wondered whom they expected and barely managed to swallow his question about it.

Hours passed, an eternity of silent vigil. To stretch his cramped muscles, Mahmoud stirred restlessly and started to get up. By the time he was on his knees, however, both his captors had sprung to their feet, apparently expecting him to make a dash. One look at the rifles they stroked so casually and he resumed his seat. Presently the man near the window made one more of his periodic trips to peer out. "Dark enough," he announced. "Let's go."

As they had arrived, so they retraced their steps back out to the main street, now nearly deserted. Still maintaining silence they plodded on until, to Mahmoud's amazement, they turned in at the palace, where the gates were opened to them without challenge. "Why are we coming here?" he demanded, breaking his self-imposed vow.

"You'll see."

"So now I'm a prisoner of the Khan."

"As you like."

"My own fault. I should have known better than to trust him. It just never occurred to me he would be a traitor to his word."

At that, one of the guards whirled and grabbed Mahmoud by the neckline of his kurta, twisting it so tightly a button cut into his throat. "We've treated you well so far," he snarled. "One more word about our Khan and you'll find out how we could treat a prisoner." Shifting his grip back to his captive's arm, he marched him to the door of the reception room and shoved him inside.

Before Mahmoud could even show his defiance by failing to salaam, he was met with a blast from the Khan. "Sayed Mahmoud, you fool!" he shouted, leaping to his feet. "Whatever possessed you to commit this idiocy? Don't you realize that every place you went, every spot where you stopped and looked around, could brand you as a spy? The British have lookouts everywhere. Perhaps you imagined you'd be unrecognizable with your limp and your Southern looks. Is that it? How could the Minister have sent me such a blockhead?"

His long frame pleated onto the mat and he sat breathing deeply, as though waiting for his anger to cool down. Knowing he deserved every word of the attack, Mahmoud could only hang his head. He was wrong, dangerously so, not only for himself, but for those who had taken him in and protected him.

"You must know that rumours about foreigners are more elaborately embroidered in Kabul than anywhere. It's one of our skills," the Khan added in a more normal voice and then chuckled. "It is also the source of many of our difficulties. Well, the English may hear about you, that we can't know, but at least their agents didn't capture you. Not yet, anyway.

"However I suggest that in future you exercise more discretion. For the rest of your stay here you will keep out of sight. Enjoy the hospitality of your host, in whom we have the utmost confidence, and content yourself with only the sightseeing you can do from his garden. Aslam Sharif has no doubt been wondering whether he's lost his charge. My men will see you back there now."

Embarrassed by the thoughtlessness of his excursion as well as by his accusation of the Khan, Mahmoud obeyed his instructions like a polo pony the rein. Matter-of-factly, he resumed the friendly but impersonal time with Sharif. The guide, when he had cleaned and tidied their quarters, sometimes picked up the tray that had arrived with food and used the occasion of returning it to set out on his own. Mahmoud assumed this was one of the ways he maintained the local contacts that made him a safe guide. He envied him the freedom to come and go, but only briefly.

In fact, he thrived during the following days, with the relaxed feeling that the most risky part of his mission had been accomplished, and with resting in the bracing mountain air. Daily exercise, even the limited exercise of counting the paces on each path through his host's spacious gardens, strengthened Mahmoud's leg and he began once again to feel fit for the return journey.

That began with a knock on their private entrance late one evening. Sharif answered it cautiously. Finding there a big stocky man in workman's clothing, generous turban shading his face and almost falling off over one ear, a dagger in his belt and his rifle slung casually over the shoulder, Sharif managed only a squeaky, "Yes?"

"Your Master in?" whispered a husky voice.

"I'll see," Sharif said and closed the door, then quickly opened it again and inquired, "Who shall I say wants him, if he's here?"

"Tell him the stranger inquires 'dosti or kutti.'"

His face an uncomprehending blank, Sharif again closed the door and turned towards the inner room. "Dosti or kutti," he muttered to himself; "friendly or hostile. Who would that be? Or does he mean the old Khan, Dost Mohammed? But then who is kutti?" Made none the wiser by his brief word with Mahmoud, he reopened the door a moment later and reported, "My Master says if you are a Sufi from a Sufi, you are welcome."

Without waiting for more formality, the stranger entered the room, dropped his rifle onto a couch and his turban on top of it, while his laugh boomed to the rafters. "Salaam, salaam, sahib," he said to an embarrassed Mahmoud, who had bounced to his feet and was busy salaaming his eminent guest. Sharif, embarrased at not recognizing the Khan, joined Mahmoud in the six salaams.

"Did you like my little trick? We Afghans are fond of intrigue, as you may know. We're rather good at it, don't you agree? I thought it would be safer for me to come here than for you to risk being seen again at the palace."

"Most gracious of Your Excellency to do this honour to our humble quarters. Spacious and comfortable they are for us, but hardly to the Khan Sahib's standards. But what can your slave offer as hospitality to one of Your Excellency's taste?"

"Wah, Mahmoud, drop this flowery language. The thin air of these mountains has long since diluted whatever we may once have had of Persian ancestry. Our usage is more direct. So now let us talk man to man."

With a wave of the hand to dismiss Sharif, the Khan sat down on the charpoy and motioned Mahmoud to join him there. When they were comfortable, he taught Mahmoud the message he was to take back for the Minister. "The northwest wind may puff out a man's clothes till he looks twice his size, without blowing him off his course." After Mahmoud demonstrated that he had learned it, the Khan turned to the question of the return journey.

Mahmoud summoned Sharif to hear the plans. The Khan estimated it would take five days to the border if they pressed hard, more depending on how much allowance had to be made for the emissary's leg. Mahmoud protested his fitness and the Khan merely nodded.

"You may start tomorrow," he instructed. "You need not worry about Khushal Gaffar; I'll take care of him. You will not return by the way you came, but head in a southerly direction. Sharif, my friend, you are known here so you need no escort. Return to your Akhund, who will by now be wondering what has become of you." Clearly pleased, Sharif salaamed and left the room.

Scarcely pausing for breath, the Khan continued. "As for you, Mahmoudbhai, my men have organized your supplies on the basis of seven days, two extra to allow for your pace. They will see you to the borders of Afghanistan and if possible turn you safely over to the Waziris, who are a trifle touchy about strangers arriving without an introduction. I had deputed two good men to accompany you. One is Aziz, who is to my own knowledge completely trustworthy. Unfortunately the other learned only this afternoon that his father is no more, so he cannot go. He has sent his badli, for whom he stands assurance so I cannot refuse to accept him. May Allah go with you."

With little more formality than he had arrived, the Khan resumed his sloppy turban, picked up his rifle, and stepped out into the night.

24

About the time that Mahmoud had completed his mission to the Khan and headed out of Kabul, his brother Hamidullah, in Khandipur, was also heading into a new state. His business had flourished, expanding beyond the mere brokering of raw cotton. Through a contact in Bombay he had been put in touch with a merchant who was going out of business and had bought his entire stock of military-grade cloth. He had also taken a risk that paid handsomely: he contracted with the mill that made such cloth for a regular percentage of its output. Now, in more than a few of the princely states and the number expanding steadily, both the regular and irregular armies wore his cotton drill.

Prosperity had enabled him to arrange advantageous marriages for Tyaba and Razia, his two remaining sisters, and to secure a seat in a good school for Kabir, the baby of the family. All that accomplished, he decided that he himself could now take a wife. With a last lingering glance at his dream of Anees, he asked his mother to find a bride for him. In view of the fading likelihood that Mahmoudbhai would ever return, this was a strategic move, another step in preserving the family. Sons would keep the family properties intact and in due course inherit his now-thriving business. For his mother it was a different matter.

"Oh, Hamid, Hamidbeta, if only you knew how I have longed for this. For your sake, of course, but for mine also."

"For yours, Amma?"

"Mine. You are out and about all day. You cannot imagine how lonely it has been since the girls went to their husbands' families. This old zenana has never been so quiet."

"Oh, Ammijan, I am ashamed. I should have—"

"Hush. There will be an end to it now. First, a daughter-in-law. I'm so happy. She will supply the companionship I've missed. Then, Insh'Allah, grandchildren to bring laughter back into the house. How I shall fuss over them! Well, beta, my son, leave it to your mother. I shall find a good wife for you."

She had long fancied Surayya, daughter of one of her friends, for a daughter-in-law, and she meant to lose no time in proposing it. Not that she could achieve anything binding, for that was the business of the men, but once the two mothers had agreed, she would summon Nur Jehan's husband to handle the official arrangements. Off she bustled to give instructions for the day's work, to send the smallest servant child for a conveyance, and at the last moment to slip the heavy burqa over her head. Then, followed by an ayah, she stepped through the slit in the felt purdah curtain and into the waiting jutka, the horse-drawn closed carriage in which women in purdah travelled.

"Come sit here and have a cool sherbet," Surayya's mother greeted her friend after helping her remove her burqa.

"No, no, Fatima, I don't need anything. Don't bother," Amina protested, while carefully folding the burqa and laying it beside her.

"What nonsense. Of course you need something cool. That cage of a jutka is always sweltering."

"Yes, but fortunately, it's a very short ride between our houses."

"Here you are," Fatima said when they had settled themselves on comfortable cushions on the balcony, where a faint breeze was stirring. "You're looking well, Amina, happier, in fact, than I've seen you for some time. What have you to tell me?"

"Such news, Fatima. You'll never guess."

"Your elder son has returned."

Amina's smile faded. "No, that fortune has not found my address. We've never believed he did anything wrong, of course, but it's hard for a mother not to know where her son is. Or even if..."

"Don't say it, Amina." Fatima put her fingers on her friend's lips. "Don't ever say such a thing; the devil might overhear and take it for a suggestion." Her hand dropped into her lap and she resumed her eager, smiling expression. "Now, what is the good news? Tell me."

161

Amina's expression changed as completely as though someone had twisted the end of a kaleidoscope in which she existed. Her face became radiant. "Hamidullah says he is ready to take a wife."

"Is that so? No wonder you're pleased. I'm so happy for you." Fatima clapped her hands, then could not resist giving her friend a hug. "And is there a candidate?"

"Oh, Fatima, you must let me have Surayya for him."

"Surayya is still young."

"You know I'll be a mother to her. And just think how much better for you both to have her near by. My own girls, fortunate as they are with their mates, are so far away. How often do I see them?"

"True. I've dreaded the moment of sending Surayya away. Still, as you point out, your household is not far from here. That's a big help."

"Hamid is a good boy, Fatima. No one could ask for a better son, and he will be as good a husband."

"And Surayya is ready. I've taught her all the things a girl should know and you'll find she's been an apt pupil, as she will be for you."

"Will you speak to her father, then?"

"I will, certainly."

"Oh, Fatima, I'm sure the Ferishtas on our right shoulders will count this as a good deed for each of us."

All afternoon, Fatima had laid her plans and prepared carefully for how she would break this news to her husband. That evening, Sadiq opened the subject himself by an abrupt question to his wife, "What are you fidgeting about?"

"Am I fidgeting?" Fatima responded. "I'm sorry. I didn't mean to irritate you."

"I know. Ever since you made my favorite rann of lamb this evening and followed it with kulfi, I've suspected—well, what else could I think?—that you wanted something."

"You're so clever, Sadiq. I can never hide anything from you."

"So out with it."

"I'm thinking about Surayya."

"What about her?"

"It's really time to arrange her marriage."

"She's young yet."

"Not that young, my dear. I know we both like having her around, but if we keep her beyond marriageable age we may have much to regret on her account."

"Are you suggesting that we need to start looking?"

"There has been a proposal."

"A proposal? From whom? Why didn't it come to me?"

"My friend Amina, the late Magistrate's widow, was here today. She says that her son, Hamidullah, is ready to take a wife."

"Hamidullah! But that's a tainted family."

"Not any more. Hamid has done so well in business he's earned a good reputation."

Declaring that Surayya would marry a family, not a business, Sadiq drew a firm line under any discussion about Hamid. He promised to start making some inquiries for a suitable match, if his wife felt so strongly about it, but could see no reason to hurry the question. Their daughter was still young.

"Would you like to play chess?" They sat down at the chess table, whose top was inlaid with rosewood and mango wood to form the board, and she began to set out the figures. They had been carved long ago of soapstone and were now, after years of careful handling, as smooth and lustrous as polished marble. Seeing and touching them was Fatima's chief satisfaction in the game, which she had learned as a bride in order to please her husband.

She was, however, not through with the question of Surayya and Hamidullah. Some days later she told her husband, "My friend Amina was here today. I feel sorry for her. She gets so lonely for her daughters, because they're married in families that live so far away. It frightens me to think of sending Surayya away like that."

"Hmph. They probably couldn't have found husbands closer to here for those girls. Not that family."

"You're wrong, my dear. Hamid found respectable husbands, more than respectable, real catches, for his sisters."

"Still, he does have a brother who was convicted of a crime. That's not something I want for our daughter."

Clearly there was nothing to be gained by pursuing the question while Sadiq was in this frame of mind. Fatima decided to change her tactic, and the next day enlisted her daughter in the struggle. "Surayya, dear, do you remember Amina Auntie's son at all?"

"Which one?"

"He's just a few years older than you. But perhaps it's too long ago; you were still so little when the boys reached the age when they were banished from the zenana if there were visitors. His name is Hamidullah."

"But I do remember Hamid! Razia adored him, so of course I did too."

"His mother would like to see you marry Hamidullah."

"Oh, Mother, how marvelous. Is it agreed?"

"Your father is very much against it."

Surayya bent over her needlework and her mother went on to mundane topics, satisfied that the seed had been planted.

Several days later Sadiq came into the zenana for his customary tea time relaxation with the family. "What are you so busy with, Surayya?" he asked his daughter.

"I'm just looking at my jewellery to see what else I'll need for my wedding. Isn't this a pretty setting?"

"Very. And why are you thinking about weddings now? Aren't you happy here at home?"

"Oh, yes, Bapa, but I'm not a child anymore, you know. I mustn't be a spinster, must I?"

"Well, well, so we must save you from that fate. We'll have to start looking for someone for you."

"There's no need to look, Bapa. I want to marry Hamidullah."

"We'll find you someone better than that."

"Please, Bapa, don't send me away to strangers. Not like Razia. She gets homesick and is too far away even for a visit now and then. Please, Bapaji, I want to stay here, near you and my mother."

"Perhaps a suitable boy exists in Khandipur. I can't think of one at the moment."

"Hamidullah is a suitable boy, Bapa. And they live so near I could visit often." In her eagerness, Surayya failed to notice her father's increasing irritation.

"He is not a suitable boy. Don't forget his brother went to prison."

"People don't think of Sayed Mahmoud any more. It's the old Magistrate they remember, and how he was looked up to. Hamid reminds them of him. Please, Bapa, don't hold that against Hamid. Please."

"Put him out of your mind, Surayya. Now please pour out my tea."

By tacit agreement, neither woman mentioned the matter again, but Fatima was frequently brusque with her husband and their daughter was not her usual sunny self.

One day, Sadiq mentioned visitors to his wife. The Nawab of Dinagadh was coming through Khandipur on his way South and had indicated he would stop off to talk with Sadiq about some business they had begun correspondence about. The fact that the Nawab would take it up in person indicated his serious purpose; to Sadiq it looked like a heaven-sent opportunity, possibly a major increase in their fortunes.

"There's something you can do to help things along," he told Fatima, fingers drumming on his thigh. "I would like you to entertain his women."

An important Nawab's family were not exactly every-day guests, and Fatima took her responsibilities as hostess seriously. On the appointed day, she was satisfied with her preparations and was able to greet her elegant guests calmly and graciously. What made her nervous as the visit progressed was the way the Begum kept eyeing Surayya.

"How old is your daughter?" she enquired almost as soon as they were introduced. On hearing the reply, the Begum glanced at her sister and nodded. "Come here, Bibi. Show me your needlework."

Surayya did as she was bid and even volunteered an explanation of some of the stitches, but presently excused herself to go supervise the making of the tea.

"Please tell me about your journey," Amina hastened into the opening. "Was your train comfortable?"

"Dirty places, trains. Hot. And when the ice in the bucket melted, our stupid servant splashed it around so we were quite discomfited."

"What a pity. Do you travel much?"

"The Nawab has to travel a good bit to see to his lands. I do not usually go with him then. But I go to a hill station every year, as now. Unfortunately I have no daughters, so as you see, I have to rely on my sister and some of these women for companionship."

"A daughter is generally considered a blessing only by her mother."

"Is your daughter promised?"

"Not definitely. Her father and I want to keep her at home for a while longer."

"I have only a son. But Khandipur cannot produce many good prospects, I should think. No doubt you would be grateful for a good offer."

"Khandipur is a pleasant place. I hope you find it so. The climate is good, not at all humid."

"A little humidity is good for the complexion. But the dryness here doesn't seem to have harmed hers, at least." She nodded at Surayya, who turned away modestly.

It was over at last. Time for the visitors to leave. "Your husband will hear from us," the Begum said as she made her farewells.

That evening Sadiq and Fatima relaxed in the comfortable zenana over their nightly cup of tea. Aware that they had both had a strenuous day, Fatima had prepared a special blend, flavoured with cardamom. "I had a very satisfactory discussion with the Nawab Dinagadh," Sadiq reported, stirring an extra spoonful of sugar into his cup. "The lawyers are drawing up the papers. How did you get on with the ladies?"

"Oh, Sadiq, they should never have come here. Why did you make me bring them?" Fatima was near tears.

"Why? What did they do to offend you so?"

"The Begum has her eye on Surayya for her son."

"Impossible!"

"It's so, I tell you. She kept on about her all afternoon. Then the last thing she said was that you would be hearing from her husband. That can't be about his business with you, you know. She couldn't take her eyes off our daughter."

"I never imagined—I should have thought about it. The boy has a terrible reputation: arrogant, cruel, careless about his debts."

"And a terrible womanizer."

Sadiq looked at his wife quizzically. "Tell me, my dear, how does a woman like you learn such a thing?"

"Even our boys, young as they are, know about him. One of them asked me whether his mother was very ugly. He wondered whether that's why the young man has to have every pretty woman he can see."

"I've heard the same thing. No decent girl would be safe with him."

"Why does she have to want our daughter, anyway?"

"Perhaps she hopes we wouldn't have heard of the boy's reputation."

"We can't let Surayya be caught in that net!" Fatima's hands, clasped in an imploring gesture, trembled slightly.

The parents continued to talk about this threat. Sadiq was concerned that if an offer should come, the newly signed business connection would make it difficult to turn down. If the refusal were regarded as insulting, the Nawab could ruin them, a disaster for the sons as well as Surayya and her parents. No business was more important than the child, but how to escape the dilemma was certainly not clear.

"If only she could be married before the offer comes!" Fatima exclaimed.

"Hmm, that's one way out. The only one I can see, in fact. How much time do you think we have?"

"Not much. The Begum sounded very clearly as though she'd made up her mind. With a son like that, I suppose they're wild to get him married."

"So what's our next step?"

"Oh, Sadiq, dear, we must hurry. Do think again about Hamidullah. That could be accomplished before the Nawab could approach you."

Sadiq covered his face with his hands. He had always assumed he would find someone very special for his beloved daughter.

"The drawbacks of that family are nothing compared to the Nawab's son," Fatima persisted.

"We don't have much choice. If I decide to consider it, I'll have a talk to the young man and then make up my mind."

"Talk with Hamidullah! That's hardly done. Your brother would speak for you, I'm sure, and Amina would have her first son-in-law take care of arrangements from her side."

"So now you know better than your husband! I thought you wanted me to accept this young man. Don't expect me to consent unless I can see him and judge for myself."

Only two days later, Hamid received a rather formal invitation to call on Sadiq. It was clear that he was to be vetted as a suitor for the daughter, since his mother had told him of her visit to Fatima. Unusual as that direct contact was, he felt not at all nervous when he presented himself at Sadiq's compound. He was not received in the mardana drawing room but in the office, a signal not lost on him. After the usual initial courtesies, his host went straight to the point. "I cannot give my daughter to a family that has been touched by scandal without knowing whether it is likely to recur, nor to a man who may have been involved in that scandal, however innocently. Did you know that the ring your brother gave you was stolen goods?"

"I have never had reason to think that it was come by dishonestly."

"Then how do you account for Sayed Mahmoud's conviction?"

"I have always believed that he was innocent."

"Then why did you not appeal? Why not fight an injustice?"

"Begging Sahib's pardon, how could I fight the most powerful man in the area, and I a mere junior clerk in his office? Besides, how could I know how many other innocent people might have suffered?"

"Yes, a good thought. Still, with your brother's imprisonment you became the head of the family. Do you now ever think of him?"

"Often, Sahib. We were not told either where he was incarcerated or the date of his release. Presumably he left the prison but he has disappeared. We have had no word from him, no trace of his whereabouts. I often pray that things are well with him."

"Do you expect to see him back here some day?"

"If I could know that, then wouldn't I feel happier about him? But he's been away for close to three years now. I should think if he were going to return he would have done so by now. Or at least sent us some word."

"So you do not expect him."

"All of us in the family care deeply about him, as he has always done about us. Perhaps that explains his silence. He was always so careful of the family honour that it would be like him to stay away to protect us. If so, then there is no chance he will come back."

"Why should I not disclose my heart to you? I find this last statement of yours reassuring, for I will not put my daughter in a situation where she would have to face renewed gossip."

"If my brother should return, I could only welcome him. If that occasioned gossip, we should have to face it. But I believe we are strong enough to do so."

"Well, Hamidullah, this is not what I wanted for my only daughter. Still, still, it does seem to me you have shown a responsible attitude. We know your Mother's hopes. Have you yourself agreed to accept my daughter as your wife?"

"I should be honoured."

"Then, reluctantly but, yes, wholeheartedly, I give you my blessing. Bismillah, in the Name of God."

Invitations went out at once, including one to the Nawab and his party at the hill station which included an apology for not delivering it in person. A wedding was a joining not so much of two individuals as of two families, and both had an active part in it. For three weeks the zenanas of both houses worked frenetically, reinforced by the relatives who had been sent for. Making gifts of clothing for the bride's family and jewellery for the bride kept Amina happily occupied, while elegant sherwanis to be presented to the groom and his young brother were stitched under Fatima's critical supervision. In both households many tradesmen were sent for to supply the trousseau. Not least demanding of attention were the trays of sweetmeats and other delicacies that must be exchanged between the two houses.

All three of Hamid's sisters and their families came for the festivity. The house rang with shrieks of joy at the reunions, laughter at shared memories and stories of new adventures, the teasing that is part of loving relationships. The nearer the marriage day approached, the less Hamid took part in these happy exchanges, withdrawing more and more into himself. "Don't give it a thought," his brothers-in-law reassured their wives when they worried about it. "Every man is terrified when he's about to marry."

It was not the forward look that frightened Hamid, however; it was the recurrence, waking and sleeping, of the image of Anees that all through the intervening years he had repeatedly told himself must be firmly banished from his mind. She had never really been absent from his dreams, but now that he was about to ally himself with another woman, she moved again to the forefront. Once again the moon-crowned beauty ravished his being; he dared not join in the jollity lest the others sense his enchantment and know it could not be with the bride he had never seen. Nor would he see her until they had been pronounced husband and wife. Surayya may have remembered him from their childhood, but he certainly had no early memory of her.

Instead he remembered Anees's hand on the purdah curtain; the passionate love for a fantasy woman who became real during his brief disguise as a Hijra; the poetic message; the ring and its explanation from the ayah. Even what he knew of the ayah's fate: Khatija, who had sent her son-in-law to warn him about Narasimha, doing him a favour even after he had caused her to be banished from Anees. Always Anees' face was there. The exquisite beauty, leaning so casually against the pillar but intense, too, for the message of the ring was that he also was important to her. Somehow. He was a part of her dream, as she of his. The dream that was all they could have.

In reality, there was no possibility that her father would ever have given her to Hamid. They could never have married. But in his heart—ah, that was a different matter. He would try to build an honest life with this woman his mother had chosen for him. But of the delirium of his first love, still his love, there was not the slightest trace.

This marriage was a calculated move. He owed it to his family, those present as well as the forebears whose proud name he had so often invoked in establishing his business, to produce a son. When he first talked with his mother about the prospect, he had thought he could accept a wife. Now, despite these fears that overwhelmed him, he knew he must go through with the wedding. The family had surmounted their earlier disgrace; he could not fail them again.

But would that mean failing the young woman who was meant to be his wife? How could he be a proper husband to one woman when he yearned for another? Perhaps the ancients were right to establish purdah; had he not violated it, he might have been able to forget the fantasy. Now it was burned on his memory, as ineradicable as a scar. In fact, as the scar that was Mahmoud. How could he make a woman happy, with all these secrets in his soul?

The preparatory ceremonies were over. Now was the day for taking the irrevocable step. "You must be happy, Hamidbeta," his mother whispered, taking a last look at his solemn face as she fastened on his head the traditional turban with its veil of jasmine and roses. "She will make you a fine wife, Insh'Allah."

"I was thinking of my brother," Hamid dissembled.

"So right. If Mahmoud were here this would be a perfect day."

25

As he said the last prayers of the day and made his nest, Mahmoud again felt thankful for being on his way back to India. Well as he had been treated in Kabul, being confined to a space still awoke some anxieties in him. Here, six days' march out, the mountains, the clear air, the vast vistas, the rugged defiles, made him feel a little larger than life. Tonight the mountains embraced the high meadow like a lover bringing a necklace of stars. Scanning the sky, Mahmoud reflected that the 'Hunter,' with the Dog Star at his heels, had never seemed more alive. He hoped they were hunting with him and not for him on this journey.

Mahmoud lay back, content with his mission so far: the risks taken, the shoals negotiated, the message delicately offered and received on the platter of gifts and the return message stowed safely in his memory. The Minister would not be happy with it but that was not the emissary's concern. Tomorrow they would cross into Waziristan and change guides. It would mean a new set of bargaining and rewards, but it also meant he could almost count the days until he reached home again. How good it would feel to speak his own tongue, sleep among his own things, eat the widow's delicious and familiar food, resume their evening conversations. In a mood of tranquillity he pulled his shawl over him. Two deep breaths and he slept.

During the night some faint alarm in his brain caused him to raise himself on one elbow. Out of nowhere a flying body landed on him, knocking him back onto the ground. As he fell, he recognized his brother Hamid's mischievous grin. Struggling to free himself enough to respond to the playful encounter, he realized it was not Hamid but Major Naughton on top of him. That the Major turned out to be a woman did not lessen his strength.

Mahmoud twisted and struggled, using the lessons his wrestling tutor had taught him when he was a child in Khandipur, until he succeeded in bringing his feet up to his assailant's stomach. As he sent him flying, he caught sight of the face of his guide, Zaki. A foot lock, a break, a half nelson, a…the fight went on until both parties panted and gasped. With a final effort, Mahmoud sent his jailer from Benur rolling down the slope, leaving him alone in his cell, which had sides like the high mountains.

Mahmoud woke, chilled through and aching throughout his body. He reached for the shawl he must have cast off, felt all around him for it, then sat up more puzzled than frightened. Perhaps an animal had carried it off. An animal. He reached for the rifle Sharif had bought for him in Kabul. It also was not there, nor was Zaki. Now thoroughly alarmed, he took inventory. His shawl, his gun, and their last package of food were the casualties. His remaining watches and money were safely in the deep pocket which a protesting tailor had inserted in his loose pyjama.

As soon as it was light, he woke Aziz, the second guide. Aziz tried to be cheerful. "Zaki gone home. No matter. Today we come to the end of my tribe's mountains. You anyway need new guides. Aziz also will go home."

They gathered up their remaining possessions and set off, in no mood to waste time hunting for game, with the rest of their supplies missing. As the minutes became hours, however, Aziz set a slower pace. "This territory strange to me, too," he explained to an impatient Mahmoud. "Must watch carefully, must meet the Waziri before he shoots."

Wise as these precautions sounded, they proved to be vain. The constant rhythm of walking stealthily down a defile, across a narrow valley, then trudging up and over the next ridge, over and over again, was wearisome. Halts were not restful, only brief pauses to scan every rock and outcropping for any sign of human presence. Nerves and senses strained to their limit. The sun was on its downward slide when suddenly, out of the silence, came the sharp crack of a rifle. A bullet whizzed past their noses to ricochet off the rock they had just passed. The Waziris had spotted them first and they must now fight.

"Keep down," Aziz whispered to Mahmoud. "No gun. All you can do is stay out of way." Aziz peered carefully around the boulder which sheltered them, pulling back quickly at the sound of a rifle being cocked. After each shot, he changed his position to get a better view of the spot from which the shot had come and fired when he thought he had seen a movement in the near distance.

After an hour, he whispered, "Best now you hide yourself. Ammunition almost finished. Dark coming soon. You can't move in dark; these mountains strange to you. Do what you can for yourself and may Allah protect you. I'll keep them occupied as long as my bullets hold out."

Frightened, exposed, terribly alone, Mahmoud crept as far as possible within the shadows and caromed from rock to rock. In this fashion he managed to slip far enough away so that the sound of the gunshots became fainter. They were still being exchanged, however, which meant that Aziz was still keeping the Waziris busy.

Reassured, Mahmoud must have momentarily relaxed his vigilance, for on stealing into the shadows from behind his current rock, he was dismayed to find himself facing a cluster of houses only a few steps away. Several small children played in the spaces between them and he could see at the other end two women squatting over their cooking. Automatically, lest one of them look up and spot him, he slipped behind the nearest house, intending to slink to the boulders opposite.

No sooner had he done so than a woman with pots balanced on her head came around the corner of a farther house and started towards him. When she turned back to call to her companions, he was about to retreat around the corner whence he had come, but there, too, he heard footsteps. Nothing to do but slip through the open door of the house against which he was sheltering. He would make a dash for it when the woman had passed.

The heightened sense of danger sharpened his reflexes despite his fatigue. Just inside the doorway, brown and dusty as the boulders among which he had been dodging, he flattened himself against the whitewashed wall. From there he could take an occasional peek without exposing himself much and immediately steal out again as soon as the woman had passed. Listening to her step, which sounded brisk, though without hurry, he estimated he would have only a moment to catch his breath before having to run for it.

To his horror, she turned into the house where he stood. He held his breath hoping to slip out while her footsteps were still warm in the dust, but she stopped in the doorway to remove the pots from her head. Still blocking the exit as she bent over to set the pots on the floor, she froze at the sight of his shoes. Then slowly her gaze moved upward: legs bent in preparation for flight or attack, spare frame, slender shoulders pressed against the wall, deeply lined face.

She straightened up, at the same time adjusting her head scarf across her face. "Welcome, stranger," she said in a husky voice. The words so staggered him that he feared he would fall. "You look weary. Sit here and rest. The call from the mosque will come any moment now, and then I can pour you a cup of water."

Warily, he sank onto a low stool and leaned his head back against the wall. After the day's exertions, the chance to let go was almost too welcome. It lasted only briefly, however, for presently the evening call came from the mosque. With a quick glance at Mahmoud, the woman poured water over her hands, wrapped her head in the approved manner and began her prayers. A moment's hesitation only, and he did likewise. Silently he prayed the required prayers for forgiveness and added his thankfulness for this respite and for the food to come and implored guidance for his next step. Afterwards, both of them seemed more relaxed.

When she motioned him to sit again, he barely managed to suppress a sigh of relief. He supposed he ought to tie and gag her, then slip out while the rest of the villagers were occupied with their meal. But he couldn't bring himself to attack a woman. Anyway, he was too weary to be able to think of it.

She took a thali and dished up food from the pots she had carried in: dal, curd, vegetables and naan, which he had come to regard as the local version of chapattis. She handed it to him without speaking, a simple, staple meal, deliciously flavoured. After his day of fasting, it was ambrosia.

During the quiet of the meal, he had taken advantage of the opportunity to steal sidelong glances at his hostess: not a line showed

175

around her eyes, which was all he could see of her face; her figure was slender, ankles slim. Odd that she was only a girl, like Razia, just entering marriageable age. He wondered who might be interested in her. Did some young villager lust for her? If so, that might mean trouble for him on the morrow, when he was found in her house. Or perhaps some older man eyed her for a second wife. Better to get away before he had to face any of them.

When Mahmoud had finished his meal and begun to express his appreciation for it, his hostess readjusted her scarf over her face and turned toward him. "You cannot stay here for the night," she said, "because I live alone. I will arrange with my neighbour to take you in, but you are my guest and under my protection."

"How can I appear to your neighbours?" Mahmoud protested. "They have been shooting at me all afternoon. The men will kill me."

She laughed. "Of course. We don't welcome intruders in our territory, so naturally they will attack you. But once you enter one of our houses you become a guest, so it is our duty to protect you and treat you as a guest should be treated. If one of our men had been killed this afternoon, it would be necessary to consult the Jirga, the village council, but obviously that hasn't happened. So long as you are with us, you are quite safe."

In the morning, after the first prayers and an early cup of tea, he returned to his original hostess, intent on securing her intercession to arrange a safe-conduct for him. But she would not hear of it. "You are still exhausted," she insisted. "Stay here in Chalab and rest for a few days. Then we can discuss arrangements for you. What kind of hospitality would it be if we sent you off before you're fit?"

Gratefully, he stayed. The first day he spent by himself, strolling among the rocks or simply sitting in the sun; that evening, not yet feeling quite confident about his relations with the men, he sat and watched Shaheen, his hostess, prepare the food. She had tucked in the end of the dupatta with which she veiled her face in his presence so that it could neither impede her movements nor drop into the fire when she bent over.

He had not watched women cook since he was eight, old enough to join the men in the mardana. He supposed many women might be as competent as Shaheen, but he admired her long, slim fingers as they moved with practiced rhythm through the process. He marvelled at the deftness with which she built a fire in a pit an arms-length in depth and two feet in diameter: a tandoor, she said. It was one of the few words she spoke during this activity. The fire at the bottom heated the sides, which had been polished to the hardness of stone.

While they came up to the required heat, Shaheen kneaded and rolled out rounds of dough for the naan, then picked up each circle and flipped it back and forth between her fingers a few times before slapping it onto the side of the tandoor; there it stuck while it baked. Then reaching deep into the pit, she turned over the guinea fowl that a neighbor had brought as her contribution to the village's hospitality.

Shaheen's tandoor was on the protected side of the house, between it and the rock from whose shadow he had first approached the village. With a laugh, Mahmoud thanked Allah that in his preoccupied watching out for people he had not fallen into it. Shaheen smiled. Like a well-brought up Muslim woman, she did not initiate speech with men, though she responded, briefly but pleasantly, to his attempts at conversation.

The next morning, following the first prayers, Mahmoud sat with Afzal Itimad, the neighbour to whom Shaheen had turned him over for the night. Cradling a mug of hot tea gave his hands a way to disguise their nervousness. He took a sip. "So tell me," he began. "This young woman who has taken me under her wing..."

"Wonderful young woman," Afzal responded. "The way she's managed that farm all by herself."

"By herself? No family then?"

"None. Her mother died when she was born, so she's an only child. The father never married again. Odd. People say he must have been very much in love with his first wife."

"That's not so odd," his wife, Birbal, broke in. She had reappeared to replenish their tea and stayed to join the conversation. "Anyway, he was too wrapped up in his daughter to look at another woman. Took her to the field with him or wherever he went."

"Took her hunting?" Mahmoud asked, startled.

177

"Anywhere but that. The rest of us looked after her then. We taught her to cook and weave and all the things her own mother would have done." She laughed. "You could say that Shaheen's the best-trained girl in Chalab; every mother here treats her like a favourite daughter."

"The father, ah, he's in the village now?"

His host scratched his beard, as though deciding how much to reveal. "He died. Shaheen was twelve when he was killed." His tone indicated finality. Mahmoud stood up, thanked them for sharing the picture of Shaheen and excused himself to go to her house.

Early October was the end of the harvest season, and Shaheen was busy cleaning up her fields. Mahmoud worked alongside her for the day, enjoying the physical activity and the crisp air. Shaheen laughed at his pleasantries but said little, concentrating on the task. Occasionally she instructed him what to do next or how to do it correctly, and he approved. On the third day, he noticed that she was less careful about veiling her face, occasionally allowing the dupatta to hang free when it slipped off while she was working. The next day, she did not even bother to attempt it. Since he had observed from a distance that women faced the village men quite uncovered, Mahmoud concluded this change in Shaheen meant he had been accepted in the community. She would meet no disapproval by treating him like one of them.

Shaheen's big dark eyes had never been covered, but now the mobility of her facial expressions showed Mahmoud the liveliness as well as the strength in this girl. Her mild words had disguised the seriousness of her convictions, as well as the teasing of which she now began to show herself capable. Mahmoud, relaxed, was able to be helpful and solicitous and even make jokes with her, treating Shaheen as he did his sisters. To Shaheen, who had never had a sibling with whom to share so informal a relationship, it seemed Mahmoud was showing interest in her. She became freer, even flirtatious, and to cherish in her heart every generous gesture he made.

Back at the end of the second day, encouraged by the confidence his night-time hosts had shown in him, Mahmoud had felt brave enough to join the men as they squatted in a convivial circle sharing a hookah. As they passed it to him, he had felt the first stirrings of acceptance into their circle. Few Chalabi men had been outside Waziristan, and they drew him out about the places he had seen, the routes and passes he knew, and his estimate of the other tribes' areas through which he had passed.

Occasionally his description of a place was interrupted by someone who was nursing a blood feud with some person or family from that area or who knew of such a quarrel. The idea of feuds was, of course, not new to Mahmoud. He was, however, puzzled at the way some had lasted across several generations, with each score that was settled creating a new obligation to retaliate. The grudge might be held for years, waiting for an opportune moment to exact retribution.

The men seemed to delight in the stories, though they could not have been new to them; indeed the precipitating events and their consequences, sometimes gory, sometimes clever, were recounted with a freshness that suggested more excitement than bitterness.

"And of course," Mahmoud concluded the account of his travels, "this is the last place I have been. It would have saved you some ammunition if my guide and I had been able to find you first." This brought the smile he was seeking. "But what happened to him? You were still exchanging shots the last I could hear."

"Hai! It was time to break our fast. One man was not worth postponing that. He wasn't even a caravan. He's well on his way home, be sure."

At the comment about breaking their fast, Mahmoud realized with something akin to shock that his contact with the Waziris had been on the second or third day of Ramzan, the month of fasting, but he and the guides had eaten by daylight without a thought. As a traveller he was of course excused from the rigours, and eating only in the dark on the journey would in any case have involved foolhardy risks.

"Now you're here," another interrupted his thoughts, "you might as well join us tomorrow. We'll be out hunting game."

"Unless we spot a caravan," someone interjected, provoking laughter.

"But you see, I haven't a gun."

Several of the men offered to lend him one; he countered with an offer to buy it instead. Determined bargaining on both sides, enjoyed as well by the onlookers, resulted in a sale. Everyone who had witnessed it felt obliged to coach Mahmoud in its use, so that he daily became more confident as a marksman. More and more a part of the activities the men undertook day by day, he passed a fortnight pleasantly. But days increasingly brisk and nights positively cold reminded him that the onset of winter was imminent. Snow might at any time trap him where he was. He had already kept the Minister waiting too long. One evening therefore he was preparing to raise the question of a safe-conduct out of Waziristan.

"All right," he began, "I've told you where I've been so far. Now you please tell me where I should go next. What direction should I take from here?"

"Aim for Bahawalpur," they told him.

"Bahawalpur? That's quite far, isn't it?"

"It is, but we've heard there aren't many people in that area. You might possibly get through it without meeting anyone."

"Well, that depends," another objected. "That would probably be so only if one were prepared to buy a horse at the first outpost."

"But that first contact would be dangerous, wouldn't it?"

The men smiled at such naivete. "If it's known you're going to leave some gold there, no one will stand in your way."

Suddenly the outpouring of advice was interrupted by the drummer. From a position behind Mahmoud, he leaped up and waved his arms in the air, ululating wildly. For a brief moment the circle was stunned into silence, then waves of laughter. The men beat one another on the back and guffawed until they were forced to stop for breath. "Bahawalpur! Buy a horse," they gasped and held their sides. "Where next?" the others roared. Wondering why the purchase of a horse should occasion such an outburst of mirth, Mahmoud looked inquiringly into one face after the other. Sidelong glances and occasionally even a gesture in his direction accompanied the laughter.

In time, the man next to him took pity on him. "Take off your turban and look at it," the neighbor advised. The action explained very little, except that a handkerchief had been affixed to it by a woman's silver hairpin.

"What is this?" Mahmoud inquired, fingering it.

"It's a woman's handkerchief," they told him.

"So I can see. What's the point?"

"The point, friend, is that now you are caught—or selected." The comment brought a renewal of the laughter.

"What does that mean?"

"You see, among us there are two ways a woman may marry. The usual way is for her family to select a husband for her and make all the arrangements. But we provide for some freedom for our women. If she wants to choose her husband herself, she can do so by having the drummer pin her kerchief to his turban with her hairpin."

"Eligible men who don't want to be caught," another interrupted, "keep an eye on the drummer in public gatherings. But you were too innocent. That's why Shaheen could succeed."

Flustered, Mahmoud could only stammer, "And now?"

"Well, naturally a man chosen in this way is obliged to marry the woman," his neighbour informed him smugly.

"Provided," another amended the statement, "he can pay the bride price. And of course we know you can, because we saw when you bought the gun that you had some gold."

26

Mahmoud was too dismayed to respond as the men of Chalab continued their excited chatter about the marriage arrangements. They took his silence for agreement, as indeed they might, for he recognized that he had no choice: if he declined, the whole village would be his enemies. So he began the traditional haggling about the bride price. He mustn't be too generous: this was not his choice, and the gold would be important for the rest of his journey. But if the price were too niggardly, the villagers would be insulted. Better not to offer, just listen to discover what they expected.

After negotiations which were protracted only for appearances' sake, the groom-to-be agreed to a bride price of two mohars, gold coins which would go to the village for the celebrations. Shaheen herself announced publicly that since she owned her farm and had managed with no problems so far, she did not demand a meher, but the declaration was overruled by her more mature and deliberate neighbours. Normally the meher was a sum agreed upon before the marriage but paid to the wife only in case the marriage was dissolved, either by the death of the husband or by divorce. In this case, all the men agreed with the drummer's suggestion that it be deposited with Shaheen in advance. Privately, Mahmoud thought this a wise precaution, for he would abscond as soon as he was able to get away.

To a man (and woman) the Chalabis reacted to this proposed marriage with delight. Waziris were known to be ferocious to prisoners, often killing them at once, but women and even small girl children of enemies were not only not molested but were escorted safely back to their own people. How much more tenderly, then, had they looked after one of their own. From time to time, some woman in the village had murmured to her husband a question about Shaheen's future. But there was plenty of time. Only last year, Iqbal Ansari had said to his father, "I have an idea. Why don't you marry me to Shaheen?"

"Shaheen is my daughter. How could I marry her to my son?"

"She's not your daughter."

"She's the daughter of every family in this village. When the time comes, Shaheen will have to marry someone outside."

"You'd let that farm go out of Chalab?'

"If you think of it that way. Or you could think that Chalab would gain another man. She will have whatever is in her fate."

Now, on her own, Shaheen had found a man to complete her life. How could they not rejoice? It was clear, even to a newcomer like Mahmoud, that this was the most exciting event to happen in this mountain village for some years. The Chalabis were not about to forego any of it: the laughter, arguments, plans, savourings, raillery, suggestions, contributions, secrets and announcements extracted every possible drop of enjoyment.

Let's get on with this, Mahmoud fumed inwardly. *Bride price, trousseau, qazi to come and perform the marriage, feast—days are going by. And the Minister waits while his emissary gets married!*

Still, his impatience had limits. Had he been at liberty to choose a wife for himself, Shaheen would have been a very acceptable candidate. She was a good match: almost as tall as he, strong from her work in the fields. Her fair skin glowed with health. Eyes that could sparkle or twinkle, or deepen their colour when she was earnest about something. She was a pleasant companion, an excellent cook and thrifty housekeeper. Her voice, though hearty, was unusually gentle for one of her race and her manners characteristically mild and good-tempered.

So he was not displeased with the bargain and the Minister's patrician face faded a bit in his mind. Almost imperceptibly his manner changed. Head up, he looked the other men in the eye and took his place more confidently in the evening gatherings. Moreover, he exulted privately, a few more days and this would be his home. Briefly, of course, but his own. How good to feel he had a home again.

Through it all, Shaheen was radiant. An eager participant in all the planning, she remained demure despite the excitement.

Numerous fingers under her chin lifted her face for their owners to look into her eyes and decide if she was happy. Satisfied, the women settled into the pleasant task of giving her advice. All voiced opinions as she chose her wedding clothes from among those the women produced from their treasure chests. A plum-colored pyjama with gold colour in the decorative stitching on the tight cuffs caught her fancy.

"Then you must choose this to go with it," a senior insisted, holding out a green kurta with bright inset over the breast, plum, gold and green striped.

"Oh, no, Ammijan, you made that for your daughter's trousseau," Shaheen protested.

The matron would not hear of it. "You also are my daughter. Take it, love. There's plenty of time to make her something else."

A many-coloured chiffon dupatta, the modesty scarf with which a village woman covered her face in the presence of strange men, completed the outfit.

A week on, a qazi arrived from the nearest larger village to perform the ceremony. Since preparation had taken them to the very eve of Id, the feast which closed the month of Ramzan fasting, they had decided to hold the wedding on the festive day itself. That made it a doubly joyous occasion, celebrated with gusto. All twenty-two households in the village had involved themselves in the preparations. Early in the morning the tandoors were lighted, the lamb and chicken put in for roasting, dough for the naan waiting only the moment before it would be needed. Already the women had prepared mounds of dal, spicy vegetables, curd, cream, paneer, butter, ghee, and something obviously regarded as a treat, new to Mahmoud, a hardened curd called croot.

Shaheen's joy when she appeared in the chosen garments was infectious, and appreciative "wah, wahs" greeted her on every side. All the couples in the village beamed like parents of the bride. "Do you," the qazi demanded, "of your own free will voluntarily accept this Sayed Mahmoud as your husband?"

"I do." Her voice was clearly audible to everyone present.

"And do you, Sayed Mahmoud, of your own will voluntarily accept this woman, Shaheen, as your wife?"

Mahmoud glanced over his left shoulder, uncomfortably aware of the Minister standing there. Without looking, he knew that his Mother stood at his right. Taking a deep breath, Mahmoud nodded. "I do."

"And now, you will both sign the marriage document. Shaheenbibi, you first. Make your left thumb mark here. Now you, Sayed Mahmoud. You are now man and wife. May Allah, the Righteous and Compassionate One, bless this marriage." He proceeded to lead the prayers for the well-being of the new couple, in which all joined.

That was the serious part of the occasion. Mahmoud could not remember ever witnessing such an outbreak of gaiety at a wedding. Games, some of them to show the bravery of the men, some, the grace of the women, some, sly jokes accompanied with much laughter, were interspersed with songs in which everyone joined. Once the dancing began, it lasted throughout the night.

Like a dancing girl veiling and pretending to unveil as she flirted with her audience, the new moon slipped in and out of gauzy clouds. Perhaps responding to the invitation, bride and groom slipped away from the festivities. Demure no longer, Shaheen turned to her new husband with undisguised joy. He felt the quickening in his loins as he reached for her. The gunshots into the air that celebrated their nuptials became no more than crickets in the corner as their passion exploded.

In the days following the wedding, Mahmoud began to suspect he was nearly as much of a cheat as Major Naughton. He had given this woman a husband for a few weeks only, until he judged it safe for him to be off. What would happen to her then? He wondered whether they would marry her to a local man; the thought of it made him shudder. Or—she had chosen him; perhaps she would put a stone on her heart, waiting for him to come back.

That raised a different kind of question: would he want to? He thought of his mother's cooking, and the widow's, and wondered whether he could eat Afghan food for the rest of his life. But he had affirmed to the qazi that he willingly married this woman. Did he now have a right to desert her? And Shaheen herself! She was as good a wife as a man could want, and these mountains could get into a man's soul. So his thoughts went round and round, while another part of him reveled in his new status.

Some days into the marriage the first crisis occurred, showing each the mettle of the person they had married and forcing Mahmoud into more of a commitment than he had yet envisaged. It began when Shaheen warned her new husband that the next morning she would wake him with his tea earlier than usual.

He looked up from the rifle he was cleaning to ask what she had planned. The Jirga, the village council, had announced that an Indian caravan of rich traders had entered Waziri territory the day before yesterday and would be near the village before mid-morning. All the men of Chalab must be in place to attack well before the advance scouts could spot them.

When Mahmoud declared he would not take part in looting a caravan, Shaheen could hardly believe he had said that. "What do you mean, you won't? You must! That's what it means to belong here, to be part of this village."

"Not to attack innocent travellers, I won't."

"How, innocent? They're too stingy to hire Waziri guides but they flaunt their riches. They enter our land without so much as a by-your-leave."

He laid aside the gun and stood up. "Like me, huh?"

She ignored the jibe and continued to press the reasonableness of the attack and of his participation in it. "They use our land to increase their own riches. They should pay for its use, share what they gain from using our territory as a convenience. Are you too self-righteous to see the justice of that?"

He took a step towards her, his voice raised, the tone menacing as well as angry. "Are you telling me what to do, wife?"

"I'm telling you what the village expects of every man, and so of you. And so do I."

"Suppose I join the caravan instead. Those are my people."

"*We* are your people now!" She paused, gasped, clenched fist at her breast. "Or have I made a mistake? Are you, too, just a stranger who's using us?"

Truth struck him like a blow to the temple. He put out a hand to steady himself, looked up, looked down, anywhere but at her face. He took a deep breath, held it, exhaled with a force that blew the Minister from his mind. In a low voice with only a trace of truculence, he replied simply, "No."

She also was struck silent, trying to understand the turn the quarrel had taken. Then she whispered, as though she feared the answer, "And...me?"

"No, Shaheen. I couldn't leave you, now. Not now."

A moment she stood, quivering. When she could control her voice as well as her limbs, she spoke in her usual efficient manner. "All right, you needn't go this time. You will go to bed and stay there. I shall say you have too much fever; no one may see you for two days. But you must promise to use the time to come to terms with this custom of ours. I will not lie for you again, not for this."

She bent over the samovar and blew up the small coals that glowed in its middle, then poured him a mug of the strong, sweet tea that had been brewing in it. He sipped it reflectively. "I will not lie for you," she had said, but he was living a lie. For a moment, it seemed clear which way honour lay. He set down his tea only half drunk. "You're right, merijan, my darling," he said, holding out both hands. His arms held her tightly and his mouth on hers stopped any reply.

Winter caught him almost immediately, enforcing his promise to her. Snowfalls on the mountain tops, exceptionally early, sent freezing winds into the valleys. Passes were blocked and even those who knew the area intimately hesitated to venture far from the village. Shaheen wove warm clothes for him: a woollen kurta and a black blanket worn like a large shawl and clinched at the waist with a strip of the same material. And she arranged to have warm boots made for him of heavy felt, lined with lambskin. "Some men are so foolish," she teased him. "They come to the mountains with only clothes that are suitable for the plains."

"But if they came equipped," he sidestepped, "they couldn't have these handsome clothes made by a local expert."

Thus protected, he went hunting with the men, seeking any game that ventured close in. With practice and the coaching of his fellows, Mahmoud's skill as a marksman had improved to the point where they no longer made fun of him. His proudest day in Chalab was the time several of them spotted a buck at the same time. One of the men put his hand on the rifle along which his son was taking aim and gently lowered it. "Mahmoud will bring it down," he whispered.

"I saw it first," the youth insisted. "Why should he have it? He doesn't even belong here."

"Silence!" his father commanded. "Now he belongs."

"But..."

"No buts. At first he was our guest, so we had to respect him. But don't forget he married a Chalabi woman; as her husband he has a right to be here. So long as he is married to Shaheen, he is not an outsider."

Exulting in the sense of inclusion even more than in his success with the buck, Mahmoud stored the conversation in his memory.

For her part, during the worst of the winter Shaheen went out only to feed her animals or occasionally, when he had brought home a large haunch of venison or they had slaughtered a goat, to light the tandoor and roast the meat. Indoors, they passed long hours together. She teased him to tell her stories of his childhood. It was sweet to remember the happy times in his family, but he avoided mentioning Hamid. "I think I would like your sisters," she commented once, "but have you no brothers?"

"Yes," he replied, and his tone said, "Don't ask." Physically, he seemed to shrink, head down, then back, shaking off something. The upsurge of resentment that surfaced was painful and jarred with his picture of himself. He pulled on his heavy boots and, barely stopping to throw the blanket over his shoulders, dashed out into the snow.

Prisoner of his anger, he had no eye for his surroundings. He stalked through the streets of the village, branched out onto familiar paths, then off them, floundering through drifts as much as knee deep. All the while, his thoughts ran on unpleasant tracks. His family had been taken away from him and given to Hamid. Things were so easy for his brother and so hard for him; unfair, unfair. He was loaded down with questions that required dishonest answers, decisions too heavy to make, burdens that tried his endurance. He resented feeling guilty all the time. And now, worst of all, his innocent Shaheen was involved in this web of deception. Impossible to imagine how to protect her.

By now, even his bones were cold. Time to go back. It was already dark—or, fearful thought, perhaps this was the snow blindness he had heard about. He could see almost nothing, not where he was putting his feet, not the trees he should recognize, no landmarks to show him where he was. He stumbled, fell, forced himself to get up and struggle on, sure that if he took a moment's respite he would never get up again.

Doubled over with fatigue, he pushed himself forward—and cracked his head on a boulder. He tried to put his arms around it, patted his way past it, took another step. Then his foot slipped, and only by throwing himself to the side, so he sprawled on the ground, did he avoid falling into a large hole. Cautiously moving the foot that dangled in space, he explored the opening. Not too large. Square. A tandoor! He thought about the boulder, the location of the tandoor, and knew finally where he was.

When he pushed open the door, Shaheen jumped up with a cry. "Your face is frostbitten," she exclaimed before any kind of greeting. "I'll get some snow for it." Ignoring his protest that he had just had plenty of snow, she stepped out and returned with two handfuls, which she held against his nose and cheeks. When the warmth of her hands had melted it, she made him go to bed, while she laid a cloth wrung out in lukewarm water to his face. As each application cooled, she renewed it, each time stepping up the heat a bit. Soothed by both her ministrations and the warmth on his face, he succumbed to his exhaustion and fell asleep. Shaheen stayed by him until she saw the colour come back to his cheeks and, touching them, was sure they were again soft. Then she, too, slept. Neither of them ever mentioned the episode.

Daytime held welcome distractions, but at night the Minister haunted him. He had eaten the Minister's salt, so he was untrue to him by staying on in Chalab. But here he had acquired new obligations, not of his own choosing even though he found them pleasant. He agonized over which was primary. In his mind, he asked the Minister's forgiveness for lingering with his wife, even for being grateful for the snow that made it impossible to leave yet.

Wakened by his thrashing, Shaheen soothed him, stroking his forehead and humming softly. In the mornings, she sometimes referred to his disturbed nights. He dismissed them as just a nightmare and, when she persisted, claimed he had forgotten what it was about.

At quieter times she regaled him with folk tales that were traditional among her people. "A young man sat under a walnut tree in his village." "One day, just at sunset, when all was quiet and enchanting..." "The sun grew like a blown bubble, casting pale colours of blue and rose on the snow-tipped mountains." "Her breasts were ripe melons that still retained their flower at the nipple." He never tired of hearing her voice, so expressive that had he not listened to the words, he could have told where she was in the story merely by the nuances of her inflection. When he lay with his head in her lap and closed his eyes, he saw not black but bright blue.

Once he told her the old story of a man pursued by his enemies, who turned into a strange house. When he put his hand against the wall to steady himself, a snake bit him. "I was that man," Mahmoud added. "But when I turned into a strange house and leaned against the wall, a dove came and lit on my shoulder."

Sometimes, in the middle of a story, she leaned down and kissed him on the lips, on the neck, nuzzled his ear. His hand found its way to her waist, lingered to feel the rhythm of her breathing, cupped a breast, which miraculously just fitted into his hand. Then the story no longer mattered.

Those were precious moments, yet they were not what defined the marriage for him. Since the fateful day he had been taken from his family home, he had been an outsider everywhere. With Shaheen, he was beginning to understand her moods, sense her boundaries, accumulate memories to share, build little routines known to only the two of them, and believe that she did the same for him. Those were the things that made him an insider. With the loneliness staved off, he could look beyond the marriage and imagine a time when he would belong even in Chalab.

So happily occupied, he scarcely remembered to count the passing months, while, undeterred by his inattention, the weather pursued its course. Storms finally abated, temperatures moderated, engorged rivers hurtled down the mountainsides. One day, standing just outside the village, Mahmoud counted seventeen waterfalls visible from a single spot, the mist hiding their first appearance like a woman veiling her face. Presently the earth became visible again, small patches of green appeared, spreading like wet ink from spot to spot. Gradually soggy places dried and landmarks resumed their familiar shapes.

From time to time, Mahmoud promised himself that when travel again became possible, as soon as the planting was done, in truth when he had found the courage, he would tell Shaheen about his obligation to the Minister and secure her agreement to his leaving. At times the thought was a splinter irritating his conscience so that he could barely talk with his wife or his fellows. At others, the Minister faded out in the bright light of Shaheen's eager love and her needs for his help and companionship.

As everyone scurried to accomplish the planting during the auspicious days, Mahmoud too became absorbed in the work, happily assuming responsibility in his wife's farm and so postponing his departure week by week. Soon vineyards needed pruning; orchards and feuds required tending. Before Mahmoud could account for the time, harvest was upon them. Then, with Ramzan imminent, the men redoubled their hunting expeditions in order to lay in a supply of meat, for they would not feel much like going out to chase game when they were weak from fasting. Mahmoud did his share. With the lean times coming on, didn't he too need to provide for his wife?

27

The Chalabi men were ranging the slopes about two weeks later when those in advance sent back word that a caravan, the first to be encountered in this season, was approaching up the valley below them. Their laughter and joking about plunder were presently forestalled when the advance scouts recognized the Waziri guide, so the caravan was protected.

Coming abreast, it stopped: a poor straggle of three camels, led by a few men whose appearance was almost as worn as their saddle bags. They had come from Quetta and hoped to reach Kabul in time to sell their wares for the Id festivities. Although they offered mostly household wares, they also carried some of the heavy silver jewellery favoured by Baluchi women, partly oxidized so that the contrast of bright and black heightened the effect of the design. The Chalabi men pawed through the offerings and loudly debated the merits of this or that piece.

Mahmoud, to murmurs of approval from the others, bought earrings for Shaheen. It was the first real gift he had given her since their wedding on last year's Id. After that he could work up little enthusiasm for continuing the hunt, for his imagination was busy with the scene at home that evening: the way he would tease his wife, the quick widening of her eyes followed by the effulgence of her smile when he gave her the earrings. As she did not spare herself during Ramzan but performed her tasks with her usual vigour, the fasting was hard on her and she already looked a bit gaunt. He thought that this gift, a surprise at the end of a hard day and not hoarded for the holiday, would make her happy and he was glad.

That night Shaheen gratified him with as much delight in the gift as he had hoped for. She immediately put it on, arranging over her head the chain that joined the baubles, then securing the ends to her ears. The carved circlets swung freely and the little balls dangling from them tinkled as she turned her head from side to side to catch the candlelight, laughing girlishly in her pleasure.

Then, her mood changing like water in a fountain, she said earnestly, "I also have a gift for you, Beloved."

Mahmoud glanced quickly about the room but saw nothing unusual. "What is it? Show me."

"Oh, it's not ready yet. I've only just started. I'm making a son for you."

"A son!" he blurted out. "For me?"

Her laughter filled the room. "Of course for you, you foolish man. Who else should be head of this family? I'm so blessed," she went on. "How did you happen to come here just at the right moment, when I was ready for marriage but still single?"

"Perhaps Allah the Merciful had His eye on you," he teased. And kissed her. He had only just stopped himself from telling her about his mission and his need to complete it. She would need him here more than ever now.

"Still, wherever you came from, it's a long way from here. Yet you got here."

"It's a long story, too long to go into now. It began when I was sent to prison. Don't worry, darling, I didn't commit any crime; I was accused of it, though."

"What was it?"

"They said I stole a ring. A sapphire ring."

"Sheni. Evil. It was, too, for you."

"I thought so. But as it brought me here, perhaps it was a blessing."

"A ring. A sapphire ring brought you to me. I'll never call it sheni again." She held up her hand and tapped a finger. "I'll see it here and be grateful."

"Perhaps some day I can give you a real one." Her fingers touched his lips.

During the month from new moon to new moon that Ramzan lasted, Mahmoud had fallen into the habit of taking with Shaheen the sherbet with which at sunset they broke their fast. After that he joined the men outside to smoke the hookah and exchange news and stories while the women cooked the special dishes that were the reward for abstaining from eating, drinking, and smoking during daylight. Sometimes the women did the cooking together and turned the meals into village feasts lasting far into the night, with singing and dancing prolonging the enjoyment.

"This village is like an extended family," Mahmoud exclaimed to Shaheen after one such occasion. "How strange life is. Usually a son inherits his extended family and his place in life from his father, but I shall be inducted into this tribe by my son. Through him, I shall truly belong here."

A recurring dream began to tarnish his assurance, however. An eagle, claws extended to seize its prey, circled and descended upon him. Mahmoud tried to run, but his feet were rooted to the ground. He threw his arms over his head in a vain effort to protect himself. But just before the eagle reached him, its beak became a patrician nose and a mouth tight with disapproval, while the Minister's eyes were no less piercing than the eagle's. Tossing in his uneasy sleep, Mahmoud wrestled with it. *Yes, Your Excellency; you trusted me to return to Lucknow. A year ago now. You'll think me a traitor. Go, have to go!*

He jerked upright. The action brought him to himself and he plopped onto his other side, turning his back on the Minister. That only brought Shaheen into his sight. *Leave her by herself? Can't. Not now. She needs me. She does. Well, all right—truth is I want her to need me. Ferishta on my left shoulder, hello. You're the bad angel; could it possibly be you making me so happy here?*

He kicked off the covers. Tried the other side again. No good. Banged his pillow. Shook his fist at the Minister. He knew he'd failed him, no less than he'd failed his wife. He was ashamed before both of them. Anyway, by now the Minister must have guessed what the Khan's reply was. Given up hope. The other man in the hut the time he was kidnapped said the Russians wouldn't come. No northwest wind. Made sense. So it couldn't matter whether the message was delivered in person. *I promised you. I pledged Shaheen. Minister. Shaheen.* He knew that the fraying ropes of the bridge he was on would one day soon give way.

When the day came that he knew he must act, his resolve vacillated like the needle on the scale when the merchant weighs out the rice, adding a handful, taking off a pinch, restoring a few grains. He knew it was important to, no, urgent to, no, (he sighed) impossible not to tell Shaheen, if only to save his own balance. But how to begin?

One day, feeling as he had when Aziz had sent him forward alone, Mahmoud reminded Shaheen how he had always evaded her questions about what had brought him to these mountains. He added that now it was important for her to know the story. He watched her brow furrow into a worried frown.

"I'd been sent on a confidential mission. I need to say that to you now because it weighs on me that I haven't completed it. I need to go and make my report, finish off this business. Then, no more secrets."

"But where would you have to go?"

"To India, where I came from."

"To India!" She moved over and shook him by the arm. "No, darling, don't go back to India! Please. You can't go!"

Hard as it was to keep the focus on his obligation, even more distressing were Shaheen's repeated pleas and her fear of losing him. He begged her to trust him, as his patron had trusted him to do the honourable thing and complete the mission. Shaheen had trouble understanding how his sense of honour could put the distant mission ahead of his ties to her, to Chalab, and to the jirga. He belonged to Chalab now. To him, on the other hand, that would be a flawed loyalty, based on dishonour. Their views seemed irreconcilable.

"Please understand, darling. I married you because—because at the time I had no choice. I stayed here at first out of a sense of obligation to you. I shall come back because I love you. No, darling, don't cry." He knelt and took her in his arms. "Please don't. I'll come back to your smile."

The colour of her eyes was dark when she wiped her tears away. She was fighting hard; it took all his strength to hold on to his resolve. "If you go, you won't come back." She hesitated, went on, voice quivering. "You probably won't live to come back. Even if I understood this need of yours, the men here wouldn't. Waziri men don't approve of husbands who desert their wives."

"I'm not deserting you. You could tell them you know why I'm going and that I'll be back."

"They'd think you forced me to say that. Once you leave here, you no longer belong to us. You'd be an enemy again, the man they were shooting at the day you appeared in this house. They would hunt you down."

In his mind echoed the words spoken on the mountainside: So long as he is married to Shaheen, he belongs here; so long as he is married to Shaheen.

"What can I do, then, if I can't stay and I can't go?" Both studied a shadow on the floor as though it held an answer. "Help me, Shaheen!"

"We'll see," was all she would promise.

Dissatisfied as he was with this inconclusive conversation, Mahmoud could think of no plan that seemed workable. With the men, he deliberately kept up his activities. At home he sat in silence for long periods, formulating and rejecting ideas and explaining his absence to the Minister in long soliloquies in his head. So preoccupied, he scarcely noticed Shaheen's eyes on him. On the few occasions when he caught her looking at him, he was not sure whether her sad expression was a reflection of his own, or whether she was already tasting his absence, a parting experienced over and over again in advance.

Once he observed her watch a blue magpie spiraling upwards and seemingly headed south, her head swirling with it. Then the bird swerved and floated back towards them. Red legs stretched out and claws firmly fastened on a branch of a nearby tree, it gave voice. Shaheen nodded and turned back indoors.

A few days later, Mahmoud went with a group of the younger men and a couple of boys to look at a litter of panther cubs one of them had seen. The men began to choose favourites as they watched the cubs playfully attacking one another, cuffing and rolling over and spitting their miniature defiances. One of the boys begged permission to shoot them. "I can skin them, I know how to use my dagger," he pleaded. "I'll just back off enough to get a good shot."

The boy's confidence and readiness for an exploit reminded Mahmoud achingly of Hamid. *Will my son be like that?* he asked himself. *Will he take after my brother, or me?* With a flicker of jealousy quickly extinguished by the secret joy flooding his soul, he acknowledged a hope that life might lie as easily on his son as on his brother.

He was brought back to the present by the voice of one of his older companions cautioning the youngster to wait a while. "They're too small to be of any use now, but when they're grown, they'll make fine pelts for warmth against the winter. Until then, let them enjoy their lives. We can find them again, now we know where their home is."

"As for us," his neighbour said, "we better turn our faces toward our own homes."

And so, laughing and talking, they started back. For Mahmoud the laughter gradually faded into a profound sense of loss. To dispel the cloud, he commented on the beauty of the mountains to one of his companions. The other man, silent for a moment, responded, "I sometimes think that Allah himself must sit on the top of that mountain and enjoy the sunset."

It was already dark when they reached the hill above the village. "Quiet," one of them exclaimed. "What's that sound?"

"Wailing. What's happened, then?"

With one accord they ran. Before they reached the outskirts, those in the lead were intercepted by two of the elders. Fear, such as he had not felt at any point in his journey, seized Mahmoud as he heard only snatches of the news: "faint from fasting." Shaheen! "Faint." Yes, not only from fasting. No one else knew she was pregnant. "Fell into the tandoor." No, it can't be. The heat from the tandoor—that might make her faint. A scream in his soul: *Why wasn't I there?*

Frenzy powered his left foot and denial his right. Bursting into their house, even as he shouted for his wife he was aware that it was empty. Out again, hurtling toward the sound of the keening. A heart-stopping glimpse of Shaheen in the group of women just as she looked up and saw him. As he skidded around the corner of the nearest house, she ran into his arms.

"Darling, darling, ya Allah, I was so afraid it was you!"

"Come." Once in the safety of their house, she whispered, "This is your chance, merajan. Tonight, when everyone is occupied with the tragedy, you can get away."

Stunned, he could only stare at her. "You'd...help me?"

"I must. You've been so unhappy lately. Somehow, I'll manage to make a little packet of food for you to take. It can't be much or people will wonder what I'm doing. Oh, darling, promise me you'll come back!"

The funeral feast bore a double share of engagement, for it was toward the end of a long month whose austerities told on people's strength, as indeed they apparently had done on Dildar, the deceased woman. She had lived on the other edge of Chalab, mother of grown sons who lived with her and for whom she had been cooking when she grew faint and toppled in. The person charged with preparing a corpse for burial had recited the prescribed prayers as he did so, then laid it on a charpoy which the sons picked up and carried to the grave others had meanwhile dug.

That done, all the men returned to the village for the funeral feast. As the first pangs of hunger began to fade, someone began a slow and mournful melody of lament. Others joined in, their simple voices becoming stronger as they sang until the very mountains seemed to echo their farewells. One song followed another, becoming firmer, more positive, more life-affirming with each new addition.

Only Shaheen was aware that Mahmoud was no longer among them. As soon as he sensed the absorption of the villagers in their singing, he had slipped into the house and retrieved his small bundle of possessions, the packet of food which Shaheen had secreted for him, and his rifle. Then, silently as the animals he had learned to track, he crept out of the village and down the trail he knew led in the direction he must take toward Bahawalpur.

It would be dawn before anyone thought to look for him. He intended to be too far away by then for pursuit to be worth their while. He groped his way through the moon-dark night, slipped on loose rock, ignored the bruises when he stepped onto loose shale and slid for twenty feet almost straight down. So he made his uncertain way.

The hole in his heart, papered over by thoughts of Shaheen as protectress, exaggerated his fear of his former friends. Daylight meant exposure, but stopping could mean capture. He stumbled on, pausing only to catch his breath and to drink from the river. A broad valley allowed him to make good time. After that, beyond exhaustion, he braced himself for yet another climb. "Gumal Pass, Gumal Pass." His mind repeated the litany until his feet picked up the rhythm and moved him forward of their own momentum. He knew from the Chalabis that this was his destination, the outer limit of their experience. Gumal was his pass to safety.

Fortunately it was neither high nor precipitous. He managed to make his way through it by the now brightening dawn. Immediately on the down side, he found a recess protected by an overhanging rock. Too exhausted even to give thanks for his escape, he threw himself down, tucked his bundle under his head, and sank into sleep. Making up for his two nights and a day of continual movement, he nearly missed the following day as well. Just as the sun began its westward decline, he woke, rested and determinedly ignoring the pangs in his stomach. As he stretched his stiffened limbs, he resolved not to risk the kind of encounter that had introduced him to the Waziris.

"Ho, men of these mountains!" he put his remaining strength into the roar, "A stranger knocks at your portals. Ho, brothers, come!"

28

"Ho, men of these mountains!" Mahmoud shouted. "Come, by the grace of Allah, and let us benefit one another." Listening to his voice bounce from peak to peak, he smiled ruefully at his naive assumption that it would produce anything more substantial than an echo.

He was wrong. In a startlingly short time, which showed how close he had been to being captured, a man called to him from a nearby rock. "Salaam," he said. "Who is it who disturbs the peace of our mountains?"

"Sayed Mahmoud, may God forgive him. I would hire a guide for the shortest way across your fair country."

The tribesman hunkered on his rock and laid down his gun, prepared for a pleasant interlude of bargaining. "Well, now," he began, "much depends on where you wish to go."

"I have heard of Delhi and have taken a fancy to visit it," Mahmoud replied casually.

"Ah, but I think you have more than heard of it, isn't that so?"

"What makes you say that?"

"Arre bapray, listen to your accent. All that Urdu flavouring your Pushtu. Your clothing is from the mountains, that's true, but still, you're clearly not one of us." His comments marked him as an acute observer and no novice at it; that impression was reinforced by a heavy beard which made him look older than his wiry frame and vigorous voice suggested. His next question, "So what brought you to our country, if a stranger may inquire?" reminded Mahmoud to be careful.

"A man may have many reasons for travelling. Na?"

"When a man travels for such indistinct reasons, he doesn't usually do so alone. What became of the rest of your party? Have those cutthroat Waziris done away with your friends?"

"Nay, brother, the Waziris were most hospitable to me and commended me to your countrymen for equally friendly reception. Didn't you hear me call you?"

"Wah, who could be deaf to that disturbing of the peace? I myself will take you to Dera Ismail Khan on the river, just to silence that great voice of yours. Preserve the tranquillity of our mountains." He went on to ask for gold; Mahmoud countered that silver would be adequate for two days' service. Another round of bargaining and Mahmoud agreed.

"Let it be gold then. Half a tola for safe conduct to Dera Ismail Khan."

"It could be more."

"It could also be less. But half a tola is a fair price."

"So be it. But for that I will leave you in the city. You will have to find your own way across the river. After that it becomes desert, no place for a man of the mountains. At the edge of the city, I go back."

"Come," Mahmoud agreed with some relief. "Let's find a fowl to cook for our meal, before it's too dark to hunt. Then we'll take rest for the night and set out at first light."

As with the other tribesmen, once a bargain had been struck, Hasan became a cheerful and pleasant companion. These were foothills rather than true mountains. Traversing them was therefore an easy two days' march into the valley, a welcome respite after his relentless trek from Chalab.

Dera Ismail Khan was like many small frontier towns whose merchants found it to their interest to make sure that strangers were not molested. Mahmoud made his way to a serai, where for a few rupees he was given shelter and food, as well as advice about where to buy a horse. Not a high-spirited Arab but a sturdy Waler for crossing the desert. The bargaining consumed most of a day.

The balance went to the renewing of his supplies. He was tempted by a saddlebag whose bright reds and intense blue attracted him. Just in time, he realized that it had obviously been knotted by mountain women, a telltale evidence of his route, in case he should find it necessary to pretend. So, reluctantly, he bartered the clothes that Shaheen had made for ones more suitable to the desert and the continuing hot season, and a brightly-coloured turban cloth in which to tie them. In view of the prospect of a lonely ride across the desert, he also treated himself to a hookah.

Then he returned to the serai for a second night, using the opportunity to sit with the other travellers over the evening hookah and learn what he could about his onward route. Lahore seemed to him the place to aim for. As it was almost due east, the route had the advantage of allowing him to cross the Jhelum and the Chenab rivers above the confluence. This was important, for although it was months since the rivers had been in spate from the spring melt, they were still swift and places to ford were rare. Moreover, the people in the area were friendly and a safe conduct unnecessary.

In the morning he rode Beg Sahib, his new horse, down to the riverbank and paid the ferryman the rupee for each of them to cross. Beg Sahib behaved as though he had taken the trip before, for he stood perfectly still, needing very little gentling from his new master. Perhaps he, too, felt he was going home.

Disembarking on the east bank of the Indus, Mahmoud inhaled deeply and let his breath out slowly, savouring it. This was once again his own country, not yet his Urdu-speaking community, for the language here was closer kin to Hindi, but at the same time it was no longer foreign. His nerves relaxed a notch.

Though it was still early morning, he took careful note of the position of the sun and the direction of the wind, for roads here were little more than trails to small interior villages, sometimes either obliterated by the blowing sand or simply non-existent. He would have to travel by his own reckoning and had no idea how long that condition might prevail. Before setting out, he drank deeply from the river.

"Come on, Beg Sahib, have a drink. No telling when you might have another chance. Move over; I'll fill the water bags. Even Allah doesn't expect us to cross the desert during Ramzan without water. Besides, fate might yet have us fasting on Id."

So they set out, ploddingly at first, but with increasing confidence as the hours passed. Occasional clumps of scrub were about the only things to grow in the hard, dry soil. No animals were visible. Even snakes, warned by the pounding of the horse's hooves, slithered away out of sight, leaving only faint trails in the empty landscape. People were equally scarce; none of the very few he caught sight of appeared hostile.

About every two hours, he stopped to rest his mount and to offer water to both of them. Toward evening, as the emptied water bags dangled from his saddle, he began to worry about finding a place to fill them. It was then that he espied a cluster of six houses surrounded by a few sorry-looking fields. That must mean a water source existed somewhere nearby. He approached discreetly, alert for surprises, and called out. First the children appeared, dirty, scrawny, potbellied. They surveyed him gravely, unresponsive to his attempts to provoke a smile. Then two or three disappeared into the houses again, and presently women emerged, the ends of their saris pulled down over their faces. They stood silently with downcast eyes, but evidently sized him up with sidelong glances. Then a frail old man appeared, a streak of ashes that indicated devotion to Shiva across his forehead.

Mahmoud, deciding it would now be politic to speak, addressed himself to the old man. "Namaste, father," he shifted his greeting, for these people were obviously Hindus and not Muslims.

"Namasteji," the old man replied in a voice as dry and cracked as the soil on which he stood.

"I am a stranger to these parts," Mahmoud began slowly and carefully. He assumed that these poverty-stricken dwellers would neither recognize nor be curious about his accent or his dress but might find it beyond their tolerance to entertain a Mussalman in their homes, however pitiable they might seem. "Water and a little food would earn an appropriate expression of my gratitude, as would the opportunity to spread my shawl on the ground to sleep within your precincts."

"May I know your good name?"

"I am called hereabouts by the name of Shri Madan."

The adults consulted together. After some discussion, one of the women offered to guide him to the small stream from which they carried their water. It was some little distance away, so she added the condition that he take her and her pots on the horse. The other women, giggling at the temerity of her demand, helped her up behind the rider. Mahmoud kept Beg Sahib to a sedate pace so as not to frighten his passenger.

At the stream, barely a trickle in the sand, he dismounted and accepted the clay pots she handed him. The trickle was so shallow, however, that it was slow work for his unpracticed hand to catch it in a round pot. Finally, handing them up to her, he filled his own water bags, which was easier, then cupped his hands and offered the water to Beg Sahib. All that done, he washed and drank for himself.

No sooner had they returned than the meal was served: thin jawar porridge with a watery dal and a starchy vegetable. He was served first, then the old man; next the children were fed, and finally the women. Meanwhile, the old man's face came alive with anticipated pleasure when Mahmoud brought out his hookah. Sharing it, he learned that all the men of the hamlet had gone to a distant area in search of work. The women and children were left to survive as best they might until the first rains would bring the men back for a few days of plowing. Then the cycle would begin anew.

In the morning, having had again the thin porridge, Mahmoud harnessed Beg Sahib, fastened his bundles and newly filled water bags to the saddle, and made his namastes to the villagers. To the woman who had ventured to the stream with him and fed him, he gave the agreed sum; then, moved by the squalor of these people's lives, he handed an equal sum to the old man, indicating that it was to be shared somehow among all of them. It was a kind of thanksgiving for the blessings that he and Shaheen and her village enjoyed. That small ceremony completed, he set off on his second day across the Punjab.

Maintaining his sense of direction and watching for natural hazards had become a second nature to him by now. Even as he pressed on hard, covering as much ground in a day as he thought Beg Sahib could safely do, that left plenty of time for daydreaming. His mind wandered both back to his wife and forward to his destination in Lucknow. The guide there who had taken him to the Minister had also taught him the name and location of a contact in Lucknow who would get in touch with the Minister on his return. Instructions would follow; either someone in Lucknow would show up with authorization to receive the message, or someone would come from Burhan.

The question was how long all that would take, how many days or possibly even weeks before his duty would be discharged and he could return to Chalab. What a relief it would be to have this mission over with! He need never leave Shaheen again.

On the fourth day, he forded the Jhelum before making camp. At that point the doab, the tongue of land just above the confluence, was less than thirty-five miles wide. With luck, that represented a day's hard riding at his fastest. That would be worth attempting, to get out of this British-held territory as quickly as possible. From there to Lahore would probably be another four days. It felt very good indeed to be able to calculate the remaining time.

Exhausted by his strenuous pace across the doab, Mahmoud crossed the Chenab, the last of the five rivers that gave the Punjab its name, and spent the night in a village on the bank. As he left there in the morning, he was joined by a British gentleman who introduced himself as Collector of Bhawanand District; he was riding circuit and professed to be going in Mahmoud's direction.

At first, it was agreeable to have company on the long trek. Experience had taught him how to be solitary; it was only when he was once again with other people that he realized how lonely he had felt. As he and his new companion chatted, Mahmoud became increasingly aware of an undercurrent of interest in his activities that was more than casual. Remembering the warning about British suspicions of visitors in the Punjab and its neighbouring areas, he watched his words carefully and gave minimal or evasive answers to questions that cut too near the bone.

"Was the ford swift?" "How about the Jhelum?" "Are you often so far away from home?" Questions such as these were dangerous. A fleeting memory of the Minister's calling him "a convincing liar" made him search the more watchfully for answers that avoided outright untruths.

After some hours of this exercise, the Collector indicated he had to turn northward. Mahmoud, true to his upbringing, brought their association to a close with the formal expressions of regard and regret that were part of his cultural background. No doubt equally true to his, the Englishman responded with a nod and a "Well, then, goodbye."

29

Beyond the Chenab River, the desert had given way to increasingly green and fertile land. That part of the Punjab was a main source of wheat in India and the first young shoots of the winter crop were just beginning to colour the fields. The flat countryside was much easier to ride through than the desert, so Mahmoud made good time.

As he parted from the Bhawanand Collector, he felt a slight relaxation of the tension that had kept him on edge. It had been pleasant to have company on the ride, but inherently dangerous. It was safer to be alone. But the contact had gone off all right. He did not imagine any consequences from it. He was therefore startled to be waylaid on the outskirts of Lahore by a sowar, a member of the cavalry unit attached to the office of the District Collector. He said that his master desired Mahmoud to proceed directly to his office.

Without a second thought, Mahmoud wheeled Beg Sahib and kicked him into a gallop. Not back where he came from but southward, he got a good head start before the surprised sowar followed. Down the road, past peasants whose curiosity was stirred by such an uneven race. With the sowar gaining on him, Mahmoud made to cut across a field, but swerved back onto the road; a farmer himself, he simply could not destroy another's crop by having two horses trample it.

That hesitation cost him a few precious seconds. Moreover, the sowar's mount was much faster than the heavy Waler that Mahmoud rode. He pulled alongside Mahmoud, then in front to cut him off. With his military background, he was experienced enough to anticipate every manoeuvre Mahmoud attempted. A sweating, panting Beg Sahib was in no condition to race further. Mahmoud gave up.

Led there by the sowar, Mahmoud was ushered straight into the office of the Collector, as the sign on the door proclaimed. There, despite the summons, Mr. Hale continued to sign the stack of papers in front of him without so much as a glance to acknowledge Mahmoud's entrance. Mahmoud, looking around, concluded that a British office was much like an Indian one, only neater. The floor was swept, the furniture merely basic, though sound—no chance of a table leg giving way under the mound of papers it bore—and the papers were in neat piles, each held in place by a weight.

The Collector was young; he looked not much older than Mahmoud, blonde, sturdy, his every movement expressing confidence. Mahmoud studied him, determined to appear equally sure of himself, no matter what story he might be forced to fabricate. When Mr. Hale had disposed of his correspondence, he looked up at the man who stood in front of him.

"Now then," he opened the conversation in a crisp voice that was meant to carry authority and did, "supposing you tell us what you are doing in the Punjab."

Mahmoud felt a surge of anger. He no more wished to be in the Punjab than the British to have him there. "Of what transgression am I suspected, may I know, that you ask me for this accounting?"

"That is our business to find out. The Bhawanand Collector warned us that you were in the doab. What were you doing there and what brings you here?"

"Is a man not free to travel in his own country?"

"That might be a reasonable question, except that this is not your country. Whatever you may claim to be here, you are in fact a Mohammedan and presumably from one of the Nawabi states. So my question stands."

Mahmoud challenged Hale's ready identification of him as a Muslim. Hale merely nodded and replied that when the call had come from the mosque just now, Mahmoud had quivered almost imperceptibly, but Hale had noticed. "Your instinct was to respond, but you suppressed it so quickly I might have missed it. But there it was. Can you deny it?"

"Even a Mussalman may explore the possibilities of business outside his native place, is that not so?"

"And what is your business?"

"Alas, Sahib, we poor Indians do not have the education for a particular business and we must look for opportunity wherever it may arise." Although his words were duly deferential, he held himself erect and looked the questioner in the eye. "I was hoping to forge links which would help to establish my unfortunate self in trade with this area."

"Then," the Collector zeroed in, "how do you happen to carry a rifle that is typical of those used by the Afghans?"

Mahmoud shrugged. "Even the Afghans venture abroad to trade, as I am sure Your Honour knows better than I. And when they do, they are not reluctant to barter away anything they may be carrying."

"Is this a family business then?"

"No, Sahib, my family has not by tradition been traders."

"What then?"

"My father, may Allah be good to him, was a local magistrate, but due to his early demise I never had the opportunity to acquire the education necessary to follow in his footsteps. So I do now one thing and now another to satisfy my stomach."

Hale seemed to relax his inquisitorial manner and adopt a more conversational tone. "Actually, you don't sound all that uneducated. Your Urdu is pure and you are well spoken."

Mahmoud inclined his head in the suggestion of a bow. "Thank you, Collector Sahib."

"Have you never done anything to make use of that language skill? It does imply a degree of education, even though not a professional one."

The strain of this past week was beginning to tell on Mahmoud. This slight easing of manner was too much for him to resist. "Actually, I was for some time a munshi in a government office."

"And where was that?" Hale inquired sharply. Then, as Mahmoud hesitated, he added, "You know we can find out, so you might as well tell me freely and save us both time."

"In Jehanabad, Sahib."

"The office and locality?"

"Burhan. I was munshi to the Military Secretary there."

Hale leaned back in his chair, indicating he was bringing the interview to a close. "Well, Sayed Mahmoud," he said mildly, "I will send a telegraphic signal to Burhan to check out your story. Meanwhile you will be a guest of the Government in the local jail."

Mahmoud's brow furrowed. "And my horse?"

For the first time, the Collector smiled. "I believe we British have a reputation for being good to horses. We will see that yours is taken care of until we find out what is to become of you." His hand reached for the bell on his desk, but instead of touching it, Hale changed his mind and sat back. "Tell me, Sayed Mahmoud," he asked, and this time his tone was conversational, not adversarial, "when my sowar found you, he didn't give you any hint about what I might want. So what made you run away?"

Mahmoud responded to the tone. "I'm sure it's not news to Your Honour that no Indian likes to speak to an Englishman. We don't trust the British."

Hale studied the marks on his desk. "I wish it were not so," he murmured in a voice so low Mahmoud barely made out the words.

With a suggestion of a shrug, Mahmoud said, "You don't trust us, either, so I suppose that evens it."

With that, a touch of the bell on his desk brought two uniformed men. Before they led Mahmoud away, however, the Collector seemed to have an afterthought, for which he resumed his original crisp voice. "While you wait, Sayed Mahmoud, you might think over whether you have told me the truth. If we find out that you have lied, and that you have been wandering through the Punjab to gather information for someone else, you will be in serious trouble."

It took a week, seven long days in which Mahmoud's mind swung like a pendulum between anxiety about his wife and anxiety for his own future. Twinges of the despair that had assailed him once before disturbed his sleep. It began to seem he was never to be free to live his own life. When honour was so important to him, it was disheartening that his life repeatedly depended on fabricating lies and half-truths. The keen edge of his loyalty blurred a bit. If the Minister really intended him to go through all this, he had certainly minimized the risk, withheld the essential warning. Perhaps he did not really owe the Minister so much.

He tried to pass the time by figuring out his chances of being cleared, but gave it up as too faint a hope. Mr. Hale's parting shot had found its mark. The British already knew he had been not only in the Punjab, but in the doab. If they should find out that he had entered the doab from Afghanistan, he would be in for the high jump.

He knew that whether he would leave the Lahore jail by release or by hanging depended heavily on what the Military Secretary might say about him. He agonized over whether the absence of the papers that would incriminate Major Naughton had been discovered and, if so, whether their theft would be charged against him. On the other hand, the Major might refrain from accusing him for fear of implicating himself; there was no way his duplicity could be kept out of the trial. Surely there would be a trial? The British were known to be scrupulous about laws. Still, if one Englishman testified against him to another, that might be considered sufficient proof of his guilt. He wished he knew more about the British.

Allah protect me, his mind raced; *only You are my recourse! I know that no one can take my life even one minute before the time You have appointed for my death. So what have I to fear? Still, it's difficult not to wonder: is this the time? Have I used up my allotment? Will Allah protect me or will He use Mr. Hale as his instrument?*

The hours of anguish were relieved by dreaming of his wife. He wondered whether Shaheen realized how much he had come to love her. He had said she was a good wife to him, but had he told her how his step quickened when he was returning to her? Or what peace he felt in her presence? He realized sharply that the time with her was the only deeply happy period of his life and he longed to resume it before their child should arrive.

There was some relief in putting those thoughts on paper. He wrote to her:

To Shaheen, my beloved wife,

I do not know whether this will ever reach you. If I live, it need not. For me to live will be to fold you in my arms again, to feel the strength of you beneath the softness of you. To smell your hair while it still has the fragrance of the soapnuts; the sheen of it is like brocade embellished with a gold thread. Your voice is a spring waterfall in your mountains, strong, yet at times of the most delicate beauty, reflecting the sunlight. It is you, merijan, my darling, who have brought sunlight into my life.

If it should turn out that I am to be hanged for being in the Punjab, I shall make every effort to send you the money I have left. Also to ask the Minister for whom I travelled to get my reward to you somehow. Most of all, I know that you will understand that this trip is a duty I could not deny. Much as I yearn to have a long life with you, if I had simply remained with you in Chalab and ignored my obligation, another part of me would have died.

I pray to be reunited with you and our little one. If that proves not possible, may Allah the Compassionate watch over you and guide you.

Your husband, who loves you more
than you know, more than even he
knew until now.

Mahmoud folded the letter carefully into a small square and put it in the secret pocket along with his remaining gold. Then he stretched out and resumed his wait.

30

By a twist of fate, both brothers were in turmoil at the same time, although neither knew about the other: Mahmoud under arrest in Lahore and Hamid struggling with a problem firmly placed on his shoulders by Khatija, Anees's old ayah. Hamid's problem did not come to him directly, but arrived in the form of a letter to Khatija that at first looked so welcome. Muneer, her son-in-law, had been working in his fields when the postman came cycling by. At Muneer's greeting, he stopped to chat and seized the opportunity to save himself the extra distance to the house. "Got something for your respected mother-in-law," he said. "Want to take it?"

Muneer held out his hand. Deciding the heavy envelope with its precise handwriting must be important, he laid down his machete and started across the fields to the house. Contrary to custom, by which men took their wives to their own homes and villages, Muneer had elected to move in with his new wife, with Khatija her mother, and with the grandmother who had brought her up. The reason was that their house was closer to his fields and the move satisfied everyone; they were a happy family.

"I have a surprise for you, Mother-in-Law," Muneer told her, arriving home unexpectedly at mid-day. "How often do you get one of these?" From his pocket he disentangled a cream-coloured envelope of heavy, hand-laid paper and handed it to her. "Looks like a wedding invitation, but who do you know who would be sending you one of those?"

Khatija hardly listened to his good-natured raillery, for she had recognized the handwriting and pressed the envelope to her bosom. "You do know how to read it, don't you?" Muneer went on, seeing that she didn't open it.

"Of course I know!" She looked up from the letter long enough to be indignant. "Begum Sahiba had them teach me when Aneesbibi was born, so that I could read up on stories to tell the child. You might not believe it, but people like that have books of their own, a whole shelf full. Good thing I read them, too, so I'd know some stories to tell my grandchildren." She held up the envelope. "Excuse me, Muneer." He nodded and went back to his fields.

Khatija retired to her favourite spot under the mango tree behind the house. Painstakingly sliding a thumbnail under the flap of the envelope, she managed to open it without damage to the paper and slid out the letter. "My dear, dear Khatijabi," she read, pronouncing each word in a whisper. Like Indians everywhere, she had been taught to read by pronouncing the words aloud, and most still did so even as adults, but Khatija's voice now was more like a prayer. "I am in Bombay and I need to see you. Please come. You have always been my comfort and my source of wise advice. Please don't fail me now. In this letter is a packet in which I have wrapped the rupees you'll need for your train ticket and for a jutka from the station to where I am staying. It is number 28/2, Caddington Lane, near Majestic Cinema. I long to see you and will tell you all when you come. Your loving Anees."

To say that Khatija was both excited and upset was like saying that Mount Everest was both high and cold. She sat for some minutes with a hand pressed to her heart to slow its beating, suffused with pleasure at the thought of seeing again the child who had been as good as hers since birth. And worrying about what could have caused this summons. Perhaps, may the Merciful One forbid it, Anees was ill. Or, what joy that would be, she may be pregnant and need her old ayah to take care of her. But then she would have said so. The only way to find out was to obey the summons.

That evening Khatija showed the rupees to her son-in-law and asked him to buy her a ticket to Bombay. Muneer understood immediately that the request was a direct result of the letter given him that morning by the postman, but was too tactful to ask about the message itself and contented himself with making sure she would feel comfortable travelling alone.

When he came home the next evening, he reported that he had bought the first available seat, which was four days hence. The money in the packet had easily covered a second class ticket with an open date for the return. He was reassured to know she would have an assigned seat for the overnight journey. To still her anxiety after two days of futile stewing, Khatija determined to visit Nuz, the ayah at the Nawab Rahmatullah's to whom she had been closest. She knew that Nuz's own house was just outside the Nawab's compound and that Nuz usually went home for the rest period everyone had after the lunch trays had been cleared away.

So eager was Khatija for any word about that family that, although her village was very close to Khandipur, she decided to hire a rickshaw for the short trip.

Nuz, like Khatija herself, had arrived at the Rahmatullah's as a very young woman and had spent her life there. The other servants all liked her and chatted with her in their off moments, so she could be counted on to know as much as anyone about the goings-on in the household. In response to Khatija's questions, she told her story with a realism that masked her own distress at the news she was relating. Khatija's imagination could fill in the details, and she felt she was actually watching those people as she listened.

The news was not encouraging. One day the Nawab had uncharacteristically arrived in the zenana at noon time and motioned to the Begum to join him in their private apartment. They remained secluded all afternoon; when they emerged at dinner time, they both looked worn. Once everyone had been served, the Nawab motioned the servants out of the room, but naturally they had eavesdropped. In a voice heavy with sadness, the Nawab told the assembled family that Anees's husband had pronounced talaq three times and paid the meher, so she was now a divorced woman.

At that point in the story, Khatija caught her breath. That's what the letter from Anees was about. What could she say to the young matron whom she still thought of as a beloved child? Anees would have no idea how to stand up under this humiliation. She was accustomed to love and admiration, not rejection.

Nuz went on about the gossip in the family. When news of the talaq was shared with the sons and daughters-in-law, Zeenat, the second son's wife, had immediately commented that this was not the first time Anees had disgraced the family. The third son rose to his sister's defence, but Zeenat countered by reminding them of the affair of the sapphire ring. (Khatija clearly recalled how Zeenat had urged the Begum to give the ring to the jeweller; it was that action that led to the discovery of its loss. Khatija had always suspected that Zeenat could never pass up any chance to make trouble for Anees.) The brother asserted that the ring question had been solved, for the ayah had stolen it and Anees had nothing to do with it.

A battle was joined. Finally Zeenat retorted, "Do you need an abacus to put two and two together? You wouldn't, if you had seen her as often as I have standing by the purdah screen. She used to spy on all of you in the mardana; your guests, too, even men from the office. Perhaps if she hadn't violated purdah in that way..."

"You must have been so jealous," Khalid sneered.

For the first time, Rahim entered the fray with a demand that Khalid apologize to his wife.

In a thundering voice rarely heard in that household, the Nawab ordered them all to be silent. He pulled his thali close to him, stared unseeing at the food, then shoved it away and got up. Without a word he left the zenana and went to his room. The rest of them pecked at their food, then one after the other rose and silently went to their own rooms.

Nuz herself had stood outside the master apartment and listened to the Nawab talking to his wife. Though he did not really like Zeenat, this time her words had struck home. For the first time it occurred to him that his daughter might really have been involved in the unhappy affair of the ring. Anees may have been ignorant of the consequences to all those people, but he as the head of the family bore the responsibility. Ya Allah, even for sending a possibly innocent man to prison. He had ruined a man's life on account of his daughter's indiscretion: he could not bear to think it was more than that.

Nuz had heard as much as she could bear. She stole away quietly. Apparently the Nawab suffered a stroke sometime during the night, for he never spoke again and died two days later. Khatija interrupted to admit she had heard of the death, but paid no attention to it except for a momentary thought that perhaps Anees would come for the mourning period. She had not come.

Nuz went on telling Khatija the gossip in the household. "Just my opinion, you know, Khatija," she said, but then very openly accused Zeenat of responsibility for much of this trouble. She had gone around insinuating to everyone whose attention she could command even for a moment that the Nawab had died of shock at learning of Anees's perfidy. Who could say, she asked rhetorically, how much further the violation of purdah had gone? What else could explain this tragedy to a healthy man?

It did not take long for Zeenat to convince others also to blame Anees for their father's unexpected demise. The beloved daughter was no longer welcome at her parental home. Khatija could well imagine the malevolence of Zeenat's eyes as she finally triumphed over the woman who had constantly put her in the shade in the family.

"I'm glad you're not there now, Khatija," Nuz concluded. "It's a sad and solemn household, not like it used to be, and I'm not sure there will be much joy again, even when the mourning period is over."

Khatija needed time to absorb all this. Dismissing the rickshaw, she walked slowly back to her own house, head down. It would not do for the neighbours to see the tears that streaked her cheeks. Tears for her darling. Tears for the disintegration of a happy household in which she had spent nearly forty years and to which she still felt loyal despite her banishment. Tears for herself and a life that suddenly seemed wasted.

Three days later the jutka deposited Khatija at No. 28/2, Caddington Lane. It proved to be one wing of what had been a grand mahal, a palace for some nobleman or aristocrat now presumably fallen on poorer times. But the whole looked properly kept up and the garden well tended. Khatija lifted the brass knocker, in the shape of a leaping deer, and hoped the figure represented the alacrity of those who would answer it. She was not disappointed. Almost immediately the door was opened by a Marathi woman who looked older than Khatija herself.

"Salaam," she said. "If you are indeed Khatijabehin, come in. Begum Sahiba is expecting you." She led the way upstairs to a pleasant sitting room furnished in the style of Anees's home district, with low furniture painted in bright colours. The good rugs and silk cushions scattered about bespoke the taste and background of the occupant. But there were no pictures or hangings on the walls, and their absence made the room seem desolate despite the colours elsewhere.

Before Khatija had completed her survey of the room, the door burst open and there was Anees herself. She wore a simple shot silk sari of blue and turquoise, with a small floral border; it was a good choice, for the heavy silk helped to hide how thin she had become. A more delicate fabric would have made her seem even more of a wraith, echoing the strain that showed in her beautiful face. A moment's hesitation, and she flung herself into Khatija's open arms. "I knew you'd come," she said with a catch in her voice. "Oh, Khatija, I'm so happy to see you. I knew you'd come."

Khatija could not speak, just held her close until she felt the tense body relax a little, then led her to one of the low chairs. Before either of them could sit down, Anees protested. "You're just off the train and I'm sure they didn't give you anything proper to eat. First some breakfast for you and then we'll talk."

Khatija agreed and made her way to the kitchen on her own, as though she had always been there; she had noticed the direction the Marathi woman had gone. Her step was more confident than her heart. Then, strengthened by a hearty breakfast and strong South Indian coffee, she came back and seated herself cross-legged at Anees's feet. "Now talk to me," she commanded in the voice she used to use to the child. "I've heard that your husband, may his voice be a croak in his throat, pronounced talaq. What happened?"

Anees was more than ready to speak about it; as she talked, tears coursed slowly down her face. The first few months of the marriage had been happy, but tension crept in early. Any request she made seemed to send him into a rage. No, he never beat her but he criticized and made fun of her over and over.

Khatija could not restrain her indignation, but Anees shook her head at the condemnations and declared it was not entirely her husband's fault. He seemed to be taking his cue from his mother, for she complained about everything Anees did, from the way she spiced the curry to the sari she chose to wear for some family occasion. In summary, the final argument arose when Anees asked for a new tilak and her husband replied that she was always making extravagant demands; she was never satisfied. When she tried to protest, he pronounced the first talaq. The second was thrown at her almost as soon as she opened her mouth; he didn't even pretend to listen.

"I apologize," she told him through her tears. "I was only trying to please my respected mother-in-law. She said the ruby in my tilak was so small and imperfect it was a disgrace and I was not to wear it again. How can I appear without a tilak?"

"So now you blame my mother for your shortcomings. Talaq!"

By the time she had reached this point in her account, Anees was sobbing. "I gave him twin sons. What more does he want?"

Khatija concluded from the vehemence in her voice that Anees had forgotten her and was really talking to her mother-in-law. "He got so angry the next time, when I produced only a girl. My brothers never told me that men don't like daughters. Baby Gulbai was welcome in my father's house. And so was I, before that."

Khatija sat in silence, not knowing what response to make except to take Anees's hand and stroke it. Eventually deciding that a change of subject was called for, she inquired, "How did you get here to Bombay?"

"I had to leave. And of course, in Islam children belong to the father. So I had no choice. That was the hardest part, to leave my babies." Here the tears flowed again, but Anees wiped them away with an impatient hand and went on. "I had only one friend there, so I went to her. She and her husband agreed to take me to Bombay and when we got here, he very kindly negotiated with someone he knew to buy this wing of the mahal for me. Then they had to go back, so now I've been alone."

"But this must have been expensive. How did you manage it?"

"When the marriage was being negotiated, my father, may he rest in peace, knew that Rajaji's family were far richer than ours, so they were more powerful. But he held an ace and knew it: he had a beautiful daughter to bargain with. He was able to demand a meher that leaves me wealthy. I'm sure neither he nor my husband's family ever expected it would actually have to be paid, and so soon, too."

"So you will stay on here."

"I own this house and I have enough money to live on for the rest of my life. But with no man to take me into society, how will I meet anyone to make friends? I'll be a recluse in these four walls for the rest of my life. And never see my babies! How can I live, knowing they're growing up and don't even know who their mother is?"

For three days Khatija sat and listened to a stream of similar accounts and Anees's laments. At the end of that time, still not sure what to do but with a glimmer of an idea, she told Anees that she must get back to her village, but would try to think of something. Anees vowed she would accept any solution Khatija suggested. "Anything at all," she assured her again and again. "I trust you, Khatija dear; I know you'll rescue me from this terrible plight. I'll do whatever you tell me to, I promise."

The Marathi woman sent a relative to the railway station to secure the seat for Khatija's return passage. She left the next day.

31

At the end of a week in the Lahore jail, Mahmoud was again brought into Mr. Hale's presence. He stood with clenched jaw, fingers brushing the pocket where the letter to Shaheen waited. This time Mr. Hale addressed him at once. "Well, Babu, was our hospitality up to your expectations?"

"Adequate, Collector Sahib."

"We've been checking up on you, but I have to tell you we haven't learned much. Your story seems to hold together. You arrived from Bhawanand at a good clip; no time there to go wandering after contacts."

Mahmoud nodded.

"We have also had a reply from your Military Secretary. You failed to tell me he was Major Naughton. Would you be interested to know what he said?"

"If the Collector Sahib will be so good as to share that information." Mahmoud did not dare pin too much hope on the unaccustomed tone.

"Here it is, then. The Major says, 'Replying to yours of the etc. etc., I beg to state that the Police Commissioner, the Kotwal, has no information on Sayed Mahmoud, which would indicate that he has no criminal record in Jehanabad. From my own experience, I might add that he is a bit of a budmash. You would not go far wrong to prosecute him.' What do you think of that?"

Determined not to be betrayed by his fury at the Major, Mahmoud replied carefully, "It is not surprising that the Kotwal does not know my name, for I have done nothing wrong in Burhan."

"At any rate, you're in luck," Hale admonished him. "I know your Major Naughton a little, enough to know how to evaluate what he says here. On the basis of the Kotwal's reply and our own investigations, I am going to let you go." He laid the paper, carefully aligned, on a pile on a corner of his desk and replaced the paperweight that kept it from being blown off by the constant fan. Then he once more looked Mahmoud in the eye.

"My advice to you is to leave Lahore quickly. The Commissioner is not in favour of intruders in the Punjab and I cannot guarantee what he might decree if he should see this response. My chaprassi will return your possessions and show you where to collect your horse. Good luck and stay out of trouble."

Cutting short Mahmoud's attempts to thank him, he picked up his pen and turned his attention to the materials on his desk.

The Collector's warning did not go unheeded. Within the hour, Mahmoud, reunited with Beg Sahib, was on his way out of Lahore. This time he paid little attention to the passing scene, for his mind was consumed with rage at the Major. Naughton, an embezzler who shamelessly stole from his patron the Minister, to whom he owed loyalty. That despicable Major, who had all the things most men would strive for: rank, a fine living, important and varied work for an honourable employer who trusted him. Yet he betrayed it all.

Contemptible Naughton, a man of no integrity, who did not even know the meaning of the word. Termite was too kind a description for him; Naughton was a pig! He snuffled around in the dirt, but when there was an opportunity, he was dangerous. Ya Allah, he had worked for a pig! That such a man could call him a budmash almost drowned out the threat it had posed to his life. Whether he recognized it or not, Mahmoud had suddenly mixed pride with honour. He had learned on this adventurous journey that he was a man worthy of respect; he had earned it and would not allow a lesser man like the Major to dissipate it.

He rode through fertile farm land, a relief from the desert he had lately crossed. The northeast monsoon was over; farmers were planting their late autumn crops and carefully nourishing the first tender shoots of wheat. Winter was not far off, a comfortable season in this region. Blood flowed fast in the invigorating air, roses bloomed, children were conceived. People smiled at one another and at strangers. All this was lost on Mahmoud, sunk in his anger. He had not chosen the route for its scenery but to avoid cities until he was safely out of the jurisdiction of the Lahore Collector.

At the first opportunity he sold Beg Sahib and boarded a train for Delhi. During that whole journey the sound of the wheels, click click clack click, click click clack click played for him only one tune: Major Naughton, I'll get even, Major Naughton, I'll get even, until the Minister himself ceased to exist for him.

In Delhi, he should have changed to a train for Lucknow. This time those instructions did not cross his mind, nor did it occur to him to go out of the station. No longer the Minister's messenger, he became now the avenger of his own honour and of the perfidy to the Minister. He bought a ticket directly to Burhan. Then, like several hundred others—some travellers surrounded by their bundles, some the red-shirted, red-turbaned porters, some simply having no place else to go—spread his shawl on the station platform and lay down to find what sleep his churning emotions might allow him.

Entrained early the next morning, he used the time on the long trip to plan his moves, not sparing a thought for possible consequences, but carefully calculating his steps upon arrival. Since a dirty, unshaven traveller would command little respect, if he were to get further than the chaprassi at the door he must look respectable. Consequently his first action on alighting was to find, near the railroad station, a modest building whose sign proclaimed it a "Hotl" and engage a room.

Under normal circumstances he would have sought a barber on the street but, to avoid the risk of being recognized, he asked to have one sent to the room. There, enthusiastically stropping his straight-bladed razor, the fellow shaved Mahmoud, cut his hair, trimmed his nose hairs, cleaned his ears, all the while chattering away.

"What a pity you were not here a few weeks ago for His Highness' birthday celebrations. Everyone in the city ate like Nawabs that night. The premier nobles could have had nothing better than HH gave all of us. Except that I have heard they eat from thalis of silver. Can you imagine that? Still, they may have it. Silver thalis would have to be washed, and who would stand and count them while the servant washed them? Our pipal leaves can just be burned.

"But first His Highness rode through the town on his elephant. What a sight he was, enough to lift the stone off any heart, dressed all in cloth of gold, seated in the gold amari with the Minister behind him. Of course, the Minister never wears gold or anything grand. Much too modest, that one is, thinking only His Highness deserves such splendour. Too honest, too, probably, to salt away the rupees for such things. May he live a hundred years.

"There you are. All finished. Shall I come back sometime or will your honour send for me when I'm needed?" Tucking his two rupees into the fold of his turban, he pronounced a cheerful "Ram Ram, Sahib," and took his leave.

Mahmoud hesitated for a moment in his dressing, uncertain whether to break the habit of never being separated from his most precious packet, in which some gold and one watch remained. In the end he slipped them in the usual concealed pocket and set out. As he had foreseen, his new prosperity and the look of authority which he had learned on his journey how to use allowed him to sweep past the chaprassi straight into Major Naughton's office.

As he went through the outer office, he realized that the desk that had been his showed no signs of being used now. The Major seemed to be having trouble finding or keeping a munshi. Perhaps his reputation was known more widely than Mahmoud had imagined.

"What the devil, what do you mean by breaking in like this!" the Major exclaimed. As Mahmoud stood erect, head high, silent, Naughton was forced to look up. "Oh, it's you," he added with a hint of consternation and an overlay of sarcasm. "What is it *you* want?"

"Money, Major." Mahmoud rather enjoyed the effrontery of omitting the 'Sahib'. He had once seen Naughton as exalted by the fact of being British and a Department Secretary; now he thought of him merely as a criminal, more despicable than any of the felons with whom he had shared prison time at Benur.

"Major Sahib. Don't forget your manners, babu. Now just what makes you think you're entitled to some money?"

"There's my two months' salary that you kept. That you may have. But what you will not be allowed to keep is the Department's money, His Highness's, as you used to remind me."

223

"What business is that of yours?"

"A little matter of justice, that's all."

"Justice, hmm? Would you care for justice for the irregularities you left in the accounts when you resigned?"

"Closer, Major; except you forget they are not *my* irregularities." In the exchanges that followed, Mahmoud mentioned enough details of forged invoices to convince the Major he was on to the game and possessed the proof. Feint, duck, punch—he had learned that much from watching the fights at Benur and used it now. The threat to expose the Major drew blood, with its implication of reclaiming the embezzled funds. When Mahmoud decided his opponent was sufficiently rattled, he threw his biggest blow.

"You cabled the Collector in Lahore that I was a budmash who should be prosecuted. I might have been hanged on the basis of that. You thought you could remove the one person who could testify against you." Mahmoud leaned forward in a threatening stance and enunciated distinctly, "You failed because of your reputation; other people also know what kind of a man you are."

With a snarl, the Major hurled himself across his desk. Mahmoud sidestepped quickly and made for the exit. In the doorway he turned. "Do you know what you are, Major?" he taunted. "You're a liar, a forger, a thief, and a…a budmash."

He closed the door quietly.

32

Hamid had been in Khandipur for a fortnight without a trip, a rare unbroken stretch. He had enjoyed the time. Surayya was a competent housekeeper and a cook who made him look forward to home fare at the end of his trips. He missed the children when he was away and made up for it, playing with his son and bouncing the baby on his knees, when he was at home. Late one evening, this domestic scene was interrupted by a knock at the gate; Hamid went to answer it. There stood a ryot who looked vaguely familiar.

"I am Muneer. Sahib won't remember me. I'm..."

"Khatija's son-in-law. I remember you now." With the man's first words, the picture had come whole for Hamid: three years earlier, Khatija sent this man to warn him that Narasimha had arrived with his followers to threaten the villagers if they sold their cotton to Hamid. Before that, Khatija had reported his poem to Anees, and delivered her ring to him. She had been good to him; now it was apparently his turn. "What can I do for you?"

"Khatijamma respectfully begs Sahib will come to the village to see her."

"Did she say what she wants? Is there a special time?"

"She says at Sahib's convenience. Excuse me, but I hear her tone of voice. Must be rather urgent, to her anyway. Only a few days back she returned from Bombay. No talk why she went there. Perhaps something to do with that trip."

He owed her. Whatever she wanted now, he would oblige her. "Please tell her I will come the day after tomorrow. Thank you for the message. Good night, Muneer."

Good as his word, Hamid showed up at Khatija's and she immediately took him to her favourite spot under the mango tree, where they could speak in private. There, almost breathless in her eagerness to unburden herself, she reported most of what she had learned in Bombay. Hamid heard her through, looking alternately at her and at his tightly clasped hands. This was more painful than anything since he had heard of Anees's marriage. Even then, he had had the consolation of knowing the Nawab had done well by his daughter. Now, only desolation for the woman he had never ceased to idealize in his heart. When Khatija stopped, he looked her in the eyes.

"This is terribly, terribly sad, truly tragic. The death. The divorce. The pain they've all—Anees Begum—all been through. I had no idea." His voice failed him for a moment. He stared at the horizon, seeming to draw strength from the fields where green was poking up with new life. "I, I'm...shaken, as you are. But why are you telling me, Khatija? There's nothing I could do about it, as you well know."

"Oh, but I think there is. Do you remember the poem you wrote for her? That was the start of all this, wasn't it."

Hamid nodded. To him, the start had actually been the eye at the purdah curtain and the jewelled hand that straightened it again, but there was no need to mention that.

Khatija went on, her voice conveying the urgency of the message. "She can't go back to her own family. She can't come to me; that would cause a scandal in the village. But she can't live alone like that in a big city, either. A prisoner in her own house." Khatija shuddered, looked up into the branches as though waiting for a myna bird to speak the next words for her, looked back at Hamid. When she resumed, her voice had changed, become softer. "She needs a man to protect her and to take her out of that house occasionally, out of herself, too. You could be that man, Hamidullah." She paused. Hamid stopped breathing. "You could do that. Marry her."

"Khatija, what are you saying! Her family are Shias. They'd be furious at the very idea I, a Sunni, had the temerity to marry her. Even to think of it!"

"They've made it clear they don't care what happens to Anees."

"Besides, I'm married already."

"Our religion allows you to have four wives. Why not two?"

226

"Because my wife is a good woman and a good wife to me. It would make her unhappy if I brought another woman into the house."

"You needn't do so. Aneesbibi owns the house she is now in and could continue to live there. Your wife need never see her. Moreover, she is a wealthy woman now. She need cost you nothing, take nothing away from your senior wife and her children. Perhaps this is a debt the false Hijra could pay."

Hamid looked puzzled for a moment, then recalled his attempted ruse when the Hijras came to dance and bless baby Gulbai. Ever since he had pretended to be a Hijra, the stolen glimpse he had had of Anees that day had made her a constant part of his inner life. Now he had the grace to look embarrassed.

He got up and paced the small patch of garden; a walk around the little house occupied only a minute. He went out and walked the path between the fields, then stood, hands clasped behind his back, staring over the fields into the far distance. And into the not-quite-so-far past. He thought of Anees, the woman he had adored from afar, now being offered to him, no, urged on him. Apparently dreams actually could come true.

He thought of Surayya, and how she would feel about this. Although it was true he was allowed multiple wives, that rule said nothing about the feelings of the first wife. He knew Surayya would be hurt, and didn't really feel he had the right to do that to her. They had taken each other in good faith, and she had never given him cause for complaint. If he followed his heart and accepted Anees, how could he soften that for Surayya?

He thought of Mahmoud, who had paid the price for his and Anees's indiscretions. What would Mahmoud advise him to do? That much at least was clear: their youthful impetuousness, which her family now claimed to have caused the father's death, was his as well as hers. And it left Hamid with no other recourse. He must step into the breach, pay the price. His only honourable action was to marry her. Yes, that much was clear.

Hours, no, years, had collapsed into minutes. "Khatija," he said on coming back to her, "you are the matchmaker. You must go back to Bombay and make the arrangements. I'll talk to my wife, she deserves that, and then I will come."

Khatija straightened up; her bosom heaved; she seemed about to burst with relief. Quickly she reverted to her practical self. "Should I make the arrangements for the nikah ceremony also?"

"No. I mean yes. There will be no festivities, simply a qazi at her house. You can arrange for that. He will speak the formulas and declare us wed. That's all. You'll be the witness for her side and I will find a contact in Bombay to be the witness for my side. Oh, and a hundred rupees only, so that we can tell the qazi a meher has been agreed."

Khatija's face registered shock and disdain. Hamid noticed and went straight on to deal with it without allowing an interruption. "If she is as wealthy as you say, she doesn't need anything more. Between Anees and me, that sum I specified is not an insult, but an agreement that whatever small fortune I have must be kept intact for my children."

"She will understand."

"She must. You say I owe her this, and I acknowledge as much. But it has already cost me dearly. I let my brother go to prison in order to protect Anees. And he has disappeared from our lives. We have lost him. I cannot complicate life for my wife and children."

"So be it."

Telling Surayya about this decision was daunting. He would have liked to write her a letter about it, but that was an act of cowardice. Or he could ask his mother to explain it to his wife. But she had selected Surayya herself; she knew Hamid's association with the Rahmatullahs and that it was the Nawab who was responsible for Mahmoud's arrest. Impossible to involve her. There was no escape; he would have to do this thing himself.

As soon as he broached the subject, Surayya's face assumed the strained look that he had feared. She raised her chin and looked straight at him, anguish in her voice. "Oh, my husband, how have I failed you? Tell me and I'll try to change." Her earnest look was more searing than tears.

"You haven't failed. I don't want you to change at all."

"Then what do I lack, that you need someone else?"

"I don't need...no, it's not me. And it's certainly not you, Surayya. It's...think of it as a debt I owe her family." He had carefully refrained from mentioning either Anees's name or her family's.

"I've heard of women who ask their husbands to marry again, to bring a junior wife into the home to help with the work. But we're not in that situation. I don't need any help."

"She won't ever come here. She'll live only in Bombay, in a house she owns. I've been going to Bombay on business anyway. Sleeping on a charpoy in the office. This'll be more comfortable." He tried to laugh, to make light of it, but it didn't register with her. "You need never see her. You'll hardly be aware she exists."

Surayya bowed. "As my husband wishes."

During the next few days, Hamid noticed that Surayya cooked his favorite dishes, tried to anticipate his wants, was an eager partner in bed. But she did not laugh, and her smile was only polite. As he was setting out for the station, he kissed her goodbye and stroked her cheek. "Try not to mind," he whispered. And was gone.

On the train, suspended between his present and his future, Hamid relaxed the tight control he had kept on his feelings. He feared he would burst with joy. All these years he had adored an unobtainable, untouchable woman. Now she was going to be his. Unbelievable, but truly his. Fantasy become real. It was too much.

At Anees's house, with no family present on either side, the two witnesses held a large embroidered shawl between them while the qazi seated Anees on one side and Hamid on the other. He spoke to Anees first. "A man named Sayed Hamidullah is there. Do we have your permission to read the marriage ceremony?"

At her clear "Hahji," Hamid's head snapped toward the sound. It was the first time he had heard her voice, mellifluous and clear. Then the qazi came to him. "Do you accept this woman as your wife?" Hamid's Qubool (I agree) was positive, with just a slight break in his voice. The qazi had each of them sign the marriage papers, declared them husband and wife, and salaamed his way out of the room. The two witnesses dropped the shawl and also walked out, leaving the new couple alone.

229

It took a moment before Hamid could accept that it was now, finally, after years of yearning, his right to look Anees in the face. When he did, he could only stare. She was exquisite, even more beautiful than his fantasy, perfect of face and figure. Her hair was drawn softly back into a bun at her neck. Brows in a high arch emphasized the size and lustre of her kohl-rimmed eyes. Nose straight with only slightly-flaring nostrils. And her lips, full and red in the smooth copper of her skin.

He claimed the kiss that was waiting for him there, pulled her to her feet and realized she had chosen not to wear the traditional gherara but a red and gold sari. As he began to unwrap it, she retained the presence of mind to pull him into the bedroom and shut the door. "I'm not Draupadi," Anees laughed, referring to the Mahabharata epic familiar to all Indians of whatever religion. "The gods will not make my sari endless."

"Maybe not," Hamid said, savouring every movement as he undid pleat by pleat, "but I feel like Duryodhana, because I've won the prize." Draupadi's husband, having gambled away everything else, had offered her in a wager with Duryodhana, his crude cousin. When Duryodhana won, he tried to disrobe Draupadi, but the gods protected her by making her sari endless. As this story flashed through his memory, Hamid thought that at least he had won Anees honourably. He released her choli, one hook at a time, without touching her breasts. Then untied her petticoat and let it drop.

She stood naked before him in all her loveliness. "I just want to look at you," he breathed. "You are Sheba, too beautiful for even the wise King Solomon to resist."

Daily oil massages all during the pregnancies and afterward had kept her skin soft and supple, and that, along with wet nurses for the babies, had allowed her to keep her youthful figure. She was still only twenty.

He could wait no longer. Dropping his clothes in a heap, he picked her up. They spent the rest of the day in bed. And the next day. Khatija or someone set trays of food outside the bedroom door, which they occasionally remembered to collect. On the third day, passion abated for the moment, they talked, they played backgammon, they compared things they liked to do. When either one touched the other, however casually, none of those things mattered any more.

On the fourth day, Hamid woke refreshed and lay enjoying the sight of his wife, hands thrown palm up, sleeping like a child. He repressed the impulse to kiss her exposed breasts and went into the dressing room. When he came back, wearing a business suit and carrying a briefcase, she opened one eye. "Where are you going at this hour?"

"I have an appointment. I'll be back before lunch."

She sat up in bed and held her arms out. "Surely your business will run without you for another day."

He smiled. "I love having nothing in my head, or my eyes, but you. Only, I have the kind of business that wants my attention sometimes, too. I'll ask Khatija to bring you some tea." He was gone.

At the end of a week, Hamid declared that he must get back to Khandipur. Anees protested, tried to flirt with him, pouted when he was adamant, turned her back and refused a goodbye kiss. That became a pattern for her; never was there a last kiss.

Hamid spent eight days of each month with Anees, though his most important customers were not in Bombay. And eight days in Khandipur with Surayya, for the Koran specified that a man must treat all his wives equally. When he added more days in Khandipur, he told himself they were for his children, or to deal with the ryots whose cotton he handled; they had increasingly come to trust him and to depend on his advice.

The rest of the month he travelled all over India to call on his customers and solicit their orders, or to establish new contacts. When Anees asked about his trips, he said only that they were boring business. He teased her, asking whether she cared which state had just ordered 6,000 metres of cotton drill, or whether that was too little or too much.

"Absolutely not," was Anees's response. "Come put your head in my lap and I'll smooth away those nasty frowns those matters give you." But she was increasingly restive. Once when he was leaving, Anees asked, not bothering to conceal the edge in her voice, "What do you do all these weeks you say you're travelling? Visit the nautch

231

girls?" Hamid couldn't think of any reply except to kiss his fingers to her and leave. Another time she exclaimed petulantly, "I suppose you're off to see your other wife." When Hamid replied merely that he was going to Khandipur, she burst out, "She has her children with her, but I can't even see mine. It's not fair. So you should spend more time with me than with her."

As he left, Hamid reflected that a pout was beginning to be the expression that characterized Anees for him. "Other wife" was Anees's way of referring to Surayya, not "senior wife," which would have been correct. Hamid assumed it was Anees's way of avoiding recognizing that she was "junior." She had probably never in her life considered herself second to any woman. Hamid had twice taken her to the home of acquaintances in Bombay, business contacts. She had not enjoyed their wives, considering them both dull and dowdy, and made no attempt at a follow-up meeting with either one.

Left alone for nearly three-quarters of every month, Anees found her thoughts occupied more and more with her first husband and her little ones. The Raja was irritable, true, but on the other hand he was always there. Even overnight. Just occasionally he went on hunting trips for a few days, but from those he came back eager to show off his trophies and to boast about his exploits in tracking and bagging them. The baby was probably still too small to miss her mother, but Anees prayed that the twins would remember her. If he married again, would they come to regard the new woman as their mother? She didn't think she could bear that.

About five months after their wedding, Hamid was astonished one day to receive a letter addressed to him at No. 28/2, Caddington Lane. His customers wrote either to Khandipur or to the small office he had established in Bombay. Moreover this letter was on heavy hand-laid paper and bore some kind of seal he did not recognize, clearly not business correspondence.

It proved to be from Anees's first husband, asking to see him at his convenience and suggesting the Prince's Club. No hint of what he might want, but there could be only one or two things. If he was trying to reclaim her jewellery, that would be a legal issue. It was certainly hers; it had either come with her from her father's house or been given to her by her husband. What kind of man tries to reclaim a gift? Or—it was just possible he wanted her back. That, ah, that now would take some thinking.

Their meeting began with the usual social preliminaries. Then the Raja leaned forward. "Sayed Hamidullah," he said, "I want my wife back."

Hamid feigned surprise. "Is that so? What wife is that?"

"Anees Begum, as you know very well."

"Ah, yes, but you see, she is my wife now."

"Just so. That's why we're sitting here, isn't it?"

"Even assuming I were willing to give her up, which you can by no means assume, what makes you think she might want to go back to you? She was not very happy in that marriage."

"She's talked to you about it, has she?"

"Not to me, but to a confidante of both of us."

That seemed to reassure the Raja. "I've come to realize my share in that unhappiness. You must know by now that in many ways she's still a spoiled child." He paused and raised an eyebrow at Hamid, who gave a barely discernable nod. "But I could have done more to protect her from my mother's criticism. It's very difficult to try to correct one's mother, and I have been too reluctant to stand up to her, I now realize. She's spent her life bringing me up and doing things for me. And she is, after all, the head of the household; she has a right to have things done her way. She was only trying to teach Anees how things are done in our family."

Hamid interrupted. "Excuse me. I thought you were going to talk about your part in Anees's unhappiness, and now you're taking your mother's side again, simply trying to justify the unhappiness your mother created."

"Yes. Maybe...I want..." For the first time the Raja appeared to be flustered. With a flash of insight, Hamid realized his opponent did not like to admit any shortcomings, an important clue. But the Raja's next statement came as a surprise. He took a deep breath and continued, "Don't be too hard on me. I suppose I also have been a spoiled child, only my mother was there to stand up for me and hers wasn't. Since Anees Begum left, I've begun to see what she must have been through. And my mother, bless her, sees how unhappy I've been. We had several good talks about that before I came here. I could have other women, but it's Anees I want. And my mother admits that any other daughter-in-law might be equally difficult. Perhaps both she and I have changed enough for Anees to be all right in my house now."

"Of course you realize, even if I should agree to release her, and I don't know about that, she herself has the decision in her hand. She has the right to choose between us; our religion is quite specific about that."

"True, but," and here the Raja smiled, perhaps a bit smugly, "I hold two trump cards. First, her children, who want their mother back. Second, on your side, do you really believe she's cut out to be a junior wife? If she comes back to me, she'll again be number one. Can you match those?"

"Perhaps not. I'll have to talk with her. Then we'll see."

"May I see her? Plead my own case?"

"See my wife? Of course not. Let me think about what you say and I'll get back to you in a few days."

The Raja had to be satisfied with that for the present.

By their next meeting, Hamid was clear what he would do. He remembered how reluctant the husband was to be seen in the wrong, so it would not be easy to get him to accept conditions that carried that possible implication. Still, Hamid had learned from negotiating his business deals not to rush his fences, but to wait out the other, or even provoke him into impatience. He would use his experience.

At their second meeting, the Raja was eager, leaning forward in his chair, clearly expecting the news to be in his favor. Hamid leaned back and crossed his legs. "I fear you're due for a disappointment," he began in a simple conversational tone. "Anees is very expensive. I don't think you can afford her."

The Raja's face darkened. "Why of all the insolent…" He stopped, made a gesture of appeasement, as though he realized he had just damaged his case. Then he took a new breath and began again in a different tone of voice. "Let me tell you some facts which seem to have been left out of your upbringing. The territory I rule…officially my father rules, of course. I act for him, since I'm the only heir. It's small in area, that's true, probably what you think of it. But its value is high. In fact we produce some of the finest rubies in the sub-continent."

"Rubies, eh?"

"Maharajas and even kings from Europe line up to buy our gems."

"Very nice for you, or will be some day. But I believe we were talking about my wife. Her continuing to be my wife. And how badly you want her back."

"I want her back."

Hamid appeared not to be listening; he was staring out the window. "Rubies. Hmm. What is she worth to you?"

"Pardon me, Sayed Hamidullah. Is this blackmail, or are you concerned about finding funds for the meher you contracted on your marriage to her?"

"Call it what you like. I'm interested in your answer."

"And if I offer you a substantial settlement, will you then release her?"

"Depends."

The Raja sat with his chin on his fist while figures whirled through his mind. He looked up. "How about a lakh?"

The corners of Hamid's mouth turned down and he shook his head. A hundred thousand was a nice little pile of rupees but didn't come up to what he had in mind.

The Raja was having equally dissatisfied thoughts. Undignified to be bargaining about a woman like this. This Hamidullah was acting like a Marwadi money-lender. Offered a sum large enough to take the man's breath away, he might accept it and that would be the end of the matter. A ridiculous sum, but Anees was worth it. And he would not be out-manoeuvred by a mere business man. "Two lakhs."

Hamid nodded. "Step in the right direction. Still, I'd need to feel confident that she'd be better off with you. And I understand that you have a rather nasty temper."

Still feeling battered by the financial bargaining, the Raja was in no condition to dispute it. "I'm afraid that's true. But I'm learning to control it. I don't think you need to worry about that."

"Even if you gave me your word on the head of your son that you would control your temper, I have no assurance that you'd be able to do so."

"A man can only try."

"The marriage agreement would have to include a pledge that you maintain the Caddington Lane house for her, so that she has a place of her own to come to if she ever needs to get away, whether for a holiday, or for her health, or for more ominous reasons. She needs to have that security."

"Of course. It's a good property anyway. It might as well stay in her name."

"Good. Then I can tell you that I accept the two lakhs you offered me. They are for Anees's meher for this marriage to you, if it takes place. I wanted a sum so outrageous that it would force you to think very carefully before you gave in to an angry impulse again."

"You drive a hard bargain, Sayed Hamidullah. A hard bargain. Still, it's clear you have her welfare to the forefront. I'll take that lesson from you."

Finally, Hamid reminded him that if Anees did choose to go back to him, the Raja would have to arrange their marriage here in Bombay, so that she could travel home with him. With that, Hamid closed the discussion, saying he would be in touch. He would send his message here to the Club.

Hamid was amazed at himself. A mere three months ago he would have been devastated at the very idea of giving Anees back to her first husband. Now he was not even displeased by this turn of events. The patina had worn off his fantasy. Even before this development, he realized that what he had worshiped all these years was a phantom, not a flesh and blood woman. Now the phantom had dissolved in reality. Anees confirmed the distinction with her very first reaction when he reported his conversation with the Raja: "My babies! I could have my little ones back!"

Hamid went over the conversation in detail. He had done his best to build a fence that could assure her security, whether the marriage failed again or succeeded this time. In spite of her many childish ways, he respected her intelligence and believed that she had learned something about making the mature allowances for other people's failings that were building blocks in any successful marriage. Moreover, she had had a taste now of life pretty much on her own and it was clear she didn't relish it.

The mother-in-law would still have her control needs, the Raja his temper, Anees her childishness. No marriage was perfect. They would have to work it out. Hamid had done what he could.

Hamid had the marriage agreement typed up, including the business arrangements he had specified. He would get the Raja's signature on it before he would release her. Dear Anees. He was letting go a part of himself, a part he had outgrown. In the end they made love with more tenderness than passion, as if recognizing it was the last. "Thank you," she whispered afterwards. "You saved my life. I'll never forget; I will pray for you always."

In response to Hamid's message, the Raja showed up at Caddington Lane. Hamid walked him through the public rooms and he expressed his satisfaction with the house. Then Hamid established him in the drawing room and left him. A few minutes later he returned, leading Anees by the hand. She had donned her burqa, as was proper in the presence of a man who was not her husband. "Aneesbibi," Hamid said as he dropped her hand and turned to face her, "the two men who have been your husband are both here. It is your right to choose which one you will now go with."

Anees looked for a long moment at the man who had come to reclaim her, then turned back to Hamid. "Khulah (I divorce my husband)," she pronounced softly.

"Come," the Raja said. "I have a suite at the hotel and a qazi is waiting for us there. Then we will go home."

Back in Khandipur, Hamid felt a lightness he had not enjoyed for many months. Surayya met him as he came in, her expression welcoming but guarded. Skin stretched tightly over the fine bones of her face, her smile was social rather than from inside her. When she saw the happiness in his face, she dropped her eyes, sure it meant he had just come from his junior wife. Without even stopping to greet the children, Hamid put his arm around her and propelled her to the balcony, closing the door behind them.

The flaming red flowers of the potted hibiscus might have represented his mood, if he had noticed, as might the jasmine in the garden below, wafting its fragrance generously upwards. "My dearest wife," he said without preliminaries, "I have news which I trust will make you happy. You are once again not only the senior wife, but my only one."

Surayya's eyes widened. "What happened?"

"Her husband wanted her back and she chose to go with him."

"And you? How do you feel about that?"

"Relieved. I've done what I could to help her and now it's over. But you, my dear, owe her a debt of gratitude."

"Me, Hamid? How could I owe her anything?"

"I married you for family reasons. Now that I've been married to her, I realize that I love you. I've wasted a lot of time and emotion adoring a fantasy. Now I know it's you, the real you, who holds my heart in your hand. You always will."

Surayya stared at him for a moment, then put her hand on his cheek. He felt the spark from it and realized with a start what her expression meant. He had never thought of his wife as passionate. This was all new, a side of her he had never recognized. Even as he had helped Anees straighten out her domestic relations, she had taught him something that would enrich his.

It was more fun when we were young, Hamid mused: *all joy in the moment and no thought of consequences. But there are always consequences. Now I understand Mahmoudbhai was trying to teach me that. I wish there were a way to let him know I've finally grown up. Allah be praised.*

33

At the Minister's deori, whither Mahmoud made his way with a light step after his dramatic exit from the Major's office, he met more adamant resistance to his entry. The chowkidar at the gate had proved susceptible to a small tip, but the chaprassi seemed immune until finally an acceptable price had been arrived at. At the secretary's desk he thought he had met an immovable object until at length he remembered the magic formula: "Please tell the Minister that a Sufi from the North sends him a message from the beyond."

"And are you this great Sufi?" the secretary snickered. But when Mahmoud drew himself to his full height and commanded, "Tell him!" he skittered off to the next room. Immediately a man emerged whom Mahmoud recognized as the person who had originally summoned him in Lucknow and guided him into the Minister's presence. Whether this man actually knew about the mission to Kabul with which the Minister had entrusted him at that meeting, or more accurately burdened him, Mahmoud did not know. What was clear, however, was that the Minister trusted him.

"I am Ghulam Ansari, the Nawab Sahib's Personal Assistant," he introduced himself. "So you come from a Sufi," he continued conversationally. "Our great Minister is interested in Sufism and is a somewhat advanced student of it himself. Come in here, please."

Once inside his room with the door closed, however, the affable manner changed. "What are you doing here? Your instructions were under no circumstances to return to Burhan."

So he did know about Mahmoud's assignment. "I come on business of my own," Mahmoud retorted. "For that I need the Minister's help. I have carried out his instructions and for that he promised me a reward. Now I come to claim it."

"How can you claim it when you disobey so explicit an order?"

Mahmoud took several deep breaths, aware that he must not lose his temper with this underling. "I wish to speak about it with the Minister."

"I am the Minister's gatekeeper. You had better tell me."

"As Sahib commands." This man was clearly more than the ordinary munshi Mahmoud had taken him to be. There would be no access to the Minister short of confiding in him. "You may know that His Excellency warned me that he was sending me on a dangerous mission. I risked my life for him many times and did not begrudge it because of my promise. But it was no part of the bargain for Major Naughton to put me in jeopardy for no reason. I want Major Naughton punished."

Ghulam Ansari's expression adequately conveyed his puzzlement. "What has the Military Secretary to do with your mission?"

In answer, Mahmoud described the sequence of events, ending with the Major's reply to the Collector.

"Insulting, I agree," Ghulam Ansari said, "but does an insult justify ignoring your orders?"

"It's not just an insult. The penalty for spying, as Sahib no doubt knows, is hanging."

Ghulam Ansari's eyebrows shot up. Mahmoud thought he saw some subtle alteration in the other's expression. The hope that he had hit a responsive chord emboldened him to go on. "Is my life worth so little that the Minister can allow anyone else to put an end to it unjustly? Is that all my services merit? And that too before the message from the Sufi is delivered?"

Ghulam Ansari smiled. "Before I answer that, perhaps you had better tell me what the message from the Sufi is."

"My instructions are to deliver it to the Minister personally, as I did his at the other end."

"Perhaps, but the person at the other end, as you put it, does not know how closely I stand in for His Excellency. You know from Lucknow how much I am entrusted with his personal affairs. Had you returned to Lucknow as instructed, it would have been I who came to hear your message. So it will be better if you tell me now."

"If the Sahib will please to regard this office as Lucknow for the moment, I can deliver the message."

A faint smile eased the sternness of Ghulam Ansari's face.

"I fear the Minister will not be pleased with it. It is, 'The northwest wind may puff out a man's clothes till he looks twice his size, without blowing him off his course.'"

The P. A. studied his thumbs for a moment before continuing, "Anything else?"

"Not from the Sufi," Mahmoud told him with an almost imperceptible relaxation of his shoulders. "However, the Khan Sahib thanks the Minister Sahib for the gifts and particularly for the repeater watch with the amethyst in the key. Also for the rifles, which I arranged for and then barely managed to protect from the thief who pretended to be a most accommodating guide. All the gifts were delivered safely and appreciated."

"Thank you, Sayed Mahmoud. Now what was it you had intended to ask the Minister for?"

"No, Sahib, the past tense will do you no good. I do intend to see the Major punished. I have proof that he has been cheating the Minister and His Highness by the way he keeps the accounts. He has embezzled lakhs. I want to see him prosecuted and to have him lose all those misbegotten profits. That would satisfy my desire for revenge, but my loyalty to the Minister also demands it; it is the Minister he cheats. You are his trusted assistant. You would do no less."

"You have proof?"

"Yes, Sahib, forged invoices in the Major's own handwriting. A comparison of those with the books will immediately show the truth of my allegations."

"You refer to more than a single incident?"

"I have proof of repeated occurrences. The only thing I cannot now show is the extent to which he has lined his pockets, but clearly he managed to keep the lid of the Treasury open for that purpose. An examination of the accounts will reveal how much he has stolen from His Highness's Government."

"You realize, I am certain, the seriousness of what you are saying. You must be very sure, for the penalty for false accusations and for slandering a man's good name is not slight."

"I do not make these statements lightly. Why should I put myself at risk if I cannot prove my words? If I am not permitted to speak to the Minister directly, please do so for me."

"I must. This is nothing I can decide on my own. Where are you staying? The Vikas Hotel? Good. Be ready at nine tomorrow evening. I will send a man for you. Meanwhile I advise you not to go out of the hotel; I trust you can get back there safely. Major Naughton will not welcome you wandering around town, but that will be nothing compared to the Minister's displeasure when he learns you are again in Burhan."

Little as he had expected it in Burhan, Mahmoud had become accustomed to instructions to stay out of sight and accordingly he returned directly to his hotel. He did not slink, nor did he proceed with undue haste, for those attitudes would immediately have called attention to him. Still, he made his turban shade as much of his face as possible and walked purposefully, head down.

The following day passed slowly but without anxiety, so confident was he of the Minister's sense of integrity and fairness. During his activities of the previous day, the knots in his stomach had made him shudder at any thought of food. Today was different. In the more relaxed atmosphere, he had good meals sent to his room, even treating himself to a non-vegetarian dinner. Nothing like the food Shaheen had prepared for him; the unbidden thought constricted his throat momentarily. Nor as delicious as the Lucknowi food at the widow's, but more tasty than any meal on his journey homewards.

That thought brought him back to his purpose in Burhan, and roused him to bathe, dress, and sit down again to resume his wait.

34

The Minister held his place in the document under his hand while he looked up to acknowledge the interruption. "Salaam, Ghulam Ansari. Perhaps I have overlooked something. Were you expected at this hour?"

The greeting did nothing to allay the Personal Assistant's anxieties. In all the time since they had left Lucknow, now nearly eighteen months ago, the Minister had not once mentioned the mission he had sent to Kabul but the P.A. knew, from the books and papers the Minister kept near him, that he thought about it. He wished he had found his superior in a more relaxed frame of mind. "No, Your Excellency. I have come without an appointment, hoping your gracious presence would admit me."

"Presumably there is a reason."

"Yes, Sahib. There is news which I thought ought not to be kept from you. I can tell you now the Khan's reply to your mission, but I fear it will not please you."

"Please repeat it."

Ghulam Ansari repeated, word for word, the message Mahmoud had given him. Then he just sat. From the courtyard, the clip-clip of the mali's machete as he chipped away at the hard earth crowded into the silence. When the Minister finally reacted, it was with the question the P.A. most feared.

"How did you come to receive this message? You have not left Burhan."

"It turns out that Your Excellency's emissary has come back to this place on business of his own."

"Sayed Mahmoud is here? Here in Burhan? He was to return to Lucknow and send us word from there."

"Nevertheless he is in Burhan, has in fact just arrived."

"Against explicit orders he comes here?"

"He says he comes on business of his own." Inexplicably, Ghulam Ansari found himself wanting to defend Sayed Mahmoud.

The Minister looked out of the window, shaking his head as though in disbelief. "He takes a year and a half to accomplish a straightforward mission and then defies his instructions for reasons of his own." His gaze snapped back to his assistant. "Get rid of him. He must be banished at once."

The Minister was no more pleased than other men to learn unpleasant news, but honesty made him receive it soon enough, and loyalty made his servants deliver it. Ghulam Ansari took a deep breath. "It may not be so simple, Your Excellency. There is a complication. He accuses the Military Secretary of embezzling significant amounts of money from the Treasury. He wants to see Major Naughton prosecuted."

"Nonsense!"

"He claims to possess proof of his accusation. If he really does have proof, he could pursue the case from any place to which he might be banished."

"I see." The Minister folded up his document and rearranged the papers on his desk, giving himself some time to think. "Well, ten thousand rupees should pay for his mission and the return as well of any proof he claims to have."

"Excuse me, Your Excellency, that may do it. But only may, I fear."

"That is a great deal of money. What are you getting at?"

"The Military Secretary managed to endanger Sayed Mahmoud's life in the Punjab. He seems quite determined to achieve Major Naughton's humiliation. In fact, he spoke like a man possessed."

"It is not our responsibility to relieve his personal hatreds. Please pay him off and see that he leaves Burhan."

The P.A. bowed, but instead of getting to his feet to leave, sat a moment tugging at his fingers. If he had not been in this office, he would have cracked his knuckles out of nervousness. "And when the documents he refers to have been returned to our possession, should we then institute an investigation of the Military Department?"

"There is no 'we' in this matter, Ghulam Sahib. I will take care of it."

"I am to secure the documents for you?"

"Their confidentiality must not be breached."

"They were not originally confidential. They are said to consist of forged invoices in the Major's handwriting."

"Impossible." Anger was clear, underneath the control.

"One would naturally hope so. But Sayed Mahmoud asked me to remind you that he has eaten your salt. As have I. He said he owed it to you to make sure that another who has also done so is not defrauding Your Excellency."

"I do not accept these allegations against my Military Secretary."

"All I am suggesting, Your Excellency, is that you might want to speak with this Sayed Mahmoud to satisfy yourself. I believe you might well be convinced that he is telling the truth about the Major. If so, further depredations need to be prevented."

"You seem to have been convinced on very slight evidence." The Minister's gaze smouldered. His diction became even more precise than usual. "That readiness to accept the story raises a question in my mind about the reason. It should not be necessary to remind Ghulam Ansari that neither His Highness nor I will tolerate that one person who serves us in a position of trust should intrigue against another."

"Your Excellency knows my loyalty. It is not intrigue I hope I am pursuing, but trust."

"An attempt to cast suspicion on another Secretary does tend to reverse the suspicion."

"But..."

"You are very useful to me, Ghulam Ansari. I should be more than sorry to have to make a change in my personal staff."

Ghulam Ansari bowed, his face a sickly gray. "Forgive me, Your Excellency," he whispered. "It shall be as you wish."

"You are excused from any further dealings whatsoever with this matter. Out of respect for your past faithfulness, I shall consider that this conversation never took place. You would do well to do the same. Good day, Ghulam Ansari."

After the Personal Assistant crept out of the room, the Minister sat staring after him. This was most unwelcome news. He could probably trust Ghulam Ansari not to spread the story, though the P.A. was obviously in sympathy with Sayed Mahmoud. But that even one additional person was aware of the complication was very dangerous.

The Secret Account was a known account designed to cover the legitimate intelligence operations of the state. He had faced the fact that if he used it to cover a mission which the British would be bound to see as subversive, and that fact leaked out, His Highness would not be able to protect him. Even though the aim of the mission was the benefit of the state, and thus also of His Highness. But he had taken pains to prevent that leak. He had never contemplated that it might actually become public knowledge.

35

After Mahmoud's long day of waiting and of controlling his rising hopes, nine o'clock finally arrived. He was rewarded with a knock on the door. Expecting Ghulam Ansari, the Minister's Personal Assistant, he was not a little startled when a stranger brushed past him into the room without waiting for an invitation. A man somewhat past his prime, he was dressed in a simple black sherwani unrelieved by any belt or brass to indicate identity or even status.

"You are Sayed Mahmoud," the intruder stated without preliminaries.

"Correct. And who have I the honour of entertaining in my humble accommodations?"

"It is enough for you to know that I come from His Excellency the Nawab Sahib."

"The Minister Sahib?"

"None other, though why he should bother with you he has not explained to me."

"And how am I to know you are really from His Excellency?"

"By this, Sayed Mahmoud. He sends you a very substantial present. From how many people could you expect to receive Rs. 10,000?"

"You have brought it with you?"

The stranger explored an inner pocket and emerged with a packet of currency notes which he waved slowly in front of his nose. Mahmoud scarcely glanced at them. "Kindly return them to His Excellency, Vakeel Sahib, and say that this is not what I requested of him."

The vakeel scowled at this unexpected turn of events. "Allow me to warn you against greed," he said contemptuously. "His Excellency is not a common tradesman to be bargained with for a few rupees. If you refuse his generosity, the offer may not be repeated."

"Since it is not what I asked for, why should a repeat interest me? He may keep his rupees. I wish to see the punishment of the Military Secretary for patent depredations of which I have offered to produce proof. It need involve no reward for me. That is all I have to say. Salaam—good night—Vakeel Sahib."

All the next day Mahmoud again stayed in his room, but this time his mind was occupied with forward-looking questions. To be realistic, he had to admit to himself that the Minister, having now received his reply from the "Sufi," and one not likely to be pleasing to him at that, would feel under very little pressure to turn his attention urgently to Sayed Mahmoud.

But he assured himself he knew how to wait, had waited long periods before this for the fulfillment of his hopes. The Minister had promised Mahmoud a reward for his dangerous journey without specifying what it would be. Now that he had told him what he was after, the Minister owed him at least a hearing. And then he wouldn't be able to ignore the evidence Mahmoud could present.

A more daunting question was what he should do if the second reply were not more satisfactory than the first. It must be, he told himself over and over. This was an issue of simple justice. There was no basis for a refusal when all he was asking for was an examination of evidence, with appropriate action based on what he knew so well would be turned up. And it would be to the Minister's interest, as well as his own, that this should be done.

But sometimes, as day followed day with no reply, a tiny worm of doubt ate its way into his apple. Perhaps he would be more sensible to accept what the Minister offered and get back to Shaheen. Apart from her, what had his life consisted of, so far? A few years as the lowest clerk in the Tahsil office, a year in prison, a few months at the widow's house.

Ah, yes, the widow. He wondered whether she was still receiving the annual sum from the Minister, or whether that had been discontinued with his long absence. If he accepted the Minister's money he would be able to send her a substantial sum, enough to help her through her son's adolescence. And send to Kamaluddin for a sapphire ring for Shaheen. Tempting. But essential to resist. At least for now. Now only vengeance and the consequent restoration of his honour were important.

Respite from the turmoil of his thoughts came from remembering the tranquillity of the widow's home and the beauty of the gardens near it. One by one, his mind called up the blossoms he loved best: the silk cotton tree, with its golden yellow flowers, and next to that the jacaranda, lifting the heart with its blue crown cool and joyful against the hot sky. Later, the scarlet of the gul mohur. Odd how so red a blossom could be so welcome in the hottest months, almost enough beauty to justify those temperatures. Cooling were the waxy blossoms of the temple tree, the purity of their white relieved by the delicate yellow centers. He experienced a fleeting nostalgia for these beauties that stood for a way of life he had renounced. Even at this distance, they calmed him.

He dreamed at night of his wife, vividly recreating the joys of their brief marriage. Sometimes he awoke, surprised and aching to find she was not in his arms. Why did fate take him to Chalab, he asked himself; why did he have to meet Shaheen? What the eye has not seen, the heart cannot long for. He asked himself for the thousandth time whether he would truly have returned to India with the message for the Minister, had it not been for the prospect of a son. A son deserved a father whose honour was intact, but perhaps the absence from mother and child was not worth it.

Shaheen herself led him to the answer to that one, for she had wanted him to accept the values of the men of her tribe. Revenge came crashing back into his consciousness. Chalabis were fascinated by blood feuds, some of them stretching back a generation or more, but never allowed just to peter out. His Afghan brothers had taught him how to wait when honour demanded vengeance. He too would not give up.

At other times, his mind turned to the more distant past and he writhed on the bed with anger which, until now, had not been allowed to surface. Recognizing that he had always suffered for the wrongs other people had done opened the floodgates. "All my life!" he repeated, and then, his fist pounding the pillow unbidden in its own expression of violence, shouting, "All my life! *All my life!*"

Mother blamed him for weakness when it was Hamid who had transgressed. Hamid let him take the blame for stealing a ring. How *did* Hamid come by it? Not right that he still didn't know; protecting his brother and the family were what seemed important at the time. Now he would never know, but at least it had taught him never again to take the blame for someone else.

Then Lahore; only his quick recall of the rock trick and good aim saved him. Liar that fellow was, pretended to be a friendly guide, but tried to steal the rifles. And after Swat, there was the clumsy guide who shot him by accident. Why couldn't he have shot his own foot instead?

Major Naughton, above all Major Naughton, tried to stop him on his leave because he no doubt intended him to bear the blame for his falsified records. Heaven knows what intervention made him change his mind that time, at least long enough for Mahmoud to get out of Jehanabad. But now, by Allah, the Major would pay for putting his life in jeopardy. For once, he would get his own back.

Mahmoud stood up and paced the room, too quickly for the small area. He had been a victim all his life, allowed himself to be a victim. But now his self-pity was leavened by newly awakened determination to turn the tables. This time he was going to be the one to demand that others take responsibility for their actions, the one to insist on integrity in others. Shaheen had accused him of a sense of honour that was merely personal; now she would see that it had implications for the community as well. She would see why Naughton had to be stopped.

Mahmoud hated Naughton with a passion that increased whenever he thought of him. The man should be put out in the sun with red pepper in his eyes. Better still, he must learn what it feels like to stand in the dock. Yes, the trial will be the appropriate humiliation for the mighty Major.

The trial that Mahmoud longed for, when the Minister would accuse Major Naughton and call for Mahmoud's testimony, played on the backdrop of his mind like a shadow play with the leather puppets of South India. The Military Secretary, pale as he enters the room, alarmed as he hears the charges read out, more and more frightened with each false entry that is identified and demonstrated. Finally he turns to his accuser, pleading, "Say it isn't true, Sayed Mahmoud. Tell them I was always a conscientious officer. For God's sake help me!" But Mahmoud stands firm on his evidence and His Excellency is implacable.

The Major is sentenced to return the total amount that he has embezzled, and in addition he is fined one half the sum of the salary he has earned during his entire tenure in Jehanabad. "Should he be sent to prison?" the Minister murmurs, half consulting Mahmoud. The latter shakes his head. "Not necessary," he advises. "Naughton cannot now get employment anywhere in India. He will have to return Home to his family and friends, a failure, penniless, dependent on them for whatever they are willing to spare him. That is the best punishment." The Major buries his face in his hands as the tears drop through his fingers.

The scene was so sweet that Mahmoud replayed it at intervals, adding embellishments as they occurred to him, but always the central theme was the anguish of the Military Secretary and his own full exaction of retribution. For His Highness, for the Minister, and for himself, justice would be seen to be done.

For days he pondered the alternatives that might be open to him, if the unbelievable should happen and the Nawab Sahib refused to act. Should he ask the widow to forward his trunk to him here, so that he could publish the allegations and their proof in the newspapers? Not very safe, for if the trunk should be lost or waylaid, his case would collapse. Moreover, he knew enough about the newspapers to realise that with the expenditure of a bit of baksheesh he could get the whole story printed. But by the same token the Major could get a convincing refutation, complete with counter claims and insinuations which would make Mahmoud's presence in Jehanabad untenable. And all that with no need for proof.

What then? The only recourse seemed to be to sue in Magistrate's Court, but his experience with the Magistrate in Khandipur left him with little confidence in that route. Every train of thought led him back to pin his hopes on the Minister. So honourable a man would not refuse justice.

36

One night, after weeks of this way of dealing with his suspense, Mahmoud was once more rewarded by a knock on the door and the unceremonious entry of the vakeel. This time, at least, the man exercised a modicum of courtesy. "Salaam, Sayed Mahmoud."

"Salaam, Vakeel Sahib."

"You are well, I trust?"

"I am well. May I hope to hear the same of His Excellency?"

"He is well, by the grace of Allah."

"Then you have seen him." Mahmoud would not be the first to give in on this game of nerves the vakeel seemed to be playing with him.

"I have been with him this very day."

"Then he is in Burhan."

"He is here. He has been out of station for some days but returned yesterday. Perhaps you heard the shouts of rejoicing on the streets as he distributed coins to the beggars."

Mahmoud executed a slight nod which could have been mistaken for a bow of agreement.

"Well, well. Enough of that. You are perhaps wondering what brings me here again at this hour of the night."

Once more the nod.

"His Excellency has decided to forgive your impertinence in refusing his generous gift, and has sent me to offer you a reward so munificent it will take your breath away. I assure you it is genuine. He says that provided you turn over to him the papers that you claim are proof of your accusations, and that you leave Jehanabad and pledge your honour not to return, he will give you a gift of a lakh rupees." The vakeel took a deep breath. "Understand me, Sayed Mahmoud: he offers you one hundred thousand rupees. There. Was I right to say this is munificence indeed?" His chest puffed out as though he himself had bestowed this largesse on a petitioner, however undeserving.

Mahmoud's head shook slowly, weighed almost beyond supporting by the heavy burden of his disappointment. "All wrong. His Excellency has not understood me at all. I do not ask for reward or settlement, His Excellency's generosity or pledge. All I ask for is the punishment of the Military Secretary. Nothing less than justice will satisfy me."

The vakeel was incredulous. "Come, come, babu!" he expostulated. "No sensible man turns down a lakh of rupees. This will make you a wealthy man and relieve you of the necessity to work or to worry about anything for the rest of your life."

"That is not the source of the peace I crave."

"Don't play the fool. Do you think the Minister hands out such gifts every day? Would God he would offer me a moiety of it."

"That the Minister fails to understand what I am asking does not relieve me of responsibility to try also to protect him. You have my answer. Please convey it to His Excellency."

"For my sake, Sayed Mahmoud, think again. His Excellency makes you an offer the like of which he is not likely ever to make again to anyone. In his place, would you not feel humiliated if it were repudiated by a mere munshi? And that, too, for the second time? If you felt that way, how much more likely that the Minister would be angry. He may even think that his vakeel has not presented the proposition properly."

"The Nawab Sahib knows that my price is the humiliation of the Military Secretary. Nothing less."

The vakeel sighed deeply. "Then there seems to be nothing more to be said, so I bid you good night."

It was not a good night for Mahmoud. By turns disillusioned, almost weeping in his disappointment, hating the Major who seemed about to work yet another injustice on him, angry with fate for making him again a butt, and with the Minister for refusing to recognize his legitimate demand, he pounded the pillow with his fist until, worn out by his own violence, he fell into restless sleep.

By morning, his unconscious mind had decided on a plan of action. He no longer had confidence in his countrymen. For some reason, the Minister preferred to protect a foreigner rather than to listen to an Indian. Perhaps he feared that making the Major's dishonesty public would cast doubt on his judgment in appointing him. That would explain why he specified the return of the documents Mahmoud had secreted. Or did he fear the British so much that he would not charge one of their citizens with fraud? The Minister had mentioned, when he proposed the trip, that Mahmoud had a prison record; possibly that wrongful conviction cast a shadow on his reputation for integrity even here. Whatever the reason, the Minister seemed determined to deny him even a hearing.

Disillusioned, he turned his steps and his aspirations towards the British Residency. He was no longer afraid to admit that he had been in Afghanistan and the Punjab, for the Minister's perfidy in dealing with him had released him from any obligation, including the obligation of confidentiality. He was totally absorbed in how he would present his case to the Resident or whichever assistant might be told off to see him first. Inattentive to his surroundings. Unaware that he had been followed.

At the very gates of the Residency, as he was about to engage the guard in the usual bargaining about baksheesh, a man intervened. "Sayed Mahmoud," he said, "come with me."

"Who are you to command me?"

The stranger withdrew a chaprassi's brass from his pocket and displayed it quickly. Before it disappeared again into the pocket, Mahmoud had time only to recognize the Minister's seal. Accordingly he accompanied the man with no further questions, hope knocking faintly at the door of his mind. Anxiety soon competed when they went to a gate that was unfamiliar to him. Judging from the location and the construction of the wall, it must have been a part of the Minister's deori, but Mahmoud could not recall ever noticing that gate before. Once inside it, the building into which he was ushered was stark.

"Wait here," his guide ordered, gesturing to a crude bench against the wall. The only other furnishing was an equally undistinguished table which bore no evidence of being used by anyone. The guide clapped his hands twice at the open door; at this signal a man wearing the sash of the Minister's army appeared and the other departed. The newcomer leaned nonchalantly against the jamb, legs stretched out into the doorway. He showed no disposition to chat. Mahmoud, failing to elicit so much as a glance by his question about present whereabouts, contributed his own blackness to the silence.

After some time the vakeel entered. "Sayed Mahmoud," he said earnestly, "this is your last chance. You must reconsider your refusal. The Nawab Sahib will graciously extend you time to think over his offer and to make the necessary arrangements for handing over the documents. He considers the grudge you bear Major Naughton petulant and he cannot entertain it. Please accept what he so graciously offers you."

"What is the necessity of coming to me again and again with the same offer when you know I will not agree to it?"

"Don't be hasty, Sayed Mahmoud. Think carefully. Meanwhile I must ask you to remain here while you reconsider. Please feel free to send me a message if you have made up your mind to agree."

The vakeel nodded to the guard and departed. The latter led a despondent Mahmoud inside, where he locked him into a cell and also left. After several weeks there, he was transferred without explanation to the Kotwal's prison.

37

Neither the metallic sound of the key turning in the lock, nor the groan of the hinges as the heavy door swung outward, caused the man sitting cross-legged on the cotton durrie to look up. The tray placed on the floor beside him held no surprises, and no interest. Food in the Kotwal's prison was neither good nor bad; it was boring. And lack of exercise left little to whet the appetite.

Besides, Mahmoud's mind was over the walls to the city gate, thinking of the visitor he had demanded to see. He had sent for a scribe, an amanuensis who made his living by sitting at the Great Gate, board on his knee and inkwell at his elbow, writing letters for the customers who came to him. "Respected Sir." "Your slave begs to see the feet of His Excellency." The flowery phrases rolled from his pen, nicely graded according to the status of the recipient.

The customers were mostly servants and wage earners with a sprinkling of small landowners and petty officials. Even those who knew how to write their mother tongue would not have known the polite forms of address, much less the elegant court language. So they came to him, asking him not only to record, but to compose their messages.

Of all who sat at the gate dipping their quills in the hopefulness of the supplicants, Ishaq was adjudged the best. He had on more than one occasion addressed petitions to no less a personage than His Highness, and even then his pen had not faltered.

Now he had been summoned to the Kotwal's prison. He had been on the verge of a scornful refusal when the fee had been mentioned. At that his greedy eyes had contradicted the reluctance of his words as he bade the messenger say that he would come when the late afternoon breeze had begun to stir. Now, looking around the cell, he was reassured that the prisoner could pay as promised. He obviously had money for bribing the guards to bring some small luxuries, of which he himself could be considered one.

How the money was come by was another question, for the cell's occupant looked no more impressive than most of the customers at the gate. No, Ishaq corrected himself with the man's first words, perhaps a shade above the average customer. The other wasted no breath on formalities.

"You've brought your writing implements?"

"Why else would I be here?" the scribe countered with some acerbity. The prisoner, if he noticed, chose not to take offence. The Minister's refusal of justice was unthinkable. So Mahmoud, a private citizen, would do what only a few years ago he would have deemed unthinkable: he would appeal to the very top. "Then we shall begin at once. A letter to the Viceroy."

"His Excellency the Viceroy and Governor-General of India? You've taken leave of your senses! What business have you writing to him?"

"Since ancient times it's been our right to appeal for justice to our rulers. Is that true or not?"

"It's true, by the Grace of God."

"Now these foreigners say that their Empire is more mighty than the Emperor Aurangzeb's. So ought they not to hear our appeals even more readily?"

"How could the Viceroy do justice to you? He doesn't know anything about you."

"Just wait till I tell him. Then won't he know? And I'm not ashamed to tell him, for I come from a respectable family; not big people, but respectable." Before the scribe could think of a suitable rejoinder to this confidence, the prisoner resumed in a brisk voice, "Did I bring you here to dispute with me? Kindly sit down and display those talents for which your fame has reached even here."

Accordingly the scribe sat, opening his writing case and arranging his ink pot, quills, and sand in meticulous order on the floor around him. On his crossed legs he balanced a thin board and on it set a piece of hand-laid paper, thick and heavy. Then, in a flowing hand he wrote, "Burhan, 6 May 1883," and the flowery Persian phrases which he deemed appropriate for the Queen-Empress's personal representative. Only then did he indicate his readiness to receive further instructions.

Sitting in the lotus position and gazing steadily at his ankles as though meditating alone in his cell, the prisoner began. "With due respect and solicitations, I beg to present myself, Sayed Mahmoud, native of Khandipur, district town of Hingaum District. I am the son of Sayed Muzzafer, deceased, a magistrate who served in the same District for twenty years and then received his pension for two years before his death. His grandfather was Sayed Ahmed Major Subedar Bahadur, who fought for the British and received from them a medal and pension for three generations. I received my education at the Government School and was employed as a Clerk in the Tahsil office at Khandipur."

Mahmoud ceased to speak. Tipping his head back, he stared upward over his shoulder with a look of such intense concentration that Ishaq was reluctant to interrupt him. In fact, Mahmoud was far away, reliving the chain of circumstances he intended to recount, beginning with his first arrival in Burhan. His nerves quivered at the very memory of so much injustice and the need to choose words that adequately conveyed the public importance of it. He did not even notice the opening of the door, nor the jerk of the warden's head toward the entrance which prompted the scribe silently to collect his paraphernalia and leave.

"Loony, huh?" the warden remarked conversationally as he rattled his keys.

"Completely. Sat there all this time and never got beyond recounting his pedigree."

"You coming back?" the warden asked, more to prolong a conversational opportunity than for any interest in the information.

"If he can think of anything more to say, I'll come as long as he can pay. After all, how much time do I get to spend in a Class A prison? What puts him here?"

"How would I know? Does the Kotwal confide in me? Of course, one does have suspicions. This is not the first time he's been in prison."

"How do you know that?"

"One sees little things. He knew what to expect when he came here. How to make the best of it. Of course, he was in some jail, possibly at one of the nawab's, before he was sent here. He claims it was the Minister's, but what would the Minister have to do with him? Unless, of course, he was stealing something there. No, I think he's made an enemy somewhere."

"He's been here a while, then?"

"Not long. A few months. He'll still be here the next time your business is slow and you want to pick up some extra rupees from him."

"If he's not too far gone in his head to remember he wanted to write a letter, I'll probably be seeing you, then." Ishaq stepped through the doorway and breathed deeply, as though savouring the air of freedom. At the step, he turned back to the warden. "The joke's really on you, you know. You think you're holding a prisoner, but he isn't even there."

Four days later the warden again put his head into Mahmoud's cell. "The Peshi (Financial) Secretary has arrived, Your Excellency."

Mahmoud bowed slightly and responded gravely. "Please show him in." It would not do to offend the warden, especially when he was attempting to be amusing.

Ishaq, the scribe from the Great Gate, had caught the warden's tone. "Salaam, Your Excellency. Writing to the Viceroy again, are you?"

"Kindly sit down," Mahmoud directed, "and when you have arranged your implements, you may remind me where we left off last week."

The scribe did as he was bid. "Your last sentence said that you had been employed in the Tahsil office at Khandipur."

"Oh, yes, I remember now. Let's continue from there." Twenty minutes later he interrupted the steady flow of his dictation. "Scribe Sahib, why are you not writing this down?"

"Is there much more to come?"

"I've hardly begun. But I had not supposed a famous scribe would tire so quickly."

"Not I, but His Excellency, the Viceroy. He will never take the time to read so much."

"But I must relate the whole story. If I don't tell him what happened, how can he understand my petition?"

"If he doesn't read it, then also he won't understand."

"So what must I do?"

"Truly a dilemma. Let us think. Well, you...no...here's one possibility. You can tell me your story and I'll condense it for your letter."

"Ridiculous! How would you know what's important?" Mahmoud glared at Ishaq, but slowly his expression softened. "Perhaps you have a point, after all. I tend to relive the events, but you are more like the Viceroy, outside of it, I mean. You could recognize what's essential for it. Yes, that just might work."

Several sessions later, Ishaq the Scribe finished his reading. "Is it well done or not?" he demanded of Mahmoud. "Have I caught the essence of your appeal without trying the Viceroy's patience?"

"It is well done. It's not by any means the whole story, but it will do."

"So you agree that all it lacks is the proper closing?"

"Let's say," Mahmoud dictated, "Trusting in Your Excellency's well-known sense of justice and believing that loyalty to your own race will not preclude your investigation of an allegation supportable by evidence, even though forwarded by an Indian, I beg to remain your humble servant."

"Hold on, that will never do! To the Viceroy one must speak with proper respect. Those are not at all the correct phrases to use to a person of his eminence."

"Very well, Ishaq Sahib, you fix it up. After all this time, you surely know my intent perfectly. Just see that it gets posted to the Viceroy. If I try to send it through the guard here, I have no way of knowing whether it has gone or he has pocketed the postage money along with his baksheesh."

"Not so fast, Sayed Mahmoud; one doesn't just post off a letter to the Government of India, Calcutta, as though it were 27 Nizamuddin Lane."

"How then?"

"The proper channel to the Viceroy is through the Resident here. It's up to him to forward it to Calcutta. So you see, if I am to start your missive on its way, I must do so by taking it to the Residency."

"Please do, Scribe Sahib. And here is something extra for you for running around like a messenger."

It was a rare occasion, for Mahmoud actually laughed.

38

The hot season was always slow at the Residency. The Government of India had moved from Calcutta to Simla, up in the Himalayas; His Highness was at his hunting lodge in the hills; while the Residency staff droned through the short stack of papers on their desks and wished that they too could go away until the monsoon broke.

Lazily, the Resident reached for another envelope. He made a little ceremony of slitting it open with his favourite paper knife, letting the smoothness of the malachite handle soothe his hot palm for a moment. Idly, he extracted the pages and turned them, merely scanning at first, but with increasing attention. At the end he sat back in his chair, thoughtfully tapping his teeth with his thumbnail. Then his hand sought the bell on his desk.

"Ask the First Assistant to step in here," he directed.

The First Assistant, who had been doing nothing, interrupted himself promptly and reported. "Yes, Sir."

"Sit down, Ian, and take a look at this." The Resident tossed a document across the table.

Ian obeyed, whistling, clucking, even chuckling at moments. Finished, he looked up at the Resident. "Well, well! It seems our Minister has been a bad boy."

"What do you see?"

"Well, for one thing, he's not supposed to communicate with a foreign power without permission."

"He didn't actually, did he?" the Resident interposed mildly.

"Not technically, perhaps, but doing so through an agent would seem to be the same thing so far as the treaty restrictions are concerned."

"So...?"

"So I suppose we have to forward this to the Viceroy, as requested, and wait for his orders."

"Which are likely to be what?"

"Bye-bye, Minister Sahib."

"That's just what worries me, Ian. Who is there to replace him?"

"Well, there are a lot of people who would like to, but that's not the same as being qualified to, of course. There's the General, but His Highness would never agree to him. And Rai Sahib, but we would hardly agree to anyone so openly hostile to us. Then there's, uh, there's, nobody. The rest would rather play at intrigue than at governing the State."

"Exactly. Legally we ought to proceed against the Minister, but politically it's very difficult. Let's look at another angle. What about the Military Secretary?"

"If this story is true, he's a first-rate rascal."

"And the implication of that is...?"

"Unfortunately, nothing. Since he's the Minister's employee and not ours, we can't very well take any steps to prosecute him unless the Minister registers a complaint about him. And His Excellency seems to be intent on protecting him, for some reason."

"Such as?"

"I can't imagine. But it does look as though whichever one we might proceed against, the other would eventually become involved."

"So we're back where we started. That leads me to another question. You seem to believe this story. Is there any reason to do so?"

"It shouldn't be too difficult to check it out."

"And warn Major Naughton to put his ducks in a row?"

"What if we confront the Minister with it?"

"Let me make a prediction. His reply would be, 'If I am so distrusted, then my usefulness to His Highness is at an end. I shall submit my resignation in the morning.' And we just agreed that would not be the best possible outcome."

"But what if it is true? Has the Minister committed a crime? Or just a breach of faith?"

"If it could be proved, I expect the Viceroy would think of some way to remove him more or less permanently and have the State accede to British India. No more Princely State."

"Everything seems to me to hinge on whether the story is true. That's what we have to make up our minds about, first of all."

"Maybe we don't," the Resident rejoined cheerfully. "These reservations we've just specified are persuasive. Let's note them and toss this hot potato upwards. Let someone in the Viceroy's office catch it."

So they did.

39

While the Resident read Mahmoud's letter to the Viceroy, the Minister also read an unexpected letter and immediately sent for the Military Secretary.

"Please explain this." He passed the letter across to Major Naughton, who noted with some surprise that it was written in the Urdu vernacular and script, not in the Court language. It read:

Respected Sir:

Before I appeal for your assistance, please allow me to introduce myself. I am a cotton broker and in addition a specialist in the types of cloth used by the military throughout India. My company has for the past two years had dealings with the Military Department in Jehanabad. I believe our cloth has proved satisfactory, as there have been repeat orders.

Enclosed herewith is the most recent order, which I decline. Also a receipt for the payment for that order, which I am asked to sign in advance although, as Your Excellency will see, it is blank. None of our other customers throughout India engage in such offensive practices. I accepted it the first few times hoping that once my reliability was established, the practice would be discontinued. Since it is not, I do not feel inclined to continue this contact.

This appeal is for Your Excellency's intervention to secure the payment for the last invoice, which has now been pending for seven months. After the receipt of our dues, I will withdraw from all contact with the Jehanabad Military.

At the same time, I shall not fail to pray for Your Excellency's health and good fortune.

/s/ Sayed Hamidullah
Cotton and Cloth Broker

Naughton looked up and shrugged. His tone was dismissive. "New chap. Very self-righteous and self-important. The letter shows how rigid he is."

"It was not your opinion of his character that I asked," the Minister rejoined.

"As for his complaint, it is surprising that he should presume to address the Nawab Sahib himself. It also suggests that he is a novice in business. I should imagine Your Excellency's experience in dealing directly with salesmen is limited. It is characteristic of them to consider that payment in full indicates the end of a relationship. We do not usually risk that."

"And the blank receipt?"

"The integrity of Your Excellency's government is well known. This is the first objection to it that has ever been raised."

"What is the reason for so questionable a practice? Even the most naive businessman might wonder whether he was signing a receipt for more than he would actually receive."

"We began it because it greatly facilitated the carrying out of Your Excellency's confidential instructions."

"That is not acceptable. I thought I had made it clear that unaudited transfers into the Secret Account were to cease."

"Indeed so, and they have ceased. My office had got into the habit of using the blank receipt and I have, perhaps wrongly, let it go on."

"The implication is displeasing. Let this be the final occasion. Please do as the letter asks: pay the amount due immediately and show me the receipt for it when it comes back. There will be no further discussion of this matter or of the Secret Account. Is that understood?"

"Very well, Your Excellency."

Back at the office, Naughton reported the conversation to Corder, his assistant, and concluded with a sigh of relief. "Close call!"

Corder was indignant. "The nerve! Imagine a mere tradesman addressing the Minister! Brazen, that's what he is. How could we possibly have guessed he would do that?"

"The worst of it is," Naughton pointed out, "that payment was entered in the books at the time, so now you and I have to cough up the cash for it."

"That hurts! All the more since some of the local sources are drying up. God, how I wish we could get through with this and go Home!"

"If this Allah they're always calling on is as merciful as they claim, perhaps he'll arrange it for us."

"Amen to that!"

40

"Come in here, Ian, this will interest you," the Resident called out one morning several weeks later, as he saw his First Assistant passing in the corridor.

"Good morning, Sir. What's up?"

"Remember that strange letter we had, about the fellow who claimed he had been sent on a mission to Kabul? The reply has just come in from Simla. Now where did I put it? This damned heat; everything sticks to one's hands so one is constantly searching for what should be in the right pile but isn't. Ah, here it is." He passed it over to Ian.

"Hmm. 'The Viceroy and Governor General in Council'—they seem to have taken it seriously—'direct me to inform you...do not think it expedient to pursue the matter.' That would seem to let us off the hook nicely. 'Affairs in Jehanabad are on an even keel just now. The Minister has been performing efficiently and with every evidence of loyalty to the Paramount Power. Moreover your own comments verify that there is at present no one qualified to succeed him. It would therefore be most unwise to disturb this satisfactory state of affairs for the sake of an alleged crime which may in any event be impossible to prove.

'You may communicate to the Minister the conclusion of this Government that this document is the work either of an unusually clever adventurer, or of a truly deranged mind. Sayed Mahmoud, if he exists, may be released.' Well, that seems pretty final."

"Pass it along to the Minister, will you Ian, like a good fellow? If it's fiction, it may afford him a moment's amusement. If it isn't, at least he can turn Sayed Mahmoud loose without a qualm. That is, of course, if he exists."

"My pleasure. All the same, Sir..."

"Yes?"

"Well, all the same, wouldn't it be interesting to know whether it's true? Does he exist?"

"Ian, my lad," the Resident said, dabbing at his face with a damp handkerchief, "you disappoint me. I thought you would have learned by now that there are some things it's better not to know."

Neither of them could know that the letter was in any case irrelevant, for it was already too late. Sayed Mahmoud existed, but as of two days ago was no longer in Burhan.

41

A few days after Naughton's session with the Minister, the Major was once more pacing the floor in Corder's office, a place where he had spent increasing amounts of time these past few days. The clicking of his heels on the cement floor was clearly getting on the assistant's nerves. "Now what's the matter?" Corder exclaimed. "Are you still fuming about losing money to that Hamidullah fellow?"

Naughton shook his head. "That's water under the bridge."

"Well, then, for heaven's sake stop chewing your fingernails and tell me what's got into you!"

Naughton strode the width of the room and back before replying, "I've been thinking about Sayed Mahmoud, that bastard who stole our invoices. One of these days he's going to give in and turn them over to the Minister."

"But we have the Minister's own scheme to cover us."

"Not for everything. Don't forget the little munshi left before the Minister proposed his scheme, so the invoices will be dated earlier than that. That not-very-happy thought is what occurred to me only now."

"Are you saying that if His Excellency should decide to prosecute us..."

"Exactly. He could even use his own scheme against us."

"Why worry now? The chap hasn't been heard from for a long time. He must have skedaddled." After the first shock, Corder would have liked to have this problem go away.

"Wrong. He's just around the corner from here, in the Kotwal's prison."

"What! I don't believe, wait a minute, how do you know that?"

Naughton snorted. "Don't be naive, Harry. Do you think the

Minister is the only one who collects information about people that interest him?"

"So he's available, to the Minister, to..."

Without waiting for the end of the sentence, Naughton leapt to his feet and left the room. Out of breath as much from anxiety as from haste, he arrived at the Minister's deori in the hope of being received without the usual prior appointment. While he waited in the Angrezi Khana, he rehearsed to himself the plan he would present. His hopes were rewarded.

"You and I both know, Your Excellency—we are in fact the only ones to know—what it is that Sayed Mahmoud claims about the accounts, what those documents are with which he is threatening you."

"Excuse me; I believe it is you who are being threatened." The Minister had known for a long time that the Major was embezzling funds: that was his hold over him to assure the confidentiality of the deposits into the secret account and their withdrawal for the mission to Kabul. It was galling, however, that in order to do the best for Jehanabad he had to deal with a criminal and overlook his crimes. To dismiss him was impossible, for a successor would surely examine the books and find the Minister's fund. On that basis, the British might even manage to paint the State red, like all British territories on the maps.

"Correct that I am the one Sayed Mahmoud is threatening, Minister Sahib, but since the scheme for the Secret Account would be exposed, I presume that has something to do with your keeping him locked up all this time. Please forgive the impertinence. It was impetuous because I have a plan that may serve us both. May I tell it to you?"

The Minister's face was granite; he barely nodded.

"Am I correct in my understanding that you would be satisfied if two conditions could be fulfilled: one, Sayed Mahmoud should be out of Jehanabad and not able or at least not very likely to return; and two, that the documents be returned to you? Even better, they should be destroyed so that they could never again fall into the wrong hands."

The Minister considered for a moment. "If that could be accomplished," he said slowly, "yes, that would solve the problem."

"Then my suggestion is that you release him into my custody. I figure the documents must be in Lucknow, since that's where you caught up with him. I'll take him there and make him hand them over. Once his evidence is gone, he'll have no reason to come back here."

"What makes you think he will give up the documents?"

"He's a simple fellow. Once he tastes freedom again, and that back in a place where he has lived, he won't hold out. He'll want to stay there. Especially since the alternative would be to return to prison. No, I think we can manage to convince him."

"We?"

"Well, it would seem safer to have two of us travelling with him. After all, it's a long journey. If I should fall asleep he might escape and get back here, but two of us could alternate."

"Probably sensible. But I have promised him a lakh of rupees for those documents."

"This way would save you that money."

"That was not my point. Since I have offered it to him, I must pay it. Anyway, it is also the reward I promised him for something else. I shall have to make arrangements to get it to Lucknow for someone to turn over to him when the documents are secured. That should not be too difficult."

"In fact it can be done easily. Give the money to me and I will exchange it for the documents. That would no doubt make the task even easier, since Your Excellency insists on honouring your word even to a criminal."

"When would you expect to start?"

"At the Minister Sahib's pleasure."

"Well, so be it. I shall have the papers drawn up to release him into your custody and send you the sum for him, as well as some amount for your expenses. It should all be ready in a few days."

Back at his own office, the Major burst into his assistant's room. "Pack your bags, Harry!" he exulted. "We're going to Lucknow."

"Whatever for?"

"To take the little mushi and a lakh of rupees." It required only a few words to explain the plan. "And once we get our hands on those documents, we can burn them and certify to the Minister that they've been destroyed. No more danger to us."

"Good show! Pity to turn over all that lovely money, though." Since he had no contact with the officials to distract him, Corder regularly focused on the money.

"Pity? It's a tragedy! We could certainly put it to better use than that fellow."

"So right. And we need a few windfalls if we're ever going to get out of here."

"Hmmm. I was so concerned with the documents I hadn't thought about that money." Naughton squirmed in his chair, tapped his fingers against the seat, looked up when his assistant pursued an idea.

"Well, let's think about it. Would we really have to give it to him? Once we've extracted the papers from him, what's to prevent us from simply leaving him, taking the rupees along?"

"We'll have to tell His Excellency that we've paid off his patsy. Still, whether we turn it over or not, he'd have only our word for it. No way he can ask for proof."

"Sounds like a done deed. I don't see that we have to fear the Sayed himself. As you say, he'd have no reason to show up in Burhan again."

Naughton got up and paced the floor, hands behind his back, fingers moving restlessly. Suddenly he swerved.

"Wait a minute, Harry. What if he makes a fuss about not getting the money?"

Corder shrugged. "How would he know the Minister had given it to us?"

"He wouldn't have to. He might simply write to the Minister and complain about being done out of his evidence without the promised reward."

"Ye gods, you're right! If a mere tradesman can address the Minister and get through to him, what's to prevent a former employee from doing it?"

"Exactly. Or he might send someone to the vakeel to demand it. Then where would we be?"

"Yes. I see what you mean." Corder threw himself back in his chair and swiped at the perspiration dripping down his face. "Even out of Jehanabad, he continues to be a threat to us."

"He will be. So long as he lives and we are here, he could undo everything we've accomplished for ourselves."

"So long as he lives."

"So long as he lives."

They stared at one another, aware that two minds were host to the same thought. Then Corder ventured, "Who would miss him?"

"You mean, who is there who might report his absence? No one, I suppose, considering he's been incommunicado for the past couple of years."

"If there's no one to report him missing…"

"It would be quite safe. How could he be got out of the way, though?"

Corder shrugged. "People do get sick and die, even on trains."

"Not in full view of other passengers. That gives me an idea, though. How about off the train?"

"You mean shoot him on the ground or something? That could be very messy to set up—and possibly to have to explain."

"No, I mean arrange an accident. Wouldn't it be a pity if he should fall off the train?" Naughton was on his feet again, head down, pacing off his ideas.

"Interesting thought. Yes. I can see it. The vestibule is open, but no one in the cars can see into it. Yes, that might work."

"What if someone looking out the window sees the body fall and stops the train?"

"In the first place, our friend won't be in any condition to testify. In the second, as soon as he goes overboard, we'll go into the car ahead, so if necessary we can say we went there to look for an acquaintance, leaving him behind."

Naughton grinned. "He must have fallen, poor bugger."

"I think we have our lines clear. It looks like the only question left is how to get him back onto a train after we get our hands on those documents."

"We'll deal with that when the time comes. Come on. Let's declare a holiday and go toast Lady Luck."

42

Mahmoud sat up straight at the sound of the key turning in the lock. The Viceroy's answer: was it possible it could have arrived so quickly? But the door swung open to admit neither Ishaq nor the guard but, of all people, Major Naughton.

"Pick up your things, babu," he ordered without preliminaries. "You're coming with me."

"On what pretext?" the startled prisoner demanded.

"You belong to me, now." He stepped into the cell and looked at Mahmoud's possessions scattered around him on a durrie. "You've been released into my custody, so look smart and do as I say."

Mahmoud leapt to his feet. "*Your* custody?"

"That's what I said. Now get moving."

"No! No, I won't! I won't go. In the custody of a criminal! They call that release? It's not right. I refuse. I'll appeal to the Minister. Get out of my cell!" He banged on the door. "Guard! Guard! Get this man out. Guard!"

Nothing happened. No guard appeared. Major Naughton simply stood there.

"Now that you've had your little tantrum, get your things together. I have neither patience for it, nor time to waste."

"Where do you propose I should go?"

"Not you, we. To Lucknow. There you will hand over those documents you've been prating about. The Minister intends to have them and so do I."

Just then the guard did appear. "This is your morning for visitors," he said to Mahmoud. "Here's another."

The Minister's vakeel appeared from behind him. "Salaam, Sayed Mahmoud."

"You're just in time. Please tell the Minister that I refuse to go with this criminal. I will stay in prison before I'll go out in his custody."

"I'm afraid it's too late for that, Sayed Mahmoud. You should have accepted His Excellency's offer when he made it. Don't say I didn't warn you. Now he sends you this."

The vakeel handed over a paper.

Mahmoud retreated to a corner of the cell where he could break the wax seal and read the missive without anyone looking over his shoulder. It read:

Sayed Mahmoud:

You are herewith remanded into the custody of Major Naughton. You are forthwith to go with him to Lucknow and there hand over to him all of those documents which you claim constitute a case against him. After that you are never again to enter the jurisdiction of Jehanabad. In return for those papers and your receipt, Major Naughton will hand over to you the lakh of rupees offered to you earlier. HUKUM, this is an order! If you do not comply, sterner measures will have to be taken.

The order was not signed, nor did it bear an identifiable seal. Still Mahmoud would have recognized its authenticity even had it not been delivered personally by the Minister's vakeel. Quite right. He had no choice. Carefully re-folding the paper, he stowed it in his pocket and began to assemble his possessions. They were few enough: two sets of clothes and a shawl, a towel, a pencil and exercise book, his brass cup. The single watch and two gold coins left from his hoard were always in his secret pocket. Depression slowed his actions, made every movement precise, deliberate. He could think of nothing more at the moment.

The trip was even worse than he had feared, more demeaning. They travelled second class, Mahmoud facing his two captors. He kept his eyes down, for looking at them nauseated him. His mind was occupied with plans for escape: futile thoughts, flawed plans.

Thinking constantly sidetracked by new expressions of a hatred so consuming there was no room even for despair.

At first, his two sentinel escorts talked to one another in their own language, ignoring him except that one or the other constantly had an eye on him. When they felt hungry they ate the food they had carried; only after satisfying themselves did they pass the leavings to Mahmoud. Fingertips barely touching the package, he tossed it out the window.

"Peel me an orange, babu," Naughton ordered.

"I am not your servant."

"No, not even that." Naughton made as if to rise, leaning toward Mahmoud. "Do it!" he commanded in a loud voice.

Faces around the car turned in his direction but no one said anything. Mahmoud lowered his head and did as he was ordered. As his hands were thus occupied, he smiled at a small child who had toddled down the aisle and stood regarding him gravely. He held out a section of orange to the child, only to have it snatched from his fingers by the Major.

"Next time, you pay for it," he growled.

Mahmoud didn't look up, concentrated on the orange.

Apparently pleased with his success, Naughton snapped his fingers at Mahmoud as they pulled into the next station. "Tea!" His voice was loud enough to be heard several seats away; he might as well have been announcing to the other passengers the extent of his control over this insignificant brown fellow, this native. Mahmoud leaned out the window and beckoned to the tea wallah.

While he was counting out the coins for the tea, a thought hit him with a physical jolt: the written order had mentioned the Major would pay him a lakh of rupees. That meant he must have it with him. Suddenly he felt strong: he would not only get away from the Major but do so with the money the Minister had offered him. It would be due him, after all, for he was now convinced of the futility of his case, so the documents might as well stay where they were until they rotted. All the Minister wanted was that they not be used in any way. All of which was very well except for the problem of how to accomplish it, and that still eluded him. But at least, at last, he felt energized enough to keep working away at it.

When the toddler headed back in his direction and fell as the train jerked, Mahmoud jumped to pick him up. As he moved, Corder stuck his foot into the aisle and sent Mahmoud sprawling. The little one wailed; the mother glared; the two Brits guffawed.

"Keep your seat, babu; it's safer."

Hatred was in his eyes, so he looked down at hands shaking with the desire to attack his British tormentors. How gratifying it would be if he could smear honey on their legs, yes, right up to the groin, and make them stand on a trail of soldier ants. The scene was clear in his mind; he watched them squirm, jump, try to brush off those creatures with their painful bites, slap them, all in vain. To hear the victims shout and cry, then see them reduced to helpless heaps of quaking flesh—all that scene was so satisfying it make him smile. But, aware that was not an expression he should allow his captors to see, he lowered his head.

When he closed his eyes, he was so astonished to see Ajai that they popped open again. He had not thought of his prison cellmate for several years. Why did he come to him now? Seeing his hands still quivering, he realized it had been only a vision, so he closed his eyes again. There, still, not at all dream-like but looking very much himself, was Ajai, smiling at him as though saying again, "You disappoint me, baba. I thought you would have learned by now." What should he have learned? What would Ajai have done? "Pass for respectable, maybe fool a few people," Ajai had said.

Mahmoud was concentrating so hard thinking about Ajai's words that for a moment he failed to notice that Shaheen had come into his vision, with that graceful, mountain-woman walk of hers. How odd she looked, holding hands with Ajai. "Haven't you learned," she challenged him, "that all the men stick together? Acting together is what it means to be part of a community."

Slowly an idea germinated; not yet formed, but a faint hope stirred within him. It led him to keep his head up, to look around, to comply with the Major's orders without obsequiousness. He had mastered the hatred; no longer its prisoner, he looked at the other passengers, nodded at some, smiled back at those who caught his eye. Many of their expressions were sympathetic. In the evening an elderly woman strolled past him, stepping over the bundles in the aisles, and quietly slipped into his hand an omelette rolled into a chapatti. Mahmoud's mouth watered at the fragrance of the spices, as his eyes threatened to do at the kindness. He ate it with extra relish because Corder glowered.

He had still worked out only the faintest plan by about noon on the second day, when everyone seemed restless. A general rustle filled the car as people stood up to stretch, yawned, paced the aisles. Mahmoud stretched in his seat, yawned elaborately. Naughton and the assistant took turns to go stand in the fresh air of the vestibule. When the train stopped for refueling at a rural station, many of the passengers got down, chatting about the food for which this place was known.

"Let's go eat," Naughton said.

"But what about...?" Corder indicated their charge.

"We can't leave him, so he better come along. But don't try any funny stuff, like running away," he warned Mahmoud.

In the station, they pushed their way into the small buffet, the air heavy with the smell of spices, tea, sweat. Naughton commandeered a table. The Indians who had been making for the same one and been pushed aside by the Major stood, grim-faced, waiting while these latecomers were served first.

Mahmoud wore his silence like a black hood, waiting to spring the trap. People continued to stream in, not only passengers but also those who had come to meet someone, to board the train at this juncture, or to collect parcels discharged here. People stood pressed against the walls. They crowded about the serving counter so closely that those who had received their tea or thalis held them over their heads to make their way back to their tables.

Finally Mahmoud's time came, a moment when he judged the crowd was dense enough for his purpose. Tense, too, from the pushing and shoving, the waiting for service, the sense that two foreigners were getting more attention from the staff than the whole crowd of Indians. Those who had been in the carriage with them, who had seen Naughton's humiliating treatment of him, stood nearest their table. Mahmoud knew this was his last chance; if he muffed it, he would be entirely at the mercy of the Major.

He wiped the sweat from his brow with his sleeve, conscious that it could give him away but probably would not, as the crowd had made the room hot for everyone. Even the Major was perspiring. The waiting, shrinking from elbows in their ribs, having their toes stepped on, the frustration of feeling thirsty and being unable to reach the tea counter, all that had produced a general irritation in the crowd; a spark would ignite it. Mahmoud intended to provide that spark.

Clearing the fear from his throat, he began to speak in a carrying voice which he increased as he went on, louder and louder, until finally it was raised to a shout.

"Ya Allah, you have ruined me!"

Sensing a diversion, those nearest gathered more closely about the table to listen.

"What are you doing?" the Major exclaimed, seizing Mahmoud by the shoulder.

"You've cheated me. Like you always do."

"Shut up!"

"First you steal my rupees. Then you steal my Master's money."

"You bloody fool!" Naughton slapped him across the mouth.

Seeing, even as he recoiled from the blow, that the crowd in the room had begun to close in around them, Mahmoud went on.

"Kill me, then! Go ahead, kill me! My life will be worth nothing anyway when my Master finds I can't give him his dues." Giving Naughton a shove, he leaped to his feet. "You foreigners always cheat us poor Indians. You take our rupees..."

"Take our land," a voice shouted from the crowd.

"Our women," another added.

"Ya, Allah! Our very country!"

"There is a bag in your pocket and it belongs to my Master."

"Then take it," voices in the crowd shouted. "Get it back. Get it! Get it!"

Rough hands laid hold of the Major and Corder. At the first interchanges, they had sat bewildered by what was happening, but now they were on their feet. Corder picked up the chair he had been sitting on and tried to raise it high enough to use as a shield to force his way through the crowd. Mahmoud wrenched it from his hands

280

and hit him on the head with it, but managed only a glancing blow. Naughton used his fists. Thalis, cups, bags became weapons. Those who could not get close enough to attack shouted encouragement from the sidelines.

"Go to it, villagers."

"Kick, kick!"

"Kick the damn foreigners. Out of the country!"

"Hold them! Here's some rope."

The two fought as best they could. But a life of dealing out cards and counting money had not been good preparation for roughing it with sturdy country men used to wielding hoes and machetes and lifting hundred-kilo burdens daily. In a trice they were both on the floor, trussed with hempen twine brought from someone's bullock cart. Another villager tore his rumal in two and used the pieces for gags.

Panting, Mahmoud paused to salute the crowd, then bent and patted the Major's pockets until he felt an appropriate bulge: it was a brocade bag closed with the Minister's seal. When he held it up, grinning triumphantly, the crowd applauded, roaring their satisfaction. Salaaming acknowledgement, he gestured to the rest to do as they pleased and stepped back. With more space, he would have floated.

The crowd closed in; those who had been most active in the fray stood closest and so got first pickings. One man after another moved away from the trussed up figures, wearing a smug look, and another took his place. Those who came later left wearing or carrying an item of clothing; many waved them like pennants as they made their way out.

By the time Mahmoud could see his victims again, they had been stripped of wallets, cuff links, studs, rings, everything of value, even their clothes and their boots. There they lay in their underwear, twitching and thrashing and making animal-like noises through their gags, when the whistle blew. The train was about to depart. Passengers scampered back to their seats and villagers ran out of the station, cheered that just this once they had got the best of these foreigners.

The cook and his helper, as well as the station master, had all decamped as soon as the trouble began. They would return when they deemed it prudent, probably in an hour or two, for they had retreated to a safe distance to wait out the uproar. As the crowd dispersed, Mahmoud grabbed a laggard villager by the arm. "Tell the station master it's safe to come back now." The villager grinned, and Mahmoud knew he would be in no hurry to deliver the message.

Then he ran after the other passengers to board the train, head up, ramrod spine. Gesturing his appreciation to the passengers as he made his way to his seat, he alternately bowed to one side of the aisle, did namaste to the other. No one actually spoke about the event, but men patted him on the back and women smiled and nodded. A few men showed one another their bruises like badges of honour and women clucked appreciatively over rips in the clothing.

Thank you, Ajai, Mahmoud's thoughts ran. It was not precisely the kind of revenge for which he had thirsted, not the trial he had so often envisioned, but the Major was certainly humiliated, and in public! That's what he had wanted most of all. Well done! Surely now the Minister must investigate the Major. His duty was finished. His honour restored.

Some miles down the track, the train slowed to drop off a mailbag. With a jaunty wave to his fellow passengers, Mahmoud hopped off and ducked behind a pile of jute bales until the last car of the train had disappeared down the track.

Erupting into the sun, Mahmoud threw the Minister's brocade bag into the air and caught it, then followed it with a great leap, and again, and again. Up, up, up, elation raised him like a hot air balloon. Up above the humiliated Major, above his childish resentments, above his obligation to the Minister. The Minister's answer in his hand. He had won! He was free! Free even of fear, for he had the means to become as indispensable to the people of Chalab as they were to him. And it was not he, Sayed Mahmoud alone, who had achieved all that—Shaheen would say "of course"—but the villagers and passengers who had bonded with him as one in their hatred of foreigners.

Exuberance swelled his chest. He was not only free but sure. He knew how to negotiate for a horse and supplies in a strange town, even for a rifle. A sapphire ring, too, to make good an early promise. How to make his way across open country to Dehra Ismail Khan; how to hire a guide there. The guide after that would be a Waziri. And he would be home.

He could hear the voices, see the people, feel the reunion with them as clearly as though he were already there. Asalaam aleikum, dear people of Chalab! Asalaam aleikum, Shaheen, my darling! Come to papa, little one.

He flung his arms wide. "Welcome, my life! Al Hamdulillah, Praise be to God!"

Afterword

Some years ago, while we were still living in India, I got tired of teaching management and discovered the joys of archival research, which continued during our interim of a few years in America. I loved the big, domed reading room in the British Museum; the India Office Records were in a building across the Thames, in the neighbourhood of the Old Vic, whose very name was an inspiration. In the National Archives in New Delhi during the winter, my toes froze, while those century-old letters set my imagination ablaze.

In Hyderabad, the archive staff set me up in the stacks, so other readers would not be distracted by my electric typewriter, and made sure I saw every relevant document. Some were pointed out to me by that meticulous researcher, Dr. Vasanth Bawa, who was working on another aspect of the same subject. It was awesome to be the first person in a hundred years to pull some of those letters out of the original envelopes in which they had been filed and try to make sure that the crumbling at the creases did not lose any of the lettering. By the time I had done the research for my two books about Hyderabad (*The Days of the Beloved* and *My Dear Nawab Saheb*), I was more comfortable in 19th-century India than in 20th-century America.

I was very fortunate in my friends, especially during that formative time. Dr. Ziauddin Ahmed, whom I met when he was an officer of the Andhra Pradesh State Archives, introduced me to Sufism and to Urdu poetry. Ashok Katakam, of Katakam and Associates, drew the map and sketches, one of which was used for the bookmark.

Serendipity is one of the rewards of doing one's own research. I read a great deal of curious and interesting stuff that didn't quite fit into the earlier books, but I filed it away in my memory, for possible future use. I came to be so sure about the atmosphere described in *Passion in Rubies* began this story then, and I've worked on it off and on ever since. For hanging in with me through multiple revisions, I am grateful to these friends: Buff Grace, Maggie Rindfuss, Carol Hudson, Janet Edwards, and most especially Margaret who offered the aha experience that has informed my writing ever since. Most of all, my family, who did without me during the long absences when I was dusting off old records abroad instead of future at home.

Pima County
Public Library
www.library.pima.gov